A DICTIONARY OF THE
JEWISH-CHRISTIAN DIALOGUE
(EXPANDED EDITION)

Studies in Judaism and Christianity

Exploration of Issues in the Contemporary Dialogue Between Christians and Jews

Editor in Chief for
Stimulus Books
Helga Croner

Editors
Lawrence Boadt, C.S.P.
Helga Croner
David Dalin
Leon Klenicki
John Koenig
Kevin A. Lynch, C.S.P.
Richard C. Sparks, C.S.P.

A STIMULUS BOOK

A DICTIONARY OF THE
JEWISH-CHRISTIAN DIALOGUE

Expanded Edition

Edited by

Leon Klenicki
and
Geoffrey Wigoder

A STIMULUS BOOK

PAULIST PRESS ◆ NEW YORK ◆ MAHWAH

Library of Congress Cataloging-in-Publication Data

A dictionary of the Jewish-Christian dialogue / edited by Leon Klenicki and Geoffrey Wigoder. — Expanded ed.
    p. cm.
    "Stimulus book."
    ISBN 0-8091-3582-5 (alk. paper)
    1. Judaism—Doctrines—Dictionaries. 2. Theology, Doctrinal—Dictionaries. 3. Judaism—Relations—Christianity—Dictionaries. 4. Christianity and other religions—Judaism—Dictionaries.
    I. Klenicki, Leon. II Wigoder, Geoffrey, 1922-
BM50.D53   1995
261.2'6'03—dc20   95-15509
                                              CIP

Published by Paulist Press
997 Macarthur Boulevard
Mahwah, NJ 07430

Printed and bound in the
United States of America

Contents

Abbreviations in Rabbinic Literature

TB   Talmud Bavli (Babylonian Talmud)
TJ   Talmud Yerushalmi (Jerusalem Talmud)

Preface

The need for this book first struck the editors when they were participating in a group of Jews and Christians discussing the challenges to our
respective faiths from the impact of secularism in the modern world. The discussion tended at times to be beset with mutual misunderstandings because
of the different meanings and significance of "secularism." Inasmuch as
Christianity is a totally religious concept, an a-religious Christian would
appear to be an impossibility. When it comes to being Jewish, the parameters
are not necessarily religious. The Hebrew word *Yahadut* can be translated as
"Judaism" or as "Jewishness." Judaism in the religious connotation can
roughly be said to parallel Christianity. Jewishness is much broader, incorporating at its maximum identity with a faith, a people, a culture and a land—
and often only some of these. Jews can be religious or a-religious, believing,
agnostic or even atheist. Jewishness and Christianity are not two sides of the
same coin; they are different coins. In the Western world there is common
talk of the "Judeo-Christian tradition," which is understandable but misleading. Though the two spring from the same roots and cover much common
ground, the differences are basic, representing two completely different
worlds and world-outlooks.

Living side by side in the contemporary Western world, they have been
driven closer together by common challenges and common enemies. Wars of
faith should be anachronistic and the strong hostility of bygone history
should be seen in these days as a futile exercise in face of the massive
onslaught of non-believers. The understanding of this need for a joint struggle, coupled with the Christian realization that its own teachings and attitudes played a crucial role in creating the atmosphere in which the Holocaust
was possible, has led to an era of dialogue. At the highest level, this now
means that Jews and Christians of all denominations sit down to discuss their
respective traditions, in an effort to foster mutual understanding and a step
toward the establishment of a more harmonious relationship. It will take a

1

long time to eradicate centuries of prejudice; but already there are encouraging signs that long-rooted hostile stereotypes are being replaced by a more authentic picture, born of knowledge.

Yet, the dialogue is often hampered and confused because of ignorance—not necessarily willful ignorance but the result of being completely apart for so many centuries. Sometimes, the source of misunderstanding is semantic. Judaism developed in a Hebraic world, Christianity in a Greco–Latin universe. Thought patterns and directions differed considerably, and when the two groups eventually came closer to one another, they often found their differences accentuated by variants in linguistic usage. Thus in the English-speaking world, Christians and Jews have had to find terms in English for theological concepts forged in other languages. These concepts may be far from congruent in the original but both are translated into English by the same term. The Greek *nomos* and the Hebrew *Torah* and *halakha*, for instance, are all translated as "law," while in the original the meanings are very unlike. Indeed, there are many key terms for which there is no adequate English translation, e.g. *Torah* or *teshuvah* in Hebrew, or *agape* in Greek.

One object of this Dictionary, then, is to explain to Jews and Christians each faith's understanding of what in English seem to be common concepts. Terms appearing to be identical may turn out to have different connotations. Each concept, therefore, is discussed by a Christian and a Jewish author. By this arrangement, the Dictionary also presents the basic outlook of Christianity and Judaism on major topics that form the bases of discussion.

We would even be so bold as to suggest that pairs of entries in the book could form the starting point for fruitful dialogue sessions. We realize that there are many other concepts that could have been incorporated but lack of space forced us to be selective. We hope to have covered the main issues, however—those that divide us and those that unite us, so that we may confront our differences and also know where we can work together, in a world where belief in God is being increasingly challenged.

The Editors

Afterlife

JEWISH VIEW:

Judaism has always maintained a belief in an afterlife. God created human beings to have both body and soul. Earthly death does not end one's existence.

Although the belief in an afterlife is basic, Jewish tradition does not provide one systematic way of understanding this concept. It is impossible, therefore, to speak of *the* Jewish idea of afterlife; there is a variety of opinions and suggestions. Moreover, Judaism realistically recognizes that no human being can speak definitively on a subject beyond the scope of human experience and reason.

Belief in an afterlife is reflected in the Bible. Presumably, when a person died he went to *Sheol* where he continued to live in a world of shadows and darkness. The story of King Saul having the spirit of Samuel raised by a necromancer (1 Sam 28) obviously presupposes that Samuel continued to live even after his earthly death, otherwise his spirit could not have been called up. The dramatic description of the ascent of Elijah to heaven (2 Kgs 2:11) assumes that the prophet continued to live even after his life on earth had ended. A direct statement concerning the afterlife is found in Daniel 12:2: "Many of them that sleep in the dust of the earth shall awake, some to everlasting life, and some to reproaches and everlasting abhorrence." While these biblical sources do not provide a clear notion of the afterlife, they do assume its existence.

A number of Hebrew phrases relate to the idea of afterlife. These phrases themselves are subject to various interpretations. Perhaps the most popular term for afterlife is *olam haba,* the future world. Another term is *atid labo,* the future to come. A widely held view, propounded by Moses Maimonides, suggests that when the body dies, the soul returns to God. The soul is immortal and will live forever in *olam haba.* Its level of blessedness will depend on how one has lived his life on this earth. The more one has devoted his life to the spiritual pursuit of God, the greater his blessing will be in the world to come.

There are other terms which are also used in relation to an afterlife. *Tehiyat hametim,* resurrection of the dead, and *yemot hamashiah,* messianic times, relate to a future time when the souls will be returned to their bodies. Resurrection of the dead is included in the thirteen principles of faith (q.v.) formulated by Maimonides. It is also an important feature of the *amidah,* the silent prayer which serves as the basis of three daily prayer services. Some thinkers have stressed resurrection of the dead as being the ultimate blessing of the afterlife, while others have stressed the spiritual immortality of the soul, placing less emphasis on the importance of actual bodily resurrection. In ancient times the issues of resurrection and immortality were disputed by the Pharisees and Sadducees. The Pharisees maintained these concepts and believed that they were implicit in the Torah itself. The Sadducees argued that body and soul die together. The position of the Pharisees, of course, has been the mainstream position of Judaism throughout the centuries. In modern times, Reform Judaism has rejected the belief in a physical resurrection of the dead.

Rav, a leading teacher of the third century CE, described the world to come as follows: "There is neither eating nor drinking nor begetting children, neither bargaining nor jealousy nor hatred nor strife. All that the righteous do is to sit with their crowns on their heads and enjoy the radiance of the Divine Presence" (TB *Berakoth* 17a). The ideal of the world to come is for the immortal souls to be free of bodily needs, to be like angels, always enjoying the splendor of God.

Other terms relating to the afterlife are *gan Eden,* Garden of Eden, and *gehinnom.* Again, there is no clear idea of what either of these terms definitely signifies, and their equation with "heaven" and "hell" is only very approximate. In a general sense, they reflect the belief that the righteous are rewarded and the wicked punished following their earthly death.

Indeed, a practical result of the belief in reward and punishment in the afterlife is the need for proper behavior here on earth. In the fourth chapter of *The Ethics of the Fathers,* Rabbi Jacob says: "This world is like a vestibule (*prozdor*) to the future world; prepare yourself in the vestibule so you can enter the banquet hall." And if a person is righteous and yet suffers much on this earth, he may expect to receive his blessing in the world to come. At the end of the second chapter of *The Ethics of the Fathers,* Rabbi Tarfon teaches: "Know that the righteous receive their reward in the time to come."

For many centuries it has been customary for mourners to recite an Aramaic prayer known as *Kaddish,* praising God. The mourners are required to recite the *Kaddish* daily for eleven months following the death of a close relative. The *Kaddish* is also recited on the anniversary of the death of near relatives. This custom presupposes the belief that God judges the soul following the death of the body. By reciting the *Kaddish*, the mourners hope to gain God's mercy toward the soul of their departed relative.

Kabbalistic literature teaches that the souls of wicked people are punished, and then reincarnated. This gives the wicked soul the opportunity to perform good deeds on earth and gain the blessing of the afterlife. In certain cases, the soul of a very wicked person is denied this process of punishment and reincarnation, and is "exiled" without the possibility of finding rest.

Among the Jews of North Africa, as well as among Hasidic Jews, there is a belief that the souls of the righteous can intervene on behalf of the living. Prayers are recited at the graves of saintly persons. A feature of North African Jewish life was the *Hiloula*, a special celebration held at the graves of very righteous people. These events were marked by prayers, fires lit over the graves of the saints, and the chanting of holy texts. People would camp out in the vicinity of the grave overnight, offering their prayers to God, and hoping that the spirit of the saint would win God's mercy for the living.

The tenth chapter of the Talmudic tractate *Sanhedrin* begins with the statement that all Israel has a place in the world to come. But the Mishnah goes on to enumerate exceptions to this rule. In fact, throughout the Talmud examples are given of people who forfeit their place in the world to come due to their sinful actions and beliefs. The blessings of the world to come, then, must be earned. This is true not only for Jews, but also for non-Jews. The righteous individuals of all nations have a portion in the world to come, and its blessings are not reserved exclusively for Jews.

Judaism placed its overwhelming stress on *olam haseh*, this world here on earth. Speculations about the world to come are peripheral to mainstream Judaism. When the Torah speaks of blessings for the Israelites who observe God's commandments, the blessings are given for this world. They are promised good crops, prosperity, health. An interesting statement made by Rabbi Jacob in the fourth chapter of *The Ethics of the Fathers* teaches: "One hour of penitence and good deeds in this world is better than all the life of the world to come; but one hour of spiritual repose in the world to come is better than all the life of this world." This statement teaches the incredible significance of life on this earth, while expressing the greatness of the spiritual repose in the next world—a repose which will be granted to the righteous.

Marc Angel

CHRISTIAN VIEW:

Daniel 12 is the only text of the Hebrew Scriptures which speaks clearly of the individual resurrection from the dead. It may seem surprising that Israel waited so long, indeed till the second century BCE, to spell out a doctrine which would right away become so important. But, on the one hand, the Israelite hope for afterlife had traditionally a collective dimension. Furthermore, only a dramatic evolution of history prompted the apocalypticists to imagine a retribution after this life for the martyrdom of the pious ones.

This does not mean that Israel could for eleven centuries remain indifferent to the individual afterlife destiny. But the resistance to Canaanism, with its naturalistic myths and rituals, was such that one had to wait until the second century BCE for a relaxation of the orthodox caution. This coincided with the martyrdom of *Hasidim* at the hand of Antiochus IV of Syria (second century BCE), an event which dramatically raised the problem of the innocents' death.

Described in general terms, death is a sign of the fundamental weakness of the human being before God, even of his status of sinner. In other words, no one can stand Divine justice and, consequently, death is "the salary of sin," the fruit of a curse upon all creation. In this sense, death is therefore not "normal." It especially does not belong to a natural and ever-recurring cycle. That is why God is not present in the *Sheol,* in contradiction to the nature divinities for which death, as well as life, constitutes the realm of power (cf. Ps 88:13).

But what is to be said of a death-offering, *le-shem ha-shamayim* (for God's sake), i.e., not the pitiful outcome of the confrontation with the Divine, but the sign of a choice *for* being and *against* nothingness? The shift in circumstances has brought about a shift in death's nature. From deserved punishment of the culprit, death has become and undeserved fate of the innocent. Death-punishment was its own justification. Death-offering finds no justification without a Divine response which vindicates it. Such a response, according to Daniel 12, is resurrection.

In the article on Creation (q.v.) the parallel with redemption has been emphasized. Corresponding to the pair redemption-creation (cf. Second Isaiah, Ezek 37, etc.), apocalyptic literature comes with the pair recreation-resurrection. Thus, to redemption with its collective dimension, echoes resurrection with its individual dimension. It also is re-creation. As the ultimate cataclysm, in the image of the Deluge, brings about, not only destruction, but the triumph of life over death, so the individual catastrophe, viz., death, contains in itself a germ of eternity (cf. 2 Chr 9:31). The correspondence goes further. For apocalyptic literature, there is a definitive end to history. Even the Messiah (q.v.) must die, according to 2 Chronicles 7, so as to leave room for a totally new world. There is thus discontinuity between this world and the world to come. Similarly, there is no bridge between this life and the life without end.

The doctrine of resurrection (cf. Eschatology) is tied with the notion of people (the people of Israel). It cannot be understood but in the framework of Covenant. Thus resurrection is an historical event, at the antipode of the naturalistic formulation by the Canaanites. In conformity with apocalyptic thinking, resurrection is an event that reveals the secret of history which was so far hidden. The secret is the transcendent dimension of the human being, what 1 Corinthians 15:44 calls his *soma pneumatikon,* the spiritual body. The end of man is to be ultimately transfigured into a "Son of man," according to Daniel 7, or to be counted with the angels or the stars, according to Daniel 12.

The New Testament is totally faithful to such an apocalyptic vision, when it proclaims that the Messiah is the reconciliation of things of the earth with the things of heaven. He "recapitulates" history which until then was "beheaded" (cf. Col 1:15–18; Eph 1:10, 22f; 1 Cor 15:20, 23). For, until the Messiah, history is, so to speak, begging for "making sense." Christ is the coherence of all things. So, one should say that the messianic event permeates humankind as a whole (cf. Jn 1:9). History thus is never deprived of its fulfillment. But, until the ultimate moment of the apocalyptic intervention of God in history, we only see this "enthronement" of sense through "a glass darkly" (1 Cor 13:12).

The messianic event brings to its end the present world. It was a world torn between life and death, good and evil, warm and cold, cosmos and chaos (cf. Gen 8:22). It was a post-cataclysmic world, torn between heaven and hell, the tree of life and the forbidden tree, the garden of delights and the dust of "eternal horror" (Dan 12:2). Apocalyptic end resolves this ontic ambiguity (cf. Zech 14:6f; Is 30:26; etc.). From this perspective, resurrection is "a metamorphosis upward to a new beginning that is not present" (N. Frye). Present is the eschatological moment, for, here and now, there are saints, sages, righteous ones who are the presence of eternity in a corrupt and transitory history. They represent the authentic dimension of human being, as eternity is the true meaning of history.

The glorification of the martyr, both by apocalyptic literature and the New Testament, means that there is concomitance of "Easter" and "Good Friday." "Who loses his life, finds it," says the Nazarene (Mk 16:25 and parallels), while "the one who tries to save it, will lose it" (8:35 and parallels).

This logic of extravagance (cf. Law) is a stumbling block for Aristotelian reasoning. The destiny of the saints transcends death. What is achieved cultically, viz., the vision of Divine glory, is made permanent in the life of the Nazarene and of the righteous. "All is accomplished."

André Lacocque

Antisemitism

JEWISH VIEW:

Though the word "antisemitism" is of nineteenth-century coinage, Jew-hatred is a phenomenon of long standing. The Bible already reports the vicious attack by Amalek upon the stragglers who left Egypt (Dt 25:17–19) which was seen by the rabbis as the prototype of anti-Judaism, as well as the classic statement of Jew-hatred: "Then Haman said to King Ahasuerus, 'There is a certain people scattered abroad and dispersed among the peoples in all the provinces of your kingdom; their religious practices are different from those of every other people, and they do not keep the religious practices of the king; so that it is not for the king's profit to tolerate them. If it please the king, let it be written that they be destroyed, and I will pay ten thousand talents of silver into the hands of those who have charge of the king's business, that they may put it into the royal treasuries'" (Est 3:8–9).

The vigor with which Antiochus Epiphanes tried to suppress the first rebellion for religious freedom led by the Maccabees (167 BCE) earned for him the title of "madman" and for the Maccabees the reputation of freedom fighters. The anti-Jewish riots of Alexandria (38 CE), the destruction of the Jews by the Crusaders, the Chmielnitski massacres in Eastern Europe (1648 CE), the pogroms of recent times, and the Holocaust—all are expressions of this strange phenomenon called Jew-hatred.

The reasons for Jew-hatred are many and varied. Three deserve mention here: (1) Jew-hatred is a side effect of other basic social and economic troubles. Troubles arise that have nothing to do with the Jews but the Jews are a convenient object of blame, anxiety, and anger. This is the scapegoat theory. (2) Jew-hatred is the expression of a resentment felt by non-Jews at the closeness of the Jewish people to God. God chose the Jews and this makes them special, to themselves and to others. Others react to this in deep

9

envy. This is the theological theory. (3) Jew-hatred is a mental disease from which non-Jews suffer. Some say this disease is innate, the dislike of the unlike; some say it is culturally conditioned. Either way, Jew-hatred is a given of existence in a non-redeemed world, a fact with which all must learn to live. This is the psychopathological theory.

Jewish-Christian relations have a particularly difficult burden to bear in the matter of Jew-hatred. The history of actual incidents is very long and so is the history of Christian literature on the subject.

As to actual history: As soon as Christianity became the official religion of the Roman state, resistance became a form of treason, not just a type of heresy, and was prosecuted accordingly. The claim to exclusive salvation frequently prompted the Church to undertake forced conversions, e.g., during the Visigoth invasions of Spain. The position of the Church that a Crusader achieved salvation by eradicating the infidels generated many acts of Jew-murder. The Inquisition in Spain, Portugal, and elsewhere is best known in Jewish history for its killing of Jews. And, even during the Holocaust, there were elements of the Christian Church that heralded Hitler as a savior figure, rationalized his Jew-murdering as a sign of God's wrath or, more commonly, divorced Jesus from the plot of Jew-murder and sheltered the Church in indifference.

As to teaching: Very early, the Church refused to admit that some people might not want to become Christians, that some people might be happy to remain Jewish, in covenant with God and his Torah. This is already reflected in the shaping of the Gospel stories and certainly in the understanding of those stories. The so-called curse which "the Jews" accepted upon themselves at the Crucifixion is a classic example. This led to the teaching of deicide, a false teaching that was only renounced in very recent times by the Catholic Church. Another pernicious teaching was the blood libel which became current in the Middle Ages: that Jews kill a Christian child and use its blood in making Passover matzot. No shred of truth ever lay in this. Yet, the libel was preached from Christian pulpits and led to pogroms for many centuries. In recent times, Christian anti-Jewish teachings created an atmosphere in which a Holocaust became possible.

Two positive notes can be sounded in this context: First, during the Middle Ages when it was really within the power of the Church to wipe out the Jews, it did not. Some say this was for economic reasons; some say it was theologically based. Second, the attempts in very recent years by Christians of goodwill to confront this element in their own religious and historical past are praiseworthy. No one wants to know such things about oneself. Yet, if there is to be any dialogue at all, these historical and theological facts must be confronted and the phenomenon of Jew-hatred in all its forms and labels must be denounced and disavowed as a violation of God's covenant and as contrary to the teachings of Christianity.

The modern period has seen the development of two new forms of Jew-hatred: the racial and the nationalistic. We, in Western society, must remember that racism was a very commonly accepted idea until fifty years ago. Professional anthropologists, for example, studied and classified racial characteristics as a scientific discipline for two centuries. Even now this intellectual scourge has not been erased from the hearts of many. Racial Jew-hatred differed from the earlier form in that there was no escape. Previously, a Jew could convert to Christianity and then become a more-or-less fully accepted Christian. But there was no way out of racial Jew-hatred. Even conversion did not help. The moral repugnance of Western society at the practical result of this teaching in the aftermath of the Holocaust, coupled with the advances in intergroup relations made during the last decades, has rendered this form of Jew-hatred largely confined to the cranks of human society.

Nationalistic Jew-hatred has, however, surfaced to new legitimacy in recent years. Jews are constituted as a people. As such, they are entitled, theologically and historically, to a secure and vital national existence. The movement that embodies this thinking is called Zionism and all Jews, either on religious or secular grounds, subscribe to these basic tenets, though they may differ about specific policies for bringing this about.

The conflict between Zionism and Arab nationalism, whatever its resolution, has revived the ancient phenomenon of Jew-hatred in the form of anti-Zionism. Arab school systems use old Nazi stereotypes in their textbooks. Arab political cartoonists use old Nazi stereotypes in their newspapers. The Covenant of the Palestine Liberation Organization includes a clause promising to "eliminate the Zionist presence" from Palestine. The United Nations, under Arab pressure, passed a resolution condemning Zionism as racism. The PLO is now, after the agreement with Israel, in the process of changing the prose of the Covenant. And so on. This is nothing but Jew-hatred in another form. Everyone, Jews included, admits that the issues themselves are very complex and require great wisdom for their solution but the use of these issues as an expression of Jew-hatred is much to be regretted.

Unfortunately, Jew-haters in the West who feel uneasy labeling themselves "antisemites" find in "anti-Zionism" an easy way to sustain their Jew-hatred under a socially acceptable label. Even serious Christians are often confused by the complexity of the issues into making radically anti-Zionist statements, not realizing that this is just another form of Jew-hatred. It is the socially acceptable form of our day. Here, too, dialogue cannot even begin until the true nature of anti-Zionism is exposed. Only then can the issues of Jewish and Arab nationalism be discussed in the context of a broader Jewish-Christian dialogue.

David Blumenthal

CHRISTIAN VIEW:

Antisemitism is a word that suffers for lack of clear definition. However, that of the French Jewish thinker, Jules Isaac, is as good today as it was when formulated in 1965: "Antisemitism is used nowadays to refer to anti-Jewish prejudice, to feelings of suspicion, contempt, hostility, and hatred toward Jews, both those who follow the religion of Israel and those who are merely of Jewish parentage" (*The Teaching of Contempt*). As many have pointed out, the Jews are not the only semitic people, but in common parlance, antisemitism means Jew-hatred.

The most accessible history of this phenomenon can be found in Edward Flannery's *The Anguish of the Jews.* Therein, Flannery shows that antisemitism predates Christianity. Greeks and Romans resented the Jews because they would not conform to the host culture's ways. The diaspora systematically refused both to take part in the state religion and to socialize with Romans and Greeks.

The reasons ascribed for Christian antisemitism through the ages are many. Perhaps the first were sociological. The first Christians were Jews who maintained that Jesus was the Messiah, the one awaited by their ancestors for centuries. Jews who did not believe this, at first treated the "Messianic Jews" as a sect, but the breach between the two groups widened and soon it was clear that a complete separation was inevitable. In the last part of the first century, the Jews of Palestine expelled the Jewish Christians from the synagogue. This expulsion was accompanied by polemics against Jesus and his followers. One can see some of the shadows of this expulsion in the Gospel of John which was written soon after the final separation.

A second reason for early Christian antisemitism was theological. That is, early converts to Christianity began to speak in theologically anti-Jewish terms (which are not, in themselves, antisemitic, in the modern sense of "Jew-hatred"); they spoke of God as repudiating the Jewish election and choosing the Church as the new people of God. The Gospel writers emphasized the argument between Jesus and the Pharisees, which scholars tell us, these writers played up, not so much because Jesus and the Pharisees were so far apart in their teachings, but because their teachings could be confused. Third, these theological polemics in the first century of the Common Era gave way to more violent anti-Jewish tracts of the Church Fathers. In these tracts, not only were Jewish rituals and interpretation of Scripture ridiculed, but Jewish life was interpreted from a Christian perspective, e.g., the notion that God expelled the Jews from their homeland and destroyed their temple as a punishment for rejecting the Christ. Early Christian thinkers, such as Justin, John Chrysostom, and Augustine, portrayed the Jews as wandering the earth in punishment for their part in Jesus' execution. For centuries, this last charge—deicide—became the cornerstone of anti-Jewish and antisemitic diatribes.

Fourth, the Middle Ages continued the polemic begun by the Church Fathers, but a countervailing trend emerged as well: the Church's protective laws of the Jews. Paradoxically, while the Church and nations of Europe denied to Jews the right to own property, they also set up laws to protect the Jews from outright persecution. Pope Gregory I is a good example: "Just as Jews should not be accorded liberties not permitted by law, they should suffer no prejudice to whatever is conceded them by law." Nonetheless, the Jews suffered through various waves of forced baptism and harassment. It was not uncommon in Christian Spain for worshipers to leave the churches on Good Friday in order to stone whatever Jews they might find on the streets. Literature of the time portrayed the Jews as "money-grubbing"; such portrayal became a stock figure in plays and novels right up to the present century.

Other anti-Jewish and antisemitic actions marked this millennium. During many of the Crusades, Jews were massacred if they did not submit to baptism. Prejudice was fed by false charges that Jews were poisoning wells and slaughtering babies. The Jews were expelled in 1492 from Spain and in 1497 from Portugal. The Fourth Lateran Council (in 1215) required that Jews wear distinguishing badges and live in certain sections of the city.

The Reformation in the sixteenth century did not see an appreciable improvement for Jews in Europe. Martin Luther fell prey to the same stereotypes of Jews that had plagued Catholicism. It was only from the end of the eighteenth century that some degree of emancipation came for the Jews throughout Europe (with the exception of Russia and Rumania). But the change of the laws did not change people's prejudices. Indeed, many blamed Hegel's philosophy for denigrating Judaism as an inferior religion; the popularity of the forgery entitled *Elders of Zion* further inflamed the never dormant antisemitic feelings of Europe. Adolf Hitler capitalized on these centuries of anti-Jewish polemic by scapegoating the Jewish people for the German defeat in World War I. In 1935, he took away citizenship from the Jews to "purify" the Aryan race of all traces of Jewish blood and subsequently embarked on the "Final Solution." And we still live in the wake and dread of the Holocaust.

Contemporary outbursts of antisemitic activity (e.g., the Ku Klux Klan, prejudice against Jews in Argentina and persecution in what was formerly the Soviet Union, graffiti swastikas on homes, etc.) are only the surface phenomena of prejudice which seems to defy all eradication. Numerous Protestant church groups have issued statements deploring antisemitism as unworthy of Christians. In the Roman Catholic tradition, Vatican II stated, "In its rejection of every persecution against any man, the Church, mindful of the patrimony it shares with the Jews and moved not by political reasons but by the Gospel's spiritual love, decries hatred, persecutions, displays of antisemitism directed against Jews at any time and by anyone" (*Nostra Aetate,* n. 4). Later guidelines by the Vatican Commission for Religious Relations with the Jews (1975) state "that the spiritual bonds and historical links binding the Church to Judaism condemn (as opposed to the very spirit of Christianity) all forms of antisemitism...."

Discussion and honest exploration of the history and causes of antisemitism belong at the very top of the Jewish-Christian agenda. The virulence of antisemitism admits to no easy explanation; its causes demand soul-searching questioning and dialogue. Some Christians see antisemitism as one case of the moral failing of Christians who have not lived up to the Gospel call to love all people. Others think that the link between Christian theological anti-Judaism (in particular, the supersessionism theory; cf. Election) and antisemitism needs much further exploration. This latter view may be quite threatening to many Christians involved in the dialogue, for it calls into question theological categories which have come to mean so much to Christians, e.g. the Church as the new Israel, the new people of God; Christ as the absolute fulfillment of Old Testament prophecy; Judaism as only a preparation for Christianity; etc.

Whatever direction the current dialogue takes, the issue of antisemitism must be close to the heart of it. Christians need to be honest and forthright about their own prejudices and Jews need to be patient and understanding as they explore this very delicate but crucial issue.

Michael McGarry

Bible

JEWISH VIEW:

The word Bible is not a Jewish term. It is a Greek word applied only in the fourth century CE and has no normative Jewish equivalent. Jews call the Hebrew Scriptures holy writings (*kitvei kodesh*), authoritative Scripture (*mikra*), or basic teachings (*torah*). Torah, then, refers to religious instruction whereby an individual learns to structure life through religious values. These ideas show the central significance of the Hebrew Bible for Judaism. Jewish community revolves around a dialectic relationship with these writings. They are the primary content of religious life; they find their religious meaning, however, in the dynamic living which they elicit rather than as fixed dogma.

The Deuteronomic reformation of King Josiah in 621 BCE represents one of the first attempts to make Judaism a religion of the Bible. Scholars are divided in their judgment about just what books or portions of books were considered "Bible" for Josiah. It is clear, however, that from that time onward Jewish self-understanding includes a responsive relationship to a written text. Canonization of that text was a lengthy process. Even when the Bible was translated into Greek in the so-called Septuagint or translation of the Seventy about 250 BCE, the exact number and order of books included was fluid. By the time of the council of Yavneh (Jamnia) in the first century CE, a more stable consensus had been established.

The division and order of books in the Hebrew canon represents theological as well as structural concerns in the Jewish view of the Bible. The Bible is divided into three parts: Torah (Genesis, Exodus, Leviticus, Numbers, Deuteronomy), Prophets (Joshua, Judges, 1 Samuel, 2 Samuel, 1 Kings, 2 Kings, Isaiah, Jeremiah, Ezekiel, The Twelve: Hosea, Joel, Amos, Obadiah, Jonah, Micah, Nahum, Habakkuk, Zechariah, Haggai, Zephaniah, Malachi), and the Writings (Psalms, Proverbs, Job, Song of Songs, Ruth,

Lamentations, Ecclesiastes, Esther, Daniel, Ezra, Nehemiah, 1 Chronicles, 2 Chronicles). This tri-partite division reflects Jewish views about the transmission of tradition. Mosaic teaching comes first and is then transmitted to prophets and then to sages. Political leaders—kings, administrators, high priests—are given only scant attention and subsumed under prophecy. The culmination of the tradition is wisdom, not prophecy. The order of the biblical books is also significant theologically. Chronologically, 1 and 2 Chronicles should precede Ezra and Nehemiah. The rabbinic authorities canonizing the Bible decided to reaffirm both the fact of exile and the promise of a return from exile (q.v.). The Jewish Bible, therefore, ends with Cyrus' call for Jews to return to their ancient homeland rather than with the anti-climactic beginnings of the Second Commonwealth.

The issues involved in canonization reveal the double importance of the Bible for Jews. Books were evaluated according to certain ideological and doctrinal criteria. They needed to be consistent with rabbinic interpretations of Mosaic law, to be of presumed antiquity, and to have certain literary value. At the same time they had to be spiritually uplifting, to provide the basis for inspiration and continued insight. Questions were raised about Ecclesiastes because of internal contradictions it contained. Song of Songs was reputed to have been suspect as overly secular. Two different stories about the controversy over the Book of Ezekiel exist. One stresses the problem of Ezekiel's reconstruction of the Temple and temple sacrifices, a reconstruction which diverges from the picture given in Mosaic teaching. The second suggests that the visionary mysticism of Ezekiel's chariot (1:4–28), his intuition of a heavenly substance (*hashmal*), and his probing of creation are spiritually suspect; they lead to heretical ideas (TB *Shabbath* 13b, *Hagigah* 13a).

Canonization seems, at first glance, to deal only with ideological concerns; a canon establishes which books—and in what order—a community considers sacred. That was certainly one effect of the Jewish standardization of the Bible. In Yavneh after the destruction of the Jerusalem Temple in 70 CE, the necessity of an authoritative power structure led to canonization. It is no accident that finalization of the canon took place at the time when Rabban Gamaliel II was deposed. That was a period of crisis and decision in rabbinic leadership. Certain basic doctrinal concerns led to the inclusion of Song of Songs, Ecclesiastes, and Esther and the exclusion of Ben Sira (basically a work in praise of the priesthood), Maccabees (a work which the anti-Hasmonean rabbis sought to suppress) and other apocryphal writings.

The two issues in canonization—ideological consistency and spiritual value—reappear in rabbinic teachings. The early rabbis turned to the Bible as a religious resource from which and upon which they built Jewish life. The earliest hermeneutical laws are associated with Hillel the Elder (a younger contemporary of Jesus). These means of deducing new practices from the Bible were the foundation of the Oral Law, the second "bible" of Judaism. Just as Moses received the written Bible at Mount Sinai, so, according to Jewish tradition, he received the Oral Law which expands and amplifies its meaning. The written law is incomprehensive without the amplification of rabbinic thought.

The technical term for this amplification is *midrash*. The root meaning of the Hebrew term is "to search out." The Bible, for Jews, is not a transparent document. It is a multivalent text which needs to be decoded. As an anvil struck by a hammer gives off numerous sparks, each flying in a different direction, so the biblical word sends off sparks when striking the human mind. The Bible cannot be interpreted at variance with its *peshat* or authoritative legal meaning. Yet as a spiritual resource it is a multifaceted touchstone. Jewish mystics warn about taking the basic doctrinal meaning of the Bible as its only significance. While such ideological authority is important, it is only the surface of the Jewish understanding of the Bible. Behind this meaning is buried a treasure house of hints, allegories, and religious secrets.

In Jewish liturgy, the Bible is represented from the rabbinic point of view. The threefold division of the Bible is reflected in the distinction between the Torah reading (from the first five books), the Haftarah reading (from the prophetic section), and the reading of the five scrolls (from the writings). On Sabbaths and holidays each section of the Bible has its appropriate place in religious worship. The use of verses from the Bible as parts of prayers is also rabbinically determined. The most obvious example is that of the *Shema* in which three selections from the Torah are recited twice daily. The selection of these passages and their recitation morning and evening reflect rabbinic decisions. Other biblical material in the liturgy—psalms for the Sabbath, for holidays, for each day of the week, prayers culled from the historical books, prophetic citations—has been chosen with the same ideological and spiritual goals in mind.

The Jew, therefore, both liturgically and practically, reads the Bible through rabbinic eyes. Without an appreciation of this Judaic sense of the Bible a dialogue between Jews and Christians is nearly impossible. Although Jews and Christians share certain texts in common, their understanding of those texts has been shaped by different forces. Christian proof-texts have radically different meanings for Jews. While Christians are dismayed that Jews do not read the Scriptures as they do, Jews conditioned by rabbinic insights find Christian interpretations forced and arbitrary.

Yet dialogue means a willingness to recognize the other possibilities inherent in any religious text. Admitting one's own prejudices is a vital preparation for dialogue; allowing the standpoint of one's partner in dialogue the same validity one gives to oneself is an essential prerequisite of interreligious discussion.

S. Daniel Breslauer

CHRISTIAN VIEW:

The Bible is a collection of books considered by the Church to be inspired by God. The word "Bible" is derived from the Greek *biblia* ("books"). These books are considered to belong to the canon because they are inspired. The word canon, from the Greek work *kanon,* signifies a reed which was used as a rule or instrument of measurement. The books accepted as canonical are thus recognized by the Church as a rule of faith, and as normative for Christian belief and practice.

Protestants, Catholics and Orthodox differ in their consideration of the canon of the Hebrew Scriptures (Old Testament) and the deutero-canonical literature, or apocrypha. Protestants accept the same canon as Jews, although they have a different enumeration. Catholics accept those thirty-nine books, plus the deutero-canonical books of Tobit, Judith, Wisdom, Sirach (Ecclesiasticus), Baruch (including the Letter of Jeremiah), 1 and 2 Maccabees, and the Greek additions of Esther and Daniel. Orthodox accept the Septuagint (the Greek translation of the Hebrew Scriptures and the deutero-canonical books).

The difference in the canon reflects the long and complex history of its development. The Jewish canon was not fixed until the end of the second century or the beginning of the third century CE, so the Christian community did not inherit a fixed canon. Consequently, while certain books such as the Pentateuch and the Prophets enjoyed general acceptance, others were disputed for many centuries.

Martin Luther and the Reformers accepted the Palestinian Jewish canon of the Hebrew Scriptures. Luther admitted the usefulness of the deutero-canonical books, and grouped them together at the end of his translation of the Bible under the title of "Apocrypha." However, later Reformers rejected these books altogether. The Roman Catholic canon was fixed in the sixteenth century at the Council of Trent, which decided to accept the deutero-canonical books as canonical, thus following the Septuagint. While this decision was based on general Church usage, it was undoubtedly influenced by Protestant-Catholic polemics.

Orthodox Christians established their canon in the seventeenth century, when the Councils of Jassy (1642) and Jerusalem (1672) accepted the apocryphal books as canonical, basing their decision on the inclusion of those books in the Septuagint. Nonetheless, many contemporary Orthodox consider the deutero-canonical books to be of a status secondary to that of the Hebrew Scriptures.

All Christians accept the same canon of twenty-seven books of the New Testament. The New Testament canon, however, is the product of a history almost as complex as that of the Hebrew Scriptures and deutero-canonical literature. It was not closed until the beginning of the fifth century in the Latin Church, and the tenth century in the Greek Church. Certain national churches, such as the Syrian and Ethiopic Churches, continued for many years to maintain a different canonical tradition.

The Bible is normative because it is recognized to be inspired. "Inspiration" refers to the influence of God on the biblical writers. Because of that influence we call the Bible the "Word of God." The influence of God on biblical writers was internal: God worked through the intellect, affectivity, and imagination on the writer. It was external: God's influence worked on the writer through his experience and that of his community. The fact that God influenced the biblical writer, however, does not mean that the latter was necessarily aware of that fact. It simply means that he was indeed moved by God in his writing.

Closely related to the idea of inspiration is belief in the inerrancy of the Bible. "Inerrancy" expresses the conviction that the Bible can contain no error because it is the inspired Word of God. Inerrancy applies to the intention of the author and to the essential message of the book. It does not preserve the author from scientific error or from the limitations of his time and culture.

Such an understanding of inerrancy requires that one learn the intention of the author and discover the message of his book. Although this may sometimes be relatively easy, as with certain of the psalms or of Jesus' parables, it may also require more extensive investigation. Thus, scholars examine biblical texts to discover the original literary forms (e.g., hymn, parable, proverb), the historical circumstances of the origin of a text, and the editorial interests of the writer in order to determine the author's intention and the message of his book. Discovery of that intention and message allows one to recognize cultural limitations while maintaining belief in the inerrancy of the Bible. For example, one can thus understand that the message of Genesis 1 is that all creation comes from God and that it is not meant to be a scientific statement about the origin of the world.

Scripture is the Word of God. It is inspired and its message is unfailingly true. Because Scripture is the Word of God, it is normative for Christian belief and practice. Interpretation of Scripture varies, however. Protestants tend to emphasize the immediacy of the Word as addressed to the individual, and the latter's primary function is interpreting Scripture. Orthodox and Catholics emphasize the ecclesial aspect of Scripture. They understand Scripture as the reflection of the faith community's experience, and thus consider that Scripture is to be interpreted not only by the individual, but by the entire faith community represented in the Tradition.

Tradition (upper case) is the entire process through which the faith is transmitted from one generation to the next. A particular teaching is part of Tradition if it cannot be eliminated without distortion of the Gospel (e.g., the messianic identity of Jesus). It is thus to be distinguished from traditions (lower case), which are customary practices or beliefs not essential to the Gospel. Catholic understanding of Tradition has a circular aspect: while Scripture is read and interpreted in light of the Tradition, Tradition itself stands under the norm of Scripture.

The Bible is both a cause for misunderstanding and a common meeting ground in Jewish-Christian dialogue. It is a cause for misunderstanding because Christians differ among themselves on such important questions as canon, inspiration, inerrancy, and the role of the Church in the interpretation of Scripture. Furthermore, Christians often read the Hebrew Scriptures only in light of the New Testament. While this practice is as old as the New Testament itself (e.g., Mt 1:23), Christians need to be careful not to read the Hebrew Scriptures and deutero-canonical literature merely as preparatory to the New Testament. (Indeed, the very term "Old Testament" can reflect an inference that the Hebrew Scriptures and deutero-canonical literature are passé, or have a secondary importance.) Sensitized by the dialogue, Christians need to hear the message of those writings through Jewish ears, for the Christian reading does not exhaust their meaning.

An understanding of this fact provides exciting possibilities for the Jewish-Christian dialogue. The Bible is a meeting ground, for Jews and Christians share the Hebrew Scriptures. The deutero-canonical literature and, to some degree, the Gospels provide information about Second Temple Judaism. Knowledge of Jewish tradition is indispensable to an adequate understanding of the New Testament. Discussion of Scripture can thus bring to all parties a deeper understanding of the Bible's religious and social values and an encouragement in the attempt to appropriate them.

Celia Deutsch

Christ—Jesus—Son of God

JEWISH VIEW:

There appear to be references in the Hebrew Scriptures to mythological "sons of god." These references echo traditions about giants, angelic creatures coming to earth, and unusual human beings with extraordinary powers. Many texts weave into these mythological themes ideas about the divine court on high and God's assembly of angels. Traditional Jewish interpretation has explained a number of these references as exalted descriptions of human nobility or of true worshipers of God. Thus Psalm 82 with its description of the divine court was explained in terms of human judges. Later Jewish sensibility to God's uniqueness rebelled against earlier mythology and an angelology surrounding God with other divine beings.

The royal psalms have a distinctive reference of "son of God." Israel's king took on a common ancient Near Eastern tradition—that of being an adopted son of the deity. The importance of this designation was less the exalted nature of the person of the king than the exalted rank of the nation who possessed such a king. The nationalistic element involved in this designation is clear in Psalms 2:7, 89:26–27 and 2 Samuel 7:14. The royal idea of divine sonship has two implications. On the one hand it suggests the special favor with which the deity treats both the king and the nation. Both come under special divine protection. This protection brings with it military and national success. At the same time, however, adoptive sonship means that the king has certain obligations to God. The king is to serve the people in responsibility, to be a willing servant of the divine and an obedient son to the divine Father. God, as Father, demands willing submission. Calling God Father brings with it recognition of divine parental authority. The idea of divine adoption of the king protects the nation against an arbitrary exercise of royal power. Royal sonship to God is, as it were, the Magna Carta of ancient Israel.

The idea of adoptive sonship was clearly linked with Israel's independence as a nation. When Israel lost that independence the idea of adoptive sonship became particularly subversive. As a memory of the past and a promise for the future it often inspired political unrest and was associated with messianic movements for national independence. References in the apocryphal writings—like those in Enoch and 4 Ezra—may have been originally revolutionary in intent, although in their present form they have been altered by late Christian editors. The Qumran sectarians, however, were active nationalists, as their messianic speculation and use of the term "son of God" shows.

Rabbinic leadership transformed the concept of divine sonship into a general description of Jews rather than a concept restricted to kings. All Israel is understood as God's children. Israel itself is called God's son as the prophetic corpus suggests. Jews who study the Bible are God's sons, and when challenged by his sons, even God must acquiesce. God, one report says, rejoices when his sons triumph over him! The sonship involved in being a Jew is not one that can become forfeit. No matter how the Jew acts, that sonship continues. Even if Israel is a disobedient son, God's kinship with the Jew is constant and unchanging. Some rabbis suggest that only when Israel obeys God's law is it worthy to be called God's son. Other rabbis, however, reject such a contingent view of Israel's sonship.

As with the idea of royal sonship, so Israel's sonship has a twofold implication. In the first place it assures Jews of a special place in God's favor: "Beloved is Israel for being called sons of God; even more beloved for having had their sonship made known to them," said Rabbi Akiba.

Torah as responsibility represents the second side of sonship. The Jew is adopted as God's son because he accepts the Torah. The gift of Torah is also an obligation to obey Torah. Israel manifests filial obedience by observing the precepts of Torah. Torah is less a legalism than the natural response of a son to a loving father. While Israel may at times be a wayward son and thereby call down punishment, repentance and return to God is always a possibility. God is pictured as saying that the Jew who observes and teaches Torah not only follows the divine path but "is as though he had redeemed me and my son (Israel) from exile" (Deuteronomy *Rabbah* 2:14).

Redemption of God's son is, thus, in Judaism the redemption of the people of Israel. All individuals who try to usurp the prerogative of the nation as a whole are to be punished. Nebuchadnezzar, the rabbis say, was punished for having described an angelic being as "like a son of God" (Exodus *Rabbah* 21:5). Repeated polemics are addressed to those who see sonship to God as the right of a particular individual. Sonship referred to the fact of having received Torah, not to messianic claims. Not royal individuals but the collective reality of a Torah community was worthy of that title.

Torah community might seem restricted to Jews alone. Rabbinic thinkers, however, included all humanity under the concept of sons of God. When God saw the Egyptians drowning he silenced the angelic songs of praise by saying "My sons are dying" (TB *Megillah* 10b). As children of Adam all humanity is worthy of being included in divine sonship. While Rabbi Akiba restricted sonship to Jews, other thinkers, like Ben Azzai, included all human beings.

This broader view is, perhaps, reflected in the Gospel of Luke when it traces Jesus' claim to divine sonship back to Adam. Unlike Matthew this Gospel sees divine sonship less as a royal prerogative than as a human one. It is on the basis of this understanding of being God's son that Jews can dialogue fruitfully. Jewish tradition, particularly in the form of the Noahide laws—laws given not just to Jews but to all humanity—can affirm the divine sonship of all people. On the basis of this divine sonship the redemption not only of Jews but of humanity as a whole in God's basic concern. The path of such redemption is loving, filial obedience. Christians can respond sympathetically to such an approach by stressing Jesus' role as exemplar. Not only is Jesus God's Son but all human beings can discover their sonship to God through that example.

Naturally Christians follow the royal understanding of sonship as well as the rabbinic one. A recognition of Jewish restlessness with this messianic claim may help dialogue. Jews restrict sonship to obedience to Torah law. The political problems associated with the royal claim to an exclusive, individual relationship with the divine should be taken into account. A Jew cannot recognize any claim to sonship that seeks to abrogate Torah law. Even the royal understanding of sonship to God included restrictive responsibilities.

Jews, however, need to see and understand the Christian tradition as a logical extension of the royal view of adoptive sonship found in biblical and early post-biblical Judaism. They can respond favorably to Gospel themes suggesting Jesus' obediential relationship to God and his willingness to sacrifice himself. Christians can see that element of Jesus' sonship as part of a continuing tradition in Judaism. True dialogue will not mean that Jews and Christians agree on the meaning of "son of God" but that they will acknowledge the heritage they share in common and the overlapping traditions which they possess.

S. Daniel Breslauer

CHRISTIAN VIEW:

"Christ" is a title given to Jesus of Nazareth by the earliest Christian community. It is a Greek word which means "anointed," and it is the equivalent of the Hebrew *mashiah* (Messiah) (q.v.). The evidence of the Synoptic Gospels (Matthew, Mark, Luke) indicates that Jesus likely never used the title "Messiah" of himself. The few times it occurs in sayings attributed to Jesus probably reflect the faith of the early Christian community.

The two instances in which Jesus seems to accept the title are ambiguous. Peter's confession of Jesus as Christ is followed by Jesus' admonition to silence, the prediction of the Passion, and the condemnation of Peter's refusal to admit the possibility of Jesus' suffering (Mk 8:29). Jesus' response to the high priest during the trial before the Sanhedrin is very likely ironical (Mk 14:61f).

Jesus was reserved about appropriating the title "Messiah" because it could be misunderstood in terms of certain political aspects of Jewish messianic expectation, i.e., the hope of a warrior-king who would liberate his people from political oppression and foreign domination as well as inaugurate the age of universal peace and justice.

Jesus did not understand his mission in political terms. He proclaimed the immediate coming of the Kingdom of God, the reign of God in human hearts and lives. Jesus proclaimed that Kingdom in parables and proverbial sayings, which drew on daily life in first century Palestine. He manifested the Kingdom's presence in his healing ministry and in his table fellowship with the outcast and poor. Although Jesus proclaimed the presence of the Kingdom, he also described it as incomplete, to be fully accomplished in an unspecified future.

The Gospels describe Jesus as Son of God. He addressed God as Abba (Father). He depends on the Father and is obedient to him. Neither the Synoptic Gospels nor John refers explicitly to this sonship in terms of divinity. However, Jesus never refers to God as "our Father," but rather to "my Father" and "your Father." This implies a distinction in relationships, and a uniqueness in Jesus' relationship to the Father.

The early Church reflected on Jesus' life and death in light of their experience that God had raised Jesus from the dead. The community did not share Jesus' reserve about the title "Messiah" because there was no longer any danger that it would be misunderstood in political terms.

The Palestinian church changed the meaning of the biblical and rabbinic use of "messiah," understood in the first century to refer to the liberator who would inaugurate the final age of universal peace and justice. Rather, it used "messiah" to express the continuity of God's action in Jesus with his action in Israel. The Church read the Hebrew Scriptures, not in their literal meaning, but in light of their experience of Jesus, and understood him to be the fulfillment of those Scriptures.

The early Church reflected on Jesus' sonship and came to acknowledge him as divine. Such an acknowledgment is implicit in John's Gospel and Paul's epistles. It emerged explicitly by the end of the first century, in the writings of Ignatius, the bishop of Antioch. This history of Christological development until the Third Council of Constantinople (681) is one of reflection on the statement that Jesus is both God and man. It is a history of theological development in struggle with heresies which would deny either the humanity or the divinity of Jesus. The Council of Chalcedon (451) answered the question "How is Jesus both God and man?" by saying that he is God and man because he is one person with two natures, divine and human.

There have been no new doctrinal formulations about the humanity and divinity of Jesus since the Third Council of Constantinople. However, there has been a continual development in theological reflection because the Christian community must continually consider anew, in light of its ongoing historical experience, its faith in Jesus the Christ.

Christian confession of Jesus as Son of God is part of the Trinitarian understanding of God. The Son is God's eternal Word of self-communication. God communicates himself, his Word, so totally that we say that Jesus is the Son of God, the Word incarnate. In Jesus, human history becomes the history of God himself: human history with its joys and sorrows, its unfinished quality, its ultimate terror of death. In Jesus the Son, God shows us that to be truly human implies a life of loving service. In Jesus' resurrection, God reveals that his final word about human existence is not death, but life.

Christians confess the risen Jesus as Christ. They see in Jesus the one in whom the Kingdom of God has become present. There is a dialectical quality about that presence, however. Although it has been made present in Jesus' life and ministry, his death and resurrection, the Kingdom awaits in an unspecified future.

The confession of Jesus as Christ and Son of God is a matter of conversion of life as well as of verbal acknowledgment. The confession of Jesus as Christ and Son implies that one follows Jesus, assuming the pattern of his life of obedience to the Father and service of others, because love of God and love of people are linked inseparably in Jesus' proclamation of the Kingdom.

The Christian confession of Jesus' messiahship is not a political one because Jesus himself was not a political leader, nor is the Kingdom he proclaimed a political entity. However, Jesus' proclamation of the Kingdom and the Christian's confession of Jesus as Messiah can and do have political implications because (1) Jesus preached the Kingdom to all, including the socially deprived and despised, and (2) the proclamation of the Kingdom calls for loving service of others, including one's enemies. Thus, confession of Jesus is social in nature. It can and should influence one's political options, leading Christians to work for social structures which foster human growth and development, particularly among the world's poor.

Confession of Jesus as Christ is at the heart of the Jewish-Christian dialogue. Full knowledge of Jesus requires a knowledge of the Jewishness of Jesus. Lack of such knowledge opens the way to an implicit diminution of the humanity of Jesus. Thus, Jesus himself becomes a meeting-ground. The relationship of Christian confession of Jesus to Jewish-Christian dialogue is more problematic, however, than learning about the Jewishness of Jesus. Confession of Jesus as Christ is central to Christian identity. Christians may not back away from confession of Jesus as Christ if they are truly to remain within the Christian community. And yet this poses difficulties for the Jewish-Christian dialogue because misinterpretation of the historical and biblical data about Jesus' messiahship gave rise to the charge of deicide and to ensuing persecution of Jews by Christians. Furthermore, this misinterpretation and its consequences contributed to the Holocaust.

Ultimately the question is: How can the Christian confess Jesus as Christ and Son of God while allowing room for the validity of Judaism (as well as other religions)? The events of the Holocaust have led some theologians to reflect anew on the meaning of the confession of Jesus as Christ. Some would suggest that one might understand Jesus' messianic role in terms of covenant. Jesus the Christ might be understood as the link between Israel and the Gentile world. Through Jesus the covenant is opened to all people, thus making the Gentiles members in the covenant between God and Israel. Other theologians have considered the Christian confession in terms of creation, revelation, and eschatology. Theological consideration is still fragmentary for the most part because of the relatively short period of time in which people have been involved in this investigation. The present challenge for the Christian is to remain true to the confession of Jesus as Christ while exploring new understandings of that confession and respecting Jews in terms of their own self-understanding(s) and self-definition(s).

Celia Deutsch

Church and Synagogue

JEWISH VIEW:

The word synagogue derives from the Greek translation of the Hebrew phrase *Beit Keneset,* house of assembly. For thousands of years the synagogue has served as a basic institution of Jewish life—as a house of prayer, learning, social gathering, communal government. According to Jewish law, it is incumbent upon every community to establish a synagogue, and all members of a community are obligated to contribute to its establishment and maintenance. It can be fairly stated that the synagogue has played the greatest role in the preservation and development of the Jewish people and Jewish religion. Indeed, the synagogue has also served as the forerunner of institutions of communal worship adapted by Christianity and Islam.

Some traditions ascribe the origins of the synagogue to Moses himself. Synagogues would have provided people with the opportunity of hearing the reading of the Torah and reciting prayers in relatively small communal settings. However, actual historical evidence concerning the origin of the synagogue is small, and a variety of theories have been posited by scholars. It seems most likely that synagogues emerged during the period of the Babylonian exile, following the destruction of the First Temple in Jerusalem in 586 BCE. It would have been natural for the Jewish exiles in Babylonia to seek to establish an institution to replace the destroyed Temple. The synagogue served as a meeting place and it is fair to assume that the Jews met in synagogues on Sabbaths where prayers were recited and scriptures were read.

Some scholars argue that synagogues existed during the period of First Temple, while others date its origin to a much later period, during the Hellenistic period. Jewish tradition attributes the formulation of early prayers—the Amidah, Kiddush, Havdalah—to Ezra and the Men of the Great

Synagogue. This tradition might presuppose the existence of synagogues at that time.

By the first century of the Common Era, the synagogue emerges as a well-established, ancient institution. Literary and archeological evidence points to the existence of synagogues throughout the places of Jewish settlement. Josephus mentions synagogues in Tiberias, Dora and Caesarea. The New Testament has a number of references to synagogues both in Israel and in the Diaspora visited by Paul. The Talmud (TB *Sukkah* 51b) notes the existence of a synagogue in Alexandria which was so large that people in the back could not hear the words of the reader in the front. A system of flag waving was developed so that those in the back of the synagogue would know when to respond to the reader. The Talmud reports the existence of hundreds of synagogues in Jerusalem alone at the time of the destruction of the Temple (TJ *Megillah* 3:1; TB *Kethuboth* 105a). Archeologists have discovered remains of synagogues dating to Temple times in Masada and Herodion.

With the destruction of the Second Temple by the Romans, the synagogue became the preeminent institution in Jewish life. It incorporated some of the customs and rituals of the Jerusalem Temple. Whereas sacrificial ritual in the Temple was known as *Abodah* ("the Service"), the synagogue ritual was known as *Abodah Shebelev,* the service of the heart, i.e., prayer. The prayer services in the synagogue were established to parallel sacrificial services which had taken place in the Temple. Synagogue liturgy includes many references to the service in the Temple in Jerusalem, as well as prayers for its re-establishment.

Synagogues differ one from the other in terms of size, style of service, architecture, etc. Some have been large and ornate, others have been small, informal and simple. Yet all synagogues have certain common features. A holy ark known as the *Hekhal Hakodesh* or *Aron Hakodesh* contains Torah scrolls. Generally, the ark is placed against the eastern wall, so that worshipers face that direction, the direction of Jerusalem. A reader's desk, known as a *Tebah or Bimah,* stands in the center of the synagogue or toward the front, and the Torah scroll is read from there. Services generally are also led from a special reader's desk. Historically, synagogues maintained separate seating for men and for women, although in modern times the Reform and Conservative synagogues do have mixed seating. For the past several centuries it has been customary for an eternal light to hang in front of the ark, as a symbol of the eternity of Israel and of the eternal providence of God. Traditionally, this eternal light was an oil lamp, although in modern times some synagogues use an electric light to serve this purpose.

The actual structure of the synagogue is considered to have sanctity, and require respect and reverence. Jewish law forbids eating, drinking, sleeping, gossiping, or doing business in the synagogue. One may not use the synagogue as a short-cut, nor may one enter the synagogue merely to avoid bad weather outside. A synagogue must be kept clean and orderly. Discussions of money are forbidden except for matters of charity or redeeming captives.

The synagogue has served as more than a house of prayer and a house of gathering. It has also been a house of learning. Sabbath services include readings from the Torah and Prophets. Synagogues have always held classes for adults and children, and the rabbi's main duty was to educate his congregation in Judaism. In the United States and elsewhere the synagogue has also become the center for a variety of community activities

The synagogue has also served as the communal government of the Jewish people. Sephardic Jews refer to the synagogue as *Kahal*, congregation. It is seen as the corporate voice of the Jewish people. It has its own religious and lay leaders who are dedicated to fostering Jewish values and Jewish practices. The Kahal is responsible for the well-being not only of its "members," but for all the Jewish people in its domain. Each synagogue, therefore, plays its role in maintaining Judaism and the Jewish people.

Marc Angel

CHRISTIAN VIEW:

The term "Church," used some one hundred and twelve times in the New Testament, renders the Hebrew term *kahal* (community of worshipers of God; cf. Dt 4:10; 2 Chr 30:13; etc.). But another translation is *synagogue*. Therefore, already on this level, there is an emphasis on the unity of God's people. Church cannot be opposed, semantically speaking, to Synagogue.

In fact, the Church saw itself in continuity with historical Israel (cf. Rom 9:11; 11:5; 15:10; 2 Pet 1:10; Eph 2) as the New Israel, a continuation of Israel, but also its consummation. This was of enormous import for the appropriation and interpretation of the Hebrew Scriptures by the Christians. (Cf. Revelation and Tradition.) As the Septuagint had become the Bible of the Greek-speaking Christians, it is its images and metaphors for the people of God which the early Church appropriated for its use and for its self-description. The Christians were "the Israel of God" (Gal 6:16), in contrast with an "Israel by the flesh" only, i.e., a promise in need of the Christian fulfillment (cf. Rom 9:6ff). Whereas to the Israelites "belong adoption, glory, covenants, law, cult, promises, fathers," and even Christ (Rom 9:5), the Church has to demarcate itself vis-à-vis the Synagogue. Thus it is the "new covenant"—a covenant sealed with the house of Israel: Heb 8:8–10—which displays the decisive characteristic of transcending the former Jewish boundaries and of incorporating the Gentiles (cf. Rom 11:17; Eph 2:12; Rev 5:9f).

Indeed, the marks of identity and glory of historical Israel were the "shadow of things to come" (Col 2:17) and those things are now present in the Church. Thus, e.g., the circumcision in the flesh has left room for "the true circumcision" (Phil 3:3; Col 2:11–14) which is no surgical operation, but a circumcision of the heart (Rom 2:29), as the prophets had wished it to be (cf. Jer 4:4; 9:25; Dt 10:16; 30:6; cf. Sir 35:1ff). Similarly, the consummated people of God are the Temple (cf. 2 Cor 6:16), for God does not really dwell in a human made building (Acts 17:24). The latter was the provision, foretaste, promise of the Temple which is indestructible and supernatural, i.e., the full presence of God within the human (cf. 1 Cor 3:16; 6:19; 2 Cor 6:16; Rev 7:15). Such is the Church, because its Master is none else but the Incarnation of God's Word (cf. Jn 1:14). The same passage from the "carnal" to the "spiritual" applies, according to early Christianity, to all Israel's features. The Church is the true Jerusalem (Heb 12; Rev 2–3; 21–22); the twelve tribes of Israel (Mt 19:28; Jas 1:1; Rev 7:4; 21:12), "Abraham's offspring" (Gal 3:29), "the people of God" (*ho laos tou theou:* Rom 9:26; 1 Pet 2:10), etc.

All this proceeds clearly from the fundamental Christian conviction of being the eschatological community proleptically hailed by the prophets (cf. Jer 31:31ff; Ez 36:24–28) and patterned by the apocalypticians. The latter point is of special importance. It can be said that all apocalyptic thinking is underpinned by the notion of *tabnit* (model, and antitype, archetype) after which not only the Tabernacle in the desert (cf. Ex 25:9, 40), but every religious aspect of historical Israel, her features and institutions, has been tailored. The End-time is a retrieval of the origins ("Ur-Zeit") inasmuch as the types give room to the antitype(s).

Paul and his followers, however, are careful to show that one cannot speak of the substitution of Israel by the Church. But because such apostolic wisdom was not to the taste of the Gentile Church, whose influence became more and more preponderant in Christianity, the idea has prevailed of the sheer rejection by God of his former people and his adoption of a new one, non-Jewish. Thus was made one of the most far-reaching and tragic mistakes in history. The New Testament dialectics of the promise and fulfillment, represented respectively by "Israel" and the Church, was traded for the hatred of the "perfect," the enlightened, the angelic, vis-à-vis the imperfect, the blind, the Satanic (cf. already in Rev 2:9 and 3:9 "the Synagogue of Satan"). An awful historical crescendo of antisemitic outbursts wound up in the Nazi extermination camps where European Jewry was nearly annihilated. The Church carries the brunt of the greatest crime ever, committed in its name mostly by people claiming to be Christians. (Cf. Repentance.)

It is thus urgently needed that the Church reassess "antisemitic" texts in the New Testament (particularly in the Johannine Gospel), and reflect upon the much more balanced developments of Romans 9–11 and Ephesians 2. The relation of Church and Synagogue receives light from the consciousness of the Church to be the fulfillment of the people of God on three theological levels (after M. Cerfaux): (1) Eschatologically, the Church brings the Hebrew Scriptures' Israel to her plenitude; it is the "pleromatic" Israel. (2) Mystically, the Church is the Body of Christ, i.e., it is Christ continued, perpetuated, extended, and proliferated ("democratized"). (3) Apocalyptically, the Church is the heavenly City. Its feet are on the earth, while its head is already with God on high.

André Lacocque

Covenant

JEWISH VIEW:

Covenant in religious terms refers to an agreement between God and human beings. The concept that the Almighty and Eternal God would make a covenant with mortals whom he has created is itself a striking theological insight. It supposes that God maintains a relationship with human beings and is willing to bind himself in some ways to the terms expressed in covenants.

Covenants between God and human beings are a vital feature of the Jewish Bible (q.v.). Following the flood, God spoke to Noah and his sons saying: "As for me, behold, I establish my covenant with you and with your seed after you and with every living creature that is with you....And I will establish my covenant with you; neither shall all flesh be cut off anymore by waters of the flood; neither shall there anymore be a flood to destroy the earth" (Gen 9:9–11). And God set the rainbow in the sky as an eternal token of this agreement.

God made a covenant with Abraham, promising the patriarch that he would be the father of a great and numerous nation, and that his people would forever possess the land of Canaan: "I will maintain my covenant throughout the ages, to be God to you and to your offspring to come. I give the land you sojourn in to you and your offspring to come, all the land of Canaan, as an everlasting possession; and I will be their God" (Gen 17:7–8). God re-established this covenant with Isaac and Jacob (Gen 22:15–18).

God established a covenant with the entire people of Israel at Mount Sinai. He revealed himself to the people, gave his Commandments, and emphasized the special relationship between the people of Israel and God. The people of Israel accepted the responsibility to observe God's Commandments and in return God promised his blessings for the people. If Israel reneges on its responsibilities, God warns of a host of punishments and curses. But God also promises that the covenant he has established with Israel is eternal, that he will never terminate his covenant with the people of Israel. After listing numerous punishments which will befall Israel if they do not fulfill the Commandments, God reminds them: "I will remember my covenant with Jacob, and my covenant with Isaac, and also my covenant with Abraham will I remember; and I will remember the land.…When they are in the land of their enemies, I will not reject them, neither will I abhor them, to destroy them utterly, and to break my covenant with them; for I am the Lord their God. But I will for their sakes remember the covenant of their ancestors whom I brought forth out of the land of Egypt in the sight of the nations that I might be their God: I am the Lord" (Lev 26:42, 44–45).

The eternal nature of God's covenant with Israel and its irreversibility is a fundamental aspect of Judaism. Even when Israel is in exile and is suffering oppression, the Jew may never conclude that God has abandoned his relationship with Israel. The prophets of the Bible speak of a renewal of God's covenant with Israel, cf his ultimate restoration of Israel to its land, to its blessings.

It is especially important that this idea of covenant be understood in the Jewish-Christian dialogue. Any suggestion by Christians that God's covenant with Israel has been transferred to a "new Israel" is obviously offensive to Jewish beliefs. Any statement implying that God's covenant with the Jewish people has been discontinued or has been replaced by a covenant with others is totally unacceptable to Jewish religious belief, and goes against the Bible itself.

The idea of a "covenant of grace" in Christian covenant theology has its own meanings and interpretations, and is based on Christian assumptions. Judaism does not interpret Adam's sin as a "fall" which required a new covenant of grace. Rather, in the Jewish view, all human beings are confronted with good and evil, right and wrong. Everyone is expected to make the right choices, but everyone—at one time or another—will choose incorrectly, will commit sins. He is expected to repent for sins, to improve his ways. Punishment for sins may be forthcoming either in this world or in the world to come. The spiritual struggle of making proper choices and avoiding sin has been part of human nature since Adam and Eve. Each individual has the power to repent, to turn to God and to gain God's forgiveness. Judaism does not teach that one must be "saved" by a special act of God's grace.

The Hebrew word designating covenant is *Berit*. Abraham was circumcised as a sign of the covenant between himself and God. To this day, the circumcision ceremony is known among Jews as *Berit Milah*, the covenant of circumcision. For Jews, then, circumcision is not viewed merely as a medical procedure, but as a religious act which brings the baby boy into the covenant.

One born of a Jewish mother is by his or her very birth part of the people of Israel. By birth, a Jew is automatically bound to the covenant established between God and the ancient Israelites at Mount Sinai. It is not a matter of free choice. Any Jew who does not fulfill the obligations of the covenant will be held responsible by God. According to Jewish law, even if a Jew renounces the covenant or converts to another religion, he remains Jewish notwithstanding, bound to the covenant in spite of anything he says or does. He shares the covenant by destiny.

A non-Jew may choose to enter Israel's covenant with God by converting. A convert to Judaism is expected to learn and accept the terms of the covenant, i.e., the Commandments, the responsibilities, the spiritual benefits. The conversion process is not complete for a male until he has been circumcised, the physical sign of Israel's covenant with God. Both male and female converts are required to be immersed in a ritual bath, symbolic of spiritual rebirth as members of the Jewish people.

Although individuals who are born Jewish are automatically partners in the covenant with God, their upbringing and education should lead them to an intellectual awareness of the rights and responsibilities of the covenant so that they will be knowledgeable and enlightened participants. With proper education and spiritual development, a Jew learns to accept the covenant with God by choice, with free will.

Marc Angel

CHRISTIAN VIEW:

The Bible knows more than one type of covenant. But whatever its diversity in kinds, covenant in Israel is "a compact which originally grounds nature upon an ethical infrastructure. Time is initiated by a covenant, and through the ongoing experience of its renewal at each moment, time continues" (E. Amado L. Valensy). The Israelite conception that God and his people are bound by a relationship of mutuality and even intimacy is probably the most profound and far-reaching revelation in human history.

It has been shown by modern scholarship that covenant making in

Israel was on the model of the ancient Near Eastern treaties known in the region since the eighteenth century BCE. All the conditional formulas used in Israel to indicate that the people are under oath vis-à-vis God, and owe him total obedience, like a vassal to his suzerain, follow the same traditional six part pattern with specific speculations.

At the basis of the relationship which binds Israel to God, there is a *covenant of grant,* i.e., an unconditional commitment of God to his people. The paradigm is provided by the covenant with Abraham (cf. Gen 15; 17:1–14). Jeremiah 34 echoes Genesis 15: no obligation is sworn to by Abraham (circumcision is no condition, but a sign of the covenant). Similarly, the tie created by God with David (2 Sam 23:5; Pss 89; 110), or with Phinehas (Num 25:10-13), or with Noah and the whole of humanity (Gen 6–9), is without pre-condition, and, in the case of Noah as with the circumcision, there is a sign of its perenniality, the rainbow.

This exploration into the history of the covenant in Israel was necessary, because, in the New Testament, the accent is definitely on divine initiative. The Greek term used is in general *diatheke,* which indicates a disposition of unilateral will, or even of last will and testament. Therefore, it corresponds better to *natan berit* (to grant a covenant) than to *karat berit* (to make a covenant with) in the Hebrew Scriptures. Thus, spontaneously, the writers of New Testament literature emphasized this aspect of the covenant which corresponded so well to their key concept of "only by grace." Moreover, as we saw, in doing that, they stressed the genuinely Israelite version of covenant, and restored laws and prohibitions within the provisionary framework where, in their judgment, they belong (cf. Law-Halakha).

Furthermore, the granting of the covenant is made "in the blood of Christ," according to Ephesians 2:13. The Epistle to the Hebrews concurs in showing that the former purification, through levitical rites, of "the copies of the heavenly things" has now received its full significance in the purification, in Christ's blood, of "the heavenly things themselves" (9:23). This is thus "a better covenant" (7:22), for it is sealed by a "once-for-all sacrifice" (9:28, etc.), viz., the sacrifice of the man who was the Son of God, superior to any angel (ch. 1), to Moses (ch. 3), to any high priest, even Melchizedek (ch. 5–7), to any sacrificial victim (ch. 9), and whose "spiritual (i.e., authentic and definitive) worship" has been offered to God once-for-all (ch. 10; cf. Rom 12:1).

Paul goes so far as to oppose, in Galatians 4:21–28, the covenant of servitude, signified by the present Jerusalem, and the covenant of freedom, signified by the Jerusalem above. The same idea appears in 2 Corinthians 3:6 where the covenant with the Church is a covenant in the Spirit, in contrast with a written code. Here again, the crux is the opposition between a relationship regulated by decrees and prohibitions, versus a relationship whose "new commandment," as John puts it (13:34, cf. Rom 13:8–10), is love, i.e., not a command but a spontaneous response of gratitude toward God.

As is well known, Paul considers the new era inaugurated in Christ as the antitype of the covenant "of grant" we saw established by God with Abraham. It is purposely that he bypasses the covenant at Sinai whose axis is historical and temporal. The covenant at Sinai promotes an order of redemption co-terminous with the order of creation.

With the Davidic (or Abrahamic) covenant, on the other hand, the relationship between God and the king precedes history and is not subject to historical contingency. There is here no human transgression which could cancel the effect of election, for indeed there is *no law* (especially under the Abrahamic form of such a covenant).

Moreover, the Law given on Mount Sinai came four hundred years after the covenant with Abraham, and it was given by God only for a time (cf. Gal 3:15ff). For Paul, this discrepancy in time between the promise and the condition for its fulfillment emphasizes the gratuity of God's grace and, consequently, the inanity of human efforts to satisfy God's demands. True, the Sinai covenant is a divine gift to Israel, itself also a grace which the Jews are forever enjoying (cf. Rom 9:2f). But it is to be put in the light of its fulfillment in Christ to be appreciated as really liberating (cf. 2 Cor 3:16–18).

Redemption is by divine decree. The people benefit from the divine grant (grace, in the New Testament) through the mediation of the Anointed. From the historicity of the Sinai covenant, we have passed to transhistoricity, according to a mythical conception that reasserted itself in apocalypticism. The latter had a deep influence upon the New Testament religion.

We can thus conclude that, in the expression "*new* covenant" (1 Cor 11:25; 2 Cor 3:6; Heb 8:13, 9:15; cf. Jer 31:31), the term "new" means that all the events of old have received their full, total, "pleromatic," sense. They are now unimpeded by any limitation of "the flesh." It is first in the realm of the covenant that Jesus on the Cross exclaims, "All is accomplished."

André Lacocque

Creation

JEWISH VIEW:

The dramatic and mysterious creation story which opens the Bible has left a deep impact on all serious readers. As the opening of the Torah, it has certainly been of tremendous significance to Jewish thought.

The rabbis of the Talmud were not very concerned with the "scientific" aspects of the story. Rather, they drew certain moral lessons which have greatly influenced Jewish thought. Since God created the world, the world has value and meaning. The universe did not come into being by a series of random accidents of nature. God designed the universe and governs it. Human beings are morally responsible for their behavior because God is their Creator and has created them to have a moral dimension.

The creation story demonstrates God's awesome power. By his "words" alone, he was able to fashion the universe. The recognition of God as Creator leads to profound religious awareness. Maimonides, in his *Mishneh Torah* (*Fundamentals of the Torah,* chapter 2, paragraph 2), writes: "What is the way that leads to the love of him and the fear of him? When a person contemplates his great and wondrous acts and creations, obtaining from them a glimpse of his wisdom which is beyond compare and infinite, he will immediately love and glorify him, longing greatly to know the great Name of God, as David said: 'My whole being thirsts for God, the living God.' When he ponders over these subjects, he will quickly recoil, and become afraid, realizing that he is only a lowly, obscure creature, as David said: "As I look up to the heavens your fingers made...what is man that you should think of him?'" God as Creator inculcates in human beings humility and spiritual longing.

The aspect of the creation story most emphasized in rabbinic literature is perhaps the story of the creation of human beings. The Talmud (TB *Sanhedrin* 37a) teaches: why did God create only one person, Adam, rather than filling the earth with people all at once? The answer: so that no one can say that his ancestry is superior to anyone else's. All people go back to one source. No individual or group has the right to think that it is superior to any other individual or group based on ancestry. The fact is, we are all descendants of the same ancestors, and in that respect all human beings are equal.

God created human beings in his own image. Rabbinic tradition generally defines "image" to mean that people have souls, intellect, spirituality qualities. The Talmud (TB *Sanhedrin* 37a) teaches the unique quality of God's creating human beings. When a person makes a mold—an image—from which he strikes coins, each coin comes out like the other. They are uniform and without individual identity. Yet God created human beings in his own image, but all human beings differ one from the other. Each person is unique, distinguished from all others.

The creation story also provides the basis for the Sabbath. God created the world in six days and on the seventh he rested. Likewise, human beings may work for six days, but on the Sabbath they must rest. The Friday evening *Kiddush,* the prayer over wine introducing the first Sabbath meal, begins with the passage at the end of the creation story, describing the Sabbath.

There has been a general reluctance in Jewish tradition to speculate on the metaphysical aspects of creation. The Mishnah (TB *Hagigah* 2:1) rules that one is not allowed to teach *Maaseh Bereshit* (mysteries of creation) in the presence of two people. The subject is so esoteric that it may only be transmitted on a one-to-one basis, and only to individuals who have substantial intellectual ability. Rabbi Yaacob Huli, in opening his Judeo-Spanish biblical commentary on Genesis, represents the mainstream Jewish tradition when he writes: "It is important not to probe too deeply into the mysteries. We should not try to find out what the world was like before heaven and earth were created, or what it will be like after they no longer exist....The human mind obviously cannot even grasp a thousandth of all this, so it is best not to think of these things at all. If a person spends his time contemplating these things, it would have been better if he had never been born." Yet, there were always individuals who did engage in metaphysical speculation, especially philosophers and kabbalists.

The general Jewish attitude throughout the ages has been that God created the world *ex nihilo.* Medieval Jewish philosophy was particularly concerned with refuting the Greek philosophical notion that matter was eternal. In his *Guide for the Perplexed,* Maimonides concludes that it is impossible to prove by reason that matter is eternal. Since reason cannot compel us to believe in the eternity of matter, we may rely on our faith that God created matter, that God's existence preceded the creation of matter.

With the rise of modern science, especially the theory of evolution, the biblical creation story has come under attack in some circles. Yet, there is no fundamental conflict between the biblical story and the evolutionary theory. First, the Bible is not a science textbook. Its interest is to provide a moral framework for human life. It is ludicrous to analyze its verses as though they were scientific axioms. Moreover, the biblical creation story itself does present a general pattern of evolution in creation, from inanimate to animate creations, from simple to complex organisms. From a Jewish point of view, it would be perfectly acceptable to believe that God created the universe through a process of evolution. The important statement for Judaism is that God did in fact create the world; an evolutionary process did not simply happen by itself, but was set into motion by God.

When the Bible speaks of God creating the world in six days, it may be speaking figuratively. The word *yom* (day) in the creation story can hardly be proved to be referring to a day of twenty-four hours. After all, the sun itself was not created until the fourth "day," so it is impossible to argue that the first three "days" were days as we know them. A more appropriate way to understand the creation story is that God created the universe in six stages, and each of these stages may have taken millions of years, or twenty-four hours, or instants. In short, Judaism insists that God created the world, that he created it in stages, and that he continues to maintain the universe which he created. The specific details of the creation process are not central to Jewish thought.

Judaism emphasizes God's providence. He did not create the world and then abandon it. Rather, he continually is involved with his creations. The morning prayers state that God renews his creation each day, that nothing could continue to exist without God's continuous creativity and providence.

In discussing the topic of creation, we must also note the Jewish belief that God is one (cf. Dogma), that he created everything. Judaism rejects polytheism, dualism, pantheism. Whatever exists—whether it appears to us as good or evil—emanates from only one source: God.

Marc Angel

CHRISTIAN VIEW:

It is of particular interest that Israel starts its own tradition with a cry of victory. Creation is from the outset God's triumph (cf. Pss 74:12–17;

89:10–13; Jb 26:12–14; Is 27:1; 51:9); it is also what initiates history. As has been said, "the Genesis myth starts with what Aristotle called the *telos*, the developed form to which all living things grow" (N. Frye). This will prove important, especially with regard to the notion of "new creation."

Meanwhile, it must be stressed that Israel took its distance from the cosmological myths of the nations. In Chapter 1 of Genesis, which belongs to the "P" school of biblical sources (Wellhausen's concept), all traces of myth have disappeared. To the ideology of natural recurrence, Israel has substituted the historical vision of the existential relationship between the divine and the human. Therefore, creation in Israel appears as an aspect only of covenant/redemption. Paradoxically, God creates the universe because he cares for, loves, saves, the world. Or, as the rabbis put it, the world has been created for Abraham/Israel.

Creation is thus not at the center of Israel's concern. At the center is the historical-existential relationship between God and Israel, and, through Israel, humankind. It is from this perspective that creation is shown as being in process (*creatio continua*); cf. Jer 5:22, Prov 8:29; Is 44:24; Ps 104. The continuity of life on earth is the outcome of God's grace. It is one and the same thing to say that God keeps us alive, that he saves or redeems us, or that he creates us.

What is emphasized in the doctrine of creation is the unlimited divine power, and, by contrast, the preposterous human weakness (cf., e.g., Ps 33:8; Jb 10:9). It is clear that some event must sometime intervene if the course of history is to shift from failure to victory, in the image of the initial victory celebrated in Genesis 1 and elsewhere.

It is thus not surprising to learn that, like everything *in* the world—including its redeeming elements such as kingship, priesthood, prophecy, temple, and even Torah—"heaven and earth will pass away" (Mt 24:35; Mk 13:31; Lk 21:33; cf. Is 13:13; 34:4; 51:6; 65:17). In other words, the present creation is only temporary, a type of things to come. There will be a new beginning and the human being will be granted a new heart (Jer 31:31–34; Ez 36:26–28; cf. Hos 2:20–25; Is 11:6–9); a new heaven and a new earth will replace the former ones (Is 66:22; cf., in general, Second Isaiah). At last, in the new creation, there will be no sin and no death, no war and no corruption, no finitude and no evil, but only the praising of God (cf. Rev. 21:1–4; 4:8–11).

The New Testament proclaims the advent of that new world as fulfillment of existence since the beginning (Mt 25:34; Jn 17:24; Eph 1:4; etc.) and accomplishment of the *Heilsgeschichte* (Eph 1:9–10). Christ is the coherence of all things (Col. 1:15–17). that is why Christ is said to have preceded creation as he is its meaning. Similarly, the rabbis had made lists of things pre-existent to the actual world (Israel, Torah, Temple, repentance, Messiah). As wisdom literature had speculated that God created by means of wisdom (cf. Prov 8:12ff, Jb 28:12ff), seeing in the first word of the Bible an indication of the agent of creation: "by means of the prime (here: wisdom), God created heaven and earth," the Pauline and Johannine writings affirm that the Prime is indeed Christ. By means of Christ, God created.

In the New Testament, John especially identifies Christ with the Logos (1:1ff, etc.) and purposely starts his Gospel with the very words of Genesis 1:1; then he proceeds with the opposition of light and darkness. It is for him an occasion to stress the inclusiveness of Christ as the one who is before and after creation, surrounding it on all sides (cf. Rev 1:17; 22:13) and permeating it to transfigure it (Jn 8:12, etc.; cf. 2 Cor 4:6; 5:17).

An important feature of the new creation is that it is instituted by divine grace, so that "it depends not upon man's will or exertion but upon God's mercy" (Rom 9:16). So in this new world, birthright is of no currency, for the whole of humankind is reconciled in Christ (Eph 2:11–22), and, since the knowledge of God is now covering the world as waters cover the bottom of the sea (Is 11:9), there is no need any longer for one (here, Israel) teaching his neighbor or brother (the nations), for "they all know me…says the Lord" (Jer 31:34).

André Lacocque

Dogma

JEWISH VIEW:

Dogma is generally defined as a definite tenet, or a doctrine of religion formally and authoritatively stated by the heads of the religion. Dogmas so proclaimed establish the boundaries of religious belief. One who accepts the dogmas is a believer; one who rejects the dogmas is a heretic and forfeits his membership in the religious community which accepts the dogmas.

By the above definition, it is exceedingly difficult to discuss dogma in relation to Judaism. Whereas Christianity has been very concerned with dogmas and has had a host of important synods to draw up statements of Christian beliefs, Judaism has been relatively unconcerned with dogma. Jewish history reveals few examples of rabbinic conferences which were convened with the purpose of establishing permanent formulas expressing Jewish beliefs. Since every Jew is by birth automatically a partner in the covenant (q.v.) between God and Israel, membership in the Jewish community is not dependent on one's acceptance or rejection of specific beliefs.

Certainly, Judaism does have theological beliefs. Yet, the overwhelming emphasis of Judaism has been on behavior. The Torah and later Jewish law teach Jews how to behave in an ethical and spiritual fashion, how to fulfill the Commandments of God. Even if a person has intellectual difficulty affirming some of the basic beliefs of Judaism, he is still obligated to fulfill the Commandments, to behave according to the norms of Jewish law.

Historically, there have been some attempts by individual rabbis to formulate articles of faith. Generally, these formulations have come in reaction to heretical beliefs which were threatening the integrity of Judaism. The Mishnah opening the tenth chapter of the tractate *Sanhedrin* begins with the famous statement that all Israel has a place in the world to come, except those who deny resurrection of the dead or the divine origin of the Torah, or who oppose rabbinic teachings.

In his introduction to his commentary on this Mishnah, Maimonides formulated thirteen principles of faith which he considered essential to Judaism. They are:

1. God is Author and Guide of all creation.
2. God is a Unity.
3. God is free from all accidents of matter and has no form.
4. God is the first and last.
5. Prayer must be directed to God alone.
6. All the words of the Prophets are true.
7. Moses was the chief Prophet and his prophecy was true.
8. The whole Law, as it now stands, was given to Moses.
9. This Law will not be changed, and there will not be any other law from God.
10. God knows all human beings and their thoughts.
11. God rewards those who keep the Commandments and punishes those who trespass them.
12. Belief in the coming of the Messiah.
13. Belief in resurrection of the dead.

These thirteen principles have been popularized in a hymn known as *Yigdal,* which is sung in the synagogue following the evening services of festivals and Friday nights.

Another medieval rabbi, Joseph Albo, reduced Judaism to three main principles: belief in God, in the divinity of the Torah, in reward and punishment. Other medieval thinkers developed other sets of principles.

Yet, all these formulations have been of peripheral importance to Judaism, and Judaism would be perfectly intact even if none of the formulations had ever been made. Moreover, even if a Jew rejects one or more of the principles of faith articulated by a particular rabbinic authority, he still remains part of the Jewish people and subject to Jewish law. For example, there are many non-Orthodox religious leaders who would not accept such principles as the divinity of the Torah, resurrection of the dead, or the coming of an individual Messiah. Nevertheless, they do not cease to be members of the Jewish people and advocates of Judaism.

In sum, dogma does not play the same role in Judaism as it does in Christianity. In any Jewish-Christian dialogue, it is essential to recognize the great difference of emphasis between the two religions concerning dogma.

Marc Angel

CHRISTIAN VIEW:

Formulations of the tenets of Christian faith came to existence as reactions to heresies which have always abounded side by side with the Church.

Christianity, it is true, like Judaism, started by being an orthopraxis rather than an orthodoxy. Even the Greek term "dogma" in the Septuagint and the New Testament (usually translated as "decree") refers to the ethical sphere (cf. Est 3:9; Dan 2:13; Lk 2:1). Only with time did the word evolve and designate a tenet of faith. From the sense of the Greek *dokeo,* which means "it seems to me," it took over the meaning of "it is to me an established fact." At the time of St. Chrysostom (fourth century), it meant a truth above reason revealed by Christ to the Church.

The Church developed dogma along the line initiated by Chrysostom. Fending off what it considered as heresies of all kinds, the Roman Catholic Church later promulgated an ever increasing number of dogmas. This it did on the authority of Scripture and Christian Tradition so that, from the outset, there is here an equation between the authority of God and the authority of the Church. Indeed, the dogmatization of religion implies the infallibility of the Church in its magisterium. There is something of a parallel between this stance and the rabbinic law of majority as expressed, e.g., in TB *Baba Meziah* 59b where a *bat kol* (divine judgment) is "defeated" by a majority decision of rabbis. A further parallel is to be seen in the Catholic Church's consciousness of continually uncovering the meaning of what has been revealed in the founding event—in one case Sinai, in the other case Christ.

Quite a number of dogmatic beliefs are held in common by Jews and Christians: monotheism, God's care for human beings, the divine inspiration of Scriptures, the resurrection of the dead, etc. Even a non-biblical belief such as the immortality of the soul can be found in many forms of Judaism and of Christianity.

Karl Barth, who has written a multi-volume *Church Dogmatics,* has expressed skepticism as to the objective content of formulations of religious truths. In the Scriptures, as a matter of fact, God is described as revealing himself, not truths or propositions for belief. It is an invitation to enter communion with him, not a series of catechismal facts. And here we come to a fundamental *caveat*. Dogma consists in fact in extracting a general truth from the "letter" of the text. This means that the metaphoricity of biblical narrative is disregarded and twisted into a dogmatic statement. A clear example is provided by the literalness with which the Church reads the midrash of the Nativity in the Gospels of Matthew and Luke, thus seeing the miracle where it is not, and not seeing it where it actually is.

In the dialogue with Jews, the Church rediscovers that dogma is at the most a heuristic approximation to the truth. Dogma is on the same level with symbol and metaphor. Thus, in a way, dogma is but another form for the direct experience of the sacred.

André Lacocque

Election

JEWISH VIEW:

The basis of Judaism, now as in previous ages, is that God chose the Jews to be his people. Jews and non-Jews can rejoice in this, or rebel against it, but it remains one of the mysteries of creation.

In his comment to the very first verse of the Bible, Rashi, the best-known medieval Jewish commentator, asks: Why did God begin the Torah with creation? Why not with the commandment to sacrifice the paschal lamb, i.e., with the commandments that are addressed to the Jewish people and which inform the existence of that people? The answer Rashi gives, relying on the classic sources, is: so that, whenever anyone would claim that God's election of the Jewish people and the Holy Land was spurious, the Jews could reply that God's choice is rooted in his being the Creator. He created the whole universe and, by that authority, he can, and did, choose the Jews and the Holy Land as vessels of his will and holiness.

God, then, chose Adam, Noah, Abraham, Isaac, Jacob, the tribes, and their decendants, the Jews. He elected them as his people. Jews read this in the Bible and celebrate it in their liturgy. God's election of the Jews, however, has three important thrusts. The first is that chosenness is bound up with the covenant (q.v.) and, hence, with God's expectations of the Jewish people. The election is for service. In this sense, we hear the refrain of the Book of Deuteronomy (cf. 26:16–19) and of the prophets (cf. Jer 31:33; Hos 2:23): "If you do my will and observe my Torah, I shall be your God and you will be my people. And, if you do not hearken unto my voice, punishment shall come upon you." The Jew, then, is chosen, but chosen to serve, to embody the will of God on earth. The Jew is chosen to be the Torah incarnate.

Election is of the flesh, not only of the spirit. This dimension of election has been labeled racist by some. It is not at all racist in the sense that twentieth century racism has used that ideology to justify the eradication or violent suppression of other races. No such motifs can be said to inhere in God's election of the Jewish people, and any such claims are nothing but distortions.

The third thrust of the doctrine of election is that, even if the Jews disobey God and invoke his wrath, they are still chosen. Because election is of the flesh, it is parental. A child is always the child of his/her parents, even if the parents are very angry, even if they reject the child. So it is with the Jews: they are always God's elect. And, as a corollary, God's election of the Jews will reach its fulfillment in the days of the Messiah when the hearts of the children will be reconciled to the heart of the Father. God has not rejected, and does not reject, his people. Rather, they and he must wait until the time for reunion comes.

The interweaving of these themes is clearly seen in Deuteronomy 7:7–11: "For you are a holy people to the Lord, your God; you has he chosen to be a special people from all peoples upon the face of the earth. Not because you were the most numerous of all the peoples did the Lord desire you and choose you, for you were the least of all the peoples. Rather, because the Lord loved you and because he honored the oath he had sworn to your forefathers, did he take you out with a mighty hand, redeeming you from the hand of Pharaoh the king of Egypt. So that you might know that the Lord your God is God, the faithful Master, honoring the covenant and the grace for those whom he loves and for those who observe his commandments even unto the thousandth generation. He also requites those who hate him to their face, destroying them; he does not tarry with his enemy but requites him/her to his/her face. Observe, then, this command, these laws, and these statutes which I have commanded you to do."

Similarly, the terrible curse that is to fall upon the disobedient people as related in Leviticus concludes: "Even then, when they are in the land of their enemies, I will not reject or spurn them, so as to destroy them, annulling my covenant with them: for I the Lord am their God; but I will remember in their favor the covenant with the ancients, whom I freed from the land of Egypt, in the sight of the nations, to be their God: I the Lord" (26:44–45).

One of the most fascinating developments in the doctrine of the election is its secularization in the last hundred years. Jews who, for a variety of intellectual reasons, reject the supernatural election of the Jews by the Creator accept the implicit assumption of some kind of election. Usually, such thinkers root this "election" in Jewish history, pointing to the fact of

Jewish survival over five millennia. They also point to the continuing high ethical aspirations that have characterized Jewish culture throughout history. And, finally, they point to the special destiny for which the Jews seem to be fated.

Whether in its religious or in its secular form, chosenness has been perceived by many as a burden. Jonah is the classical example, the man who tries to flee God and cannot. The Jews who tried to deny the peoplehood dimension of Jewish existence in favor of religious rationalism in the modern era are another. The facticity and the demand of election remain one of the mysteries.

Christianity, while it has a clear concept of covenant, does not understand that covenant to be of the flesh. The election of the Jews as a people is thus difficult to grasp. The secularized understanding of chosenness is even more difficult to understand. For Christianity, the covenant is spiritualized into the faith and the Church. It is entered and left by an act of human will. This is not so for the Jewish understanding. Discussion of these matters is a fruitful subject for dialogue.

David Blumenthal

CHRISTIAN VIEW:

For many Christian scholars, election holds a primary place as a primary theme in the Old Testament. The Christian view sees the descendants of Abraham as the special object of God's love and promises. Often the notion of election was related to a calling to a particular task or office, as in the case of the prophets (e.g., Amos, Isaiah, Jeremiah), the king (e.g., David), and the priests and Levites.

Tied very closely to the notion of election, then, would be the notion of covenant. Covenant conjures in the Christian mind thoughts of God's faithfulness to those he has chosen and reciprocity of relationships.

But the notion of election, as beautiful as it is, has provided problems for many Christians. Sometimes Christians have seen the notion of election as difficult to transfer to the Church. Other Christians, reared in democratic or republican forms of government, have been reluctant to speak of election as a viable theological concept because of its alleged non-egalitarian character.

The first problem—the place of Christianity after, and in relation to, Jewish election—Christians addressed in their earliest writings. They asked the question: If the Jewish people are the chosen people of God and we believe that Jesus of Nazareth is the fulfillment of the promises given by God to Jews throughout their history, how does the notion of election relate to the Christian reality? Very quickly, Christians began answering their own question by stating that election has been extended, if not completely transferred, to the Christian Church. This they did by identifying Christ as "the elect of God," and Christians through faith and baptism are incorporated into him. That is, the election which Israel possessed for generations was passed on to Jesus as the Christ. The new elect are those who become part of "the Body of Christ" through entry into his Church, the new Body of Christ (cf. 1 Cor 12; Rom 12).

Problematic in such a theological construct would be the Jews' status, since their election had been passed on to someone else. Some Christians answer that the call, the choice of Israel *as a people,* has never been abrogated; the call has been extended to Christians *as individuals* (cf. Eph 1:4; 1 Pet 1:20). Others see that the election given to the Jews has been replaced by that given to the Christian Church. Certain New Testament texts have been very important in supporting this position; an example would be 1 Peter 2:4ff, which invites the newly converted Christian to "come to him (Christ), to that living stone, rejected by men but in God's sight chosen and precious.... 'The very stone which the builders rejected has become the head of the corner.'" This and other passages have been used through the ages of Christian apologetics to show that the election which was once the Jews' is no longer theirs: The Church is the new chosen people (cf. 1 Pet 2:9, 2 Tim 2:10, Rom 16:13). Furthermore, the early Christians were quick to point out the parallel of Jesus picking his followers with God's choice of Israel (compare John 15:16 with Deuteronomy 7:6). The notion of "the elect" is to be found in numerous places throughout the New Testament (cf. Rom 8:33, Col 3:12, etc.)

The second issue, that of the non-egalitarian character of election, becomes less an issue when election is seen more as a vocation than a privilege, a responsibility more than an honor. This elucidation of election can be seen in Jeremiah 31:37 where the election of Israel is intimately connected with the mission of Israel to be faithful to the one God and to be faithful to the law. Nonetheless, in the mystery of Israel, it is impossible to escape the fact that some part of election has meant the very special love which God has had for Israel, the "apple of God's eye."

In a contemporary setting, some Christians may refer to the Jews as "chosen," but feel very uncomfortable doing so—as do many Jews in being so designated. Nonetheless, some understanding of election is necessary to remind Christians of God's special love for the Jews, lest they begin to think that God reneges on his promises. If Christians are called to imitate the God they worship, then they are to have a special love for the Jews as God does. To do less is to question God's choice and to forget that our God never gives up on his chosen. The covenant which God made with Abraham has not been abrogated by Jesus.

What becomes problematic, then, for Christians is to figure out just how they can be included in the election given originally to the Jews. Has the one covenant/election, first given to the Jews as a people, been extended to Christians? Or has God, through the Jewish Jesus, entered into a new covenant with all Gentile peoples which covenant they can be part of through faith in Christ? Whatever the final answer is to these questions, Christians are guided by the words of Paul in his Letter to the Romans: the Jews "as regards election…are beloved for the sake of their forefathers" (11:28).

The notion of election is a ripe one for further Jewish-Christian dialogue. For the assertion that election has been passed on to the Christian Church, and, by implication, withdrawn from the Jews, has been a foundation for strained relations between Christians and Jews. This is called the "supersessionist theory," and it is variously expressed in the history of Christian theology. Some of these expressions are the Church as the "new (and therefore better) Israel," the Church as "the new chosen people" displacing the old, Christ as the absolute fulfillment of Old Testament prophecies (with the implicit notion that other readings of the Old Testament are ignorant or superficial), the Jewish people as merely forerunners of the Church, and the "New" Testament making the "Old" Testament obsolete or replacing it. Christians in the Jewish-Christian dialogue need to find ways of describing election which would leave room for both Christians and Jews. While Christians search for ways to understand election as their reality as well, their new understandings must not imply that God has turned his back on his election of the Jews.

Michael McGarry

Eschatology

JEWISH VIEW:

The Jewish view of the universe is well represented by the Sabbath prayer which states, "There is none to be compared to you, O Lord our God, in this world; neither is there any beside you, O our King, in the life of the world to come; there is none but you, O our Redeemer, in the messianic days; none is like you, O our Savior, for resurrecting the dead." Beyond this mundane existence Judaism posits life after death in the world to come, messianic redemption, and resurrection of the dead. This fourfold structure has only tenuous rootage in the Hebrew Bible. Biblical texts are often contradictory and show a variety of beliefs concerning life after death. One common view (found, for example, in 1 Samuel 28) was that after death a shadowy existence persisted in Sheol, the place of the "shades" wherein no praise of God was uttered. Many biblical passages deny the expectation of a meaningful life after death (Jb 14:13–15; Pss 88:10–12; 115:17–18).

In later biblical texts a more clearly eschatological expectation appears. Isaiah 24–27, held by scholars to be a later interpolation in the Isaianic tradition, introduces the idea of a post-mortem judgment. The Book of Daniel uses the same idea to justify divine justice (12:1–4). A more polemical note is sounded in 2 Maccabees where the theme of theodicy is augmented by the argument that martyrdom is incomprehensible without the hope for life after death (7:7–9, 13–14, 20–29; 12:44–46).

The ambiguity of the biblical view aggravated the tension between Pharisees and Sadducees in early post-biblical Judaism. The basis of this tension, it has been argued, is that the Pharisees sought to democratize the hope of salvation. The opponents of this view stressed class distinctions and the inherited status of the elite. Resurrection—supposedly assured for every Jew by biblical promises—equalized all classes. Ezekiel's vision of the valley of bones

(Chapter 37) was originally a parable for national revival; Pharisaic interpretation transformed it into a paradigm of individual hope for resurrection.

Because of the ambiguity of the biblical material, even Pharisees were divided about who merited resurrection. Some suggested that only martyrs would enjoy rebirth; others felt that only those dying and buried in the land of Israel would experience it. Final opinion, however, emphasized Pharisaic democracy—every Jew shares in resurrection except for those who deny its reality. The polemics in favor of the idea reveal that there were indeed those who did reject it. Rabbinic Judaism sought biblical precedent to strengthen their case for the concept of a universal resurrection. While many scholars today find the stories of Elijah and Elisha to be a self-conscious polemic which utilizes, while rejecting, pagan mythology, Pharisaic argument found in those stories prototypical examples of resurrection. Because prophets like Elijah, Elisha, and Ezekiel have already shown the possibility of bodily resurrection, the expectation of a future resurrection is not absurd. Those who reject the idea are rejecting a concept rooted in tradition.

Not only tradition but daily experience was used to bolster the credibility of the idea. Nature, according to Jewish liturgy, is recreated daily. God performs the act of creation anew each day. Nature is renewed every spring—the miracle of life-giving rain is an anticipation of the miracle of resurrection. Not surprisingly rabbinic liturgy joins the prayer for rain with the prayer praising God who "makes the dead to live again." This association of resurrection and the natural cycle has an important psychological dimension. By asserting the reality of resurrection the Jew is linked with the great chain of existence of the natural order. In direct antithesis to Job, rabbinic Judaism affirms that just as there is hope for a tree when it is cut down to send forth a new shoot, so too there is the hope of resurrection for a human being who dies. Resurrection is not only a biblical precept for rabbinic Jewish thought. It is also required because of the close ties between human beings and nature.

Human beings, however, are more than merely natural and their expectation of resurrection is linked to that difference. Many Jewish thinkers see the purpose of resurrection closely associated with the divine command to perform *mitzvoth*, to follow the precepts of Jewish law. Since these precepts demand bodily performance, one needs a body to observe them. The true fulfillment of human destiny lies in obedience to God's demands; only by a true bodily resurrection is that destiny made possible.

Other Jewish thinkers see resurrection only as a stage in the human development toward self-perfection. For them a human being is a spiritual, rational creature. The Commandments are way-stations toward fulfilling spiritual potential. After resurrection has achieved its purpose, then human beings proceed to a purely spiritual life. In this view the true enjoyment of the world to come follows the messianic period and the time of resurrection.

These two divergent views are represented in the contrast between the views of two thinkers, Moses Maimonides (1135–1204) and Moses Nachmanides (1194–1270). The former de-emphasized resurrection, although including it as one of the articles of Jewish faith. True human perfection will come only after corporeal life has been transcended. Messianic fulfillment will lead to Israel's political triumph which will be followed by resurrection. After a period of time all humanity will then die once again to be reborn to a purely spiritual existence.

Traditionalists opposed this view which seemed to reverse the order of events usually assumed. Maimonides was charged with having violated the *meaning* of resurrection, if not literally abandoning its doctrinal affirmation. Nachmanides offered a stinging rejection of a purely spiritual interpretation of human existence. Returning to the biblical view, he saw existence after death as a shadowy persistence in "the world of souls." Only with resurrection would a true "world to come" be experienced. The messianic period, resurrection of the dead, and the world to come combined in an eternal, humanly perfected, ideal. This ideal is distinctly Jewish because it takes the world of bodily action as the appropriate and inevitable arena of human life.

There are three important points about these eschatological expectations for a dialogue between Jews and Christians. The Jew, in the first place, need not turn to the Christian or the Christ-event to learn of resurrection. The eschatological hope of the Jew includes messianic politics, spiritual fulfillment, and resurrection. By looking at the Bible through rabbinic eyes and by studying the natural cycle and the human place in it, the Jew finds assurances of personal resurrection. No supernatural or extraordinary event needs to root the expectation of resurrection in human experience. Life itself and revelation as a public witness are proofs enough.

Secondly, the idea and hope of resurrection is integrated into the entire scheme of Jewish living. Liturgically the concept is unescapable, not only in prayers affirming the multi-layered nature of experience, but also in prayers combining the expectation of resurrection with such normal miracles as rain, springtime, and daily renewal. Through historical reflection the Jew is brought into contact with the hope of resurrection. The story of Jewish martyrs is witness to the power of that hope even in times of crisis. The democracy of God's justice which extends this hope to all who believe in it is clearly demonstrated throughout Jewish life.

Finally, the importance of resurrection as an opportunity to perform

God's commandments makes the particularity of the Jewish eschatological expectation comprehensible. The Jew does not focus on Jewish hopes because of a hostility to non-Jews. Non-Jews are not automatically excluded from the hope for resurrection. The messianic expectation includes the belief that non-Jews will convert to Judaism. Such conversion is necessary because without it resurrection makes no sense. Resurrection is a blessing only if corporeal living is a blessing. In Judaism the ability to perform God's commandments gives life meaning. Resurrection is a reward only for those who find performing *mitzvoth* the fulfillment of human purpose. Such a view of resurrection is indeed particular—it sees human meaning in a peculiarly Jewish way. Given that approach, however, resurrection is only meaningful to Jews and has no inherent relevance to the non-Jew.

Reform Judaism denies the doctrine of resurrection and has expunged it from its liturgy, saying it is a foreign import. Moderate Reform and Conservative Judaism sometimes identify resurrection with immortality of the soul (an idea that can be traced to Maimonides).

S. Daniel Breslauer

CHRISTIAN VIEW:

Eschatology is the division of theology which discusses the "last things." (The Greek word *eskata* means "last things.") In the biblical perspective it refers to the Kingdom of God. In the theological perspective, it refers to those matters which describe the final end of human existence: death, heaven, hell, judgment.

Eschatology refers to the Kingdom, sometimes also called "Kingdom of Heaven." Jesus appropriated the Jewish symbol of Kingdom of God to signify the reign of God in the hearts of humankind. The sayings and parables of Jesus reveal that he believed that the Kingdom of God had drawn near (Mk 1:15), and that it was present in his miracles and exorcisms (Lk 11:20). God's reign is characterized by providence and forgiveness. Thus, the Lord's Prayer indicates that one experiences the Kingdom in the granting of the petitions for bread, forgiveness and deliverance.

The presence of the Kingdom is God's initiative. Human beings do not build the Kingdom. Yet the Kingdom calls forth response on the part of human beings. Indeed, the message of the Kingdom sounds a note of crisis, of decision (Lk 9:62). It requires a radical response. People are called to conversion (Mk 1:15), which is manifest in forgiveness of others (Lk 11:4), in service of the deprived (Mt 25:31–46), and in love of others, even of one's enemies (Mt 5:44–48). The message of the Kingdom upsets established values and reverses our expectations: the first are last and the exalted are humbled (Mk 10:31; Lk 14:11).

Jesus taught that the Kingdom of God had drawn near in himself, that it was present in his teaching and ministry. He also described the process of its development, comparing it to a seed growing (Mk 4:26–29). The presence of the Kingdom does not eradicate evil, but the Kingdom exists side by side with it until the final consummation in an unspecified future (Mt 13:24–30).

The Kingdom which is present in Jesus and grows quietly also has a future aspect; it has not yet fully come. Jesus describes the future consummation of the Kingdom in apocalyptic tones. A judgment will take place at an unspecified time in the future (Lk 19:11–27). The criterion of judgment will be the acceptance or rejection of Jesus, manifest in service or lack of concern regarding one's fellow human beings (Mt 25:31–46). The Kingdom of God, in its present state and in its final consummation, is the destiny of humankind, the fullness of human existence, as indicated by Jesus' description of it as a feast (Lk 14:15–24) or as a wedding banquet (Mt 25:1–13).

Jesus' teaching about the Kingdom of God excluded any purely political interpretation of the expression; that is, the Kingdom of God was not to be associated with any particular political event, movement, or government. However, Jesus' teaching does have political implications, for Jesus embodied the Kingdom of God by going to the deprived. He called his followers to the same concern, and this sometimes implies certain political options.

The Kingdom of God is primarily a collective notion about the ultimate destiny of humankind. Systematic theology considers that destiny with respect to the individual as well as the communal in the categories of heaven, hell, and judgment. One can, however, reflect on these matters only in light of the Christian understanding of life and death.

The human person is open to the transcendent. Openness to the transcendent is such an integral part of the human person that we can call it constitutive of human existence. People are human only in the measure that they move beyond themselves in knowing and loving. They experience this, albeit unreflectively, in the act of questioning the meaning of life, in the desire to understand, in the need to love and be loved.

The human person is also limited, and experiences existence as marked off by the inevitability of death. The person faces the radical finitude of death, not only in the final moment itself, but in those lesser, daily experiences such as disappointment, illness, and separation. In a paradoxical way, not only is death that which closes off life as we know it, but it is part of life itself.

Christians believe that life is fulfilled only in the gift of self in love of God and others. Jesus shows us that a person can live in such a way that even death becomes an outpouring of love. If a person enters into death in the manner of Jesus, death becomes not simply the closing off of present life; it also becomes the way to new life. Christians believe that, just as the Father raised Jesus to new life, so too will the Father raise them. This belief in new life after death is the meaning of both Heaven and general resurrection.

"Heaven" expresses Christian belief in an afterlife with respect to the individual. Traditionally many Christians described death as the separation of body and soul, and believed that the soul went to Heaven after death. Today, however, we are more aware of the wholeness of the human person in all of its aspects: physical, affective, intellectual. Thus, such a notion of death and afterlife is unsatisfactory. We can describe the Christian belief more adequately by saying that, after death, the whole person enters into new life, a life continuous with the present in that it is characterized by love and self-transcendence. We do not know how this occurs. The New Testament itself simply tells us that the resurrection of Jesus is the guarantee that the God who is faithful brings people to new life after death, and that we have already entered into that new life in baptism.

The belief in an afterlife is expressed in a collective fashion, in the notion of a general resurrection, referred to in the New Testament as the resurrection of the dead (1 Thess 4:16), and in the early creeds as the resurrection of the body. This belief originated in the Jewish tradition. It reflects the understanding that fullness of life with God is the destiny, not only of the individual, but of humankind. Bodiliness and solidarity with others will be part of the life to come, for they are constitutive of human existence. Again, while the New Testament describes the resurrection of the dead in highly symbolic language, it does not tell us how this will happen.

Belief in judgment, both individual and general, is another concept which originated in the Jewish tradition. It does not reflect a notion of a calculating or wrathful God. Rather, it expresses the hope that, ultimately, ambiguity will be resolved and that good will indeed prevail over evil. Symbolically, we say that general resurrection and judgment will occur at "the end of the world" or "at the end of time." These are not temporal expressions, however. They express completion and consummation, and the hope that the cosmos itself will be transformed (Rev 21:1).

Heaven is the fullness of a life of love and self-transcendence. "Hell" expresses its opposite. It does not refer to divine punishment. Rather, it expresses the ultimate conclusion of a life of selfishness, of deliberate alienation from God and others. It is not God's choice for the human being, but it is the correlative of human freedom.

Orthodox Christians and Catholics in communion with Rome believe in purgatory as an intermediate state. This teaching expresses the realization that even good people end their lives with some selfishness unresolved. Purgatory is thus a state for the resolution of all ambiguity so that one can enter fully into a new life of total love and self-transcendence (cf. Afterlife).

The ultimate realities of human existence expressed in eschatology are already experienced in the present. The person experiences purification and death in limitation and suffering, and new life in the growth of love and self-transcendence. There is a dialectical quality in human existence. The inevitability of death casts a shadow over life, yet Christian hope lends the promise of resurrection. Death is already present, yet new life has begun.

Celia Deutsch

Exile

JEWISH VIEW:

Exile in its primary sense means the exile of God from the Temple, the eclipse of the physical presence of God from the Jewish people.

One of the most traumatic passages in the Bible is the story in Ezekiel contained in Chapters 10 and 11. The prophet, who has been transported to Jerusalem in a vision, sees the great chariot upon which the Glory of God is resting. The Glory is the physical presence of God and it was to be found in the sanctuary. The story continues: "And the Glory of the Lord rose up from upon the cherub (i.e., the chariot) to the threshold of the house; and the house was filled with the cloud and the courtyard was full of the brightness of the Lord's Glory" (10:4). The chariot is then described and the action resumes: "The Glory of the Lord went out from the threshold of the house and stood over the cherubim. The cherubim lifted up their wings and they rose from the earth in my sight as they left, the wheels (going) with them. And it (i.e., the chariot) stood at the opening of the eastern gate of the house of the Lord and the Glory of the God of Israel was over them above" (11:18–19). Some actions intervene and then the narrative resumes: "The Glory of the Lord lifted from the midst of the city and it stood on the mountain which is east of the city" (11:23). With this movement, God's physical presence left the Temple, the holy city of Jerusalem, and the Jewish people.

How terrifying for the prophet and for the people. God's physical presence had been with the people for centuries, in good times and in bad. And now he had left. He had abandoned them. But it is more than abandonment, for, to the ancient Israelite, the Temple was the point where Heaven and earth met, where the will of man could approach the will of God, where humankind could make true contact with the Creator. Everyone sacrificed in the Temple, even those who saw its corruption. No one advocated abolishing

59

the Temple because God was truly there. And now he was gone and no one knew when he would return.

Exile also means national disaster. The Jewish state was no more. The bodies of the people were strewn in the streets; the dead were so numerous that there were none to bury them. The leadership was in chains in a strange land. The righteous were slain with the wicked, the innocent together with the defenders. The holy city was in ruins. The very land itself had been profaned. The survivors were stunned, dazed, and depressed, not knowing what to do or where to turn. Their plaintive cry was: "The crown of our heads has fallen; woe unto us for we have sinned....You, O Lord, dwell forever; your throne is for all generations. Why have you forgotten us forever, deserting us for so long? Return us to you, O God, and we will return; renew our days as of old" (Lam 5:16–21). The Book of Lamentations paints this whole picture with great poignancy.

From that moment in 586 BCE, the Jewish people and Jewish history would not be the same. Even the second Temple did not restore the full measure of God's presence, and its destruction in 70 CE reinforced the great tragedy of Jewish existence. By 150 CE, the rabbis knew that the Exile was permanent until the eschaton. All subsequent national tragedy was a shadow of the Exile story. Today there are those who claim that even the Holocaust is of the same genre as the great Exile. Surely, Jewish liturgy sees it that way.

Exile also means the loss of certain crucial religious forms: first and foremost, the sacrificial cult. There are no more sacrifices, and prayer takes its place. As there were three daily sacrifices in the Temple, so there are three daily services in the synagogue, and so on for the Sabbath and holidays. Second, most of the agricultural laws no longer apply, though some have been restored on a partial basis in the new State. Thus, there are no tithes of agricultural products, no heave offerings, etc. Third, the complex laws of purity which envisioned the world as a set of concentric circles with the Temple and the priesthood in the center no longer apply. Some remnants remain but true ritual purity is no longer available to Jews. Life in Exile is life steeped in impurity. Fourth, the measurements of the Temple and the sequence of the services have, in large measure, been lost. Part has been reconstructed, but that is a reconstruction, not a living tradition. Finally, the ineffable Name of God which was pronounced only on the Day of Atonement in the Temple by the High Priest has been lost to history. No one knows, by authentic tradition, how to pronounce God's Name. No one knows how to address him by his Name.

Exile, then, has several layers of meaning. Nationally, it means the loss of Jewish political sovereignty in the land promised by God to the people.

Religiously, it means the loss of the sacrificial cult, the agricultural laws, the rules of purity, and the use of the Name of God. Spiritually, it means the loss of the physical presence of God, a sense of a distance between God and the Jewish people. There is, thus, an ontological and axiological sense of Exile, along with the national and the political.

Return is the counterforce. Return implies, first, a return of national sovereignty to the Jewish people, in the land promised by God. Return certainly includes a renewed presence of the Jewish people in the holy city of Jerusalem. It is there that God dwelled with the community, and it is there that Jews shall meet him again. This, in part, explains the extraordinary attachment of Jews to Jerusalem.

Most important, though, the Return implies a reconstitution of the intimate relationship with God, a time when the hearts of the children will be at one with the heart of their heavenly Father, a time when the ordinary Jew will have intimate access to God himself just by walking the streets and fields of the Holy Land. It will be a time of renewed protection and peace, a time of physical and spiritual blessing. All the sources agree on this.

It is difficult for Christians to understand the breadth and depth of this pair of value-concepts: Exile and Return. That God could be so angry as to physically leave the Jewish people yet maintain his special relationship with them remains a mystery; that God stamped his presence upon a place so deeply that the memory thereof still survives twenty-four hundred years later is an enigma.

David Blumenthal

CHRISTIAN VIEW:

In general, an exile is a deportation of a conquered people by the victors, and this occurred more than once to the Jewish people of old. When Christians use the term, they almost always mean the Babylonian exile.

Exiles in the Old Testament were often interpreted as God's way of punishing the people for their sin. The sins for which exile was the punishment included sins of the rulers (Is 8:16; 30:1f) and sins of the rich who did not share their possessions (Is 1:23).

One of the features of exile in the Hebrew Scriptures was the rise of the prophet who would interpret the reason for the exile and call the people back to conversion and repentance (cf. Hosea, Jeremiah, Ezekiel, etc.) The exile occasioned a new self-understanding for the Jews: the vocation to be a "light to the nations" (Is 42:6; 49:6). This self-understanding was later related to the Jewish diaspora as the "light to the world."

In New Testament thought, the cycle of exile and return was paralleled with death and resurrection. In the Christian churches, particularly those influenced by Platonic anthropology, Christians spoke of life in the body as an exile from the true homeland which was to be found in heaven (cf. 2 Cor 5:6).

We have already pointed out that exile was interpreted by the Jews of Old Testament times as punishment from God for unfaithfulness to the law, particularly those breaches of the law which related to how they treated the poor, the marginalized, the stranger, and the widow. In later Christian polemic, however, the dispersal of the Jews after 70 CE was interpreted as God's once again exiling the Jews for their lack of faith. From the Christian perspective, this lack of faith meant not to believe that Jesus of Nazareth was the Messiah. Even worse, some Christians interpreted the dispersal of the Jews from Palestine as punishment for having collaborated in the death of Jesus. The Jews have been cursed, so the interpretation goes, to wander the earth in perpetual exile until the return of Christ just before the cataclysm. Often the prophetic texts from the Hebrew Scriptures, as in Isaiah and Jeremiah, were used by Christian apologists to interpret the exile of the Jews from Palestine. The Book of Daniel was frequently cited to support this interpretation. Thus, the word "exile" has been applied by many Christians to the plight of the landless Jews after Christ. A return then to the promised land would be quite remarkable in such a worldview.

Because of the history of Christian polemic about the fate of the Jews after the destruction of Jerusalem, dialogue and investigation about "exile" might be a very appropriate focus for Jewish-Christian dialogue. Christians must rid themselves of the myth of "the wandering Jew," and a more biblically based understanding of exile might help them in this regard.

Michael McGarry

Faith

JEWISH VIEW:

There are two Hebrew terms to define the different aspects of the Jewish concept of faith. *Emuna* refers to faith in its mystical, traditional, and experiential dimension. The second term is *bittahon* and means faithfulness. These dimensions may overlap in any given individual but continue to be valid modes of faith in Judaism.

The Hebrew word *emuna*, in its various verb and noun forms, means "to be firm," "to be faithful." Thus: "and his (Moses') hands were firm" (Ex 17:12); "for they acted in faithfulness" (2 Kgs 12:16); "the faithful God who keeps the covenant" (Dt 7:9); "a faithful witness does not lie" (Prov 14:5). From this root, we have the word "Amen" as a response to a blessing or a prayer, meaning "May it be so" (Dt 27:15ff; Jer 28:6; etc.). The connotations which we in Western civilization attach to such phrases as "to have faith" or "to believe," however, do not seem to be present in the biblical usages, at least not in the same sense.

The Arabic term *iman* (which is linguistically related to the Hebrew term *emuna*) refers primarily to "faith through tradition." The rabbinic understanding is that the Jew should accept certain concepts as true on the basis of the "true tradition," that is, of the veracity of the community of basis of the "true tradition," that is, of the veracity of the community of faith. Such teachings as the exodus, the revelation, and the redemption were to be accepted "on faith," that is, on the word, transmitted by generations of truth-telling ancestors, that these events happened. Much was made by advocates of this type of faith from the fact that Sinai took place in the presence of very large numbers of people while the revelations to Jesus and Mohammed were either private or before very small groups. Note that the issues at stake were historical. From them however, certain theological ideas could properly be drawn, e.g., the existence of God, miracles, chosenness, etc. These, too, were to be accepted on the basis of the collective wisdom of the historical and contemporary community of faith.

By "rational faith" the rabbis meant that the Jew should have convictions about the existence of God, creation (nature), Torah (socio-moral guidance), providence (history), etc., which were to be firmly based in some form of reasoning or rational argument. The "proofs" used to support rational conviction varied through time from the Islamic Kalam, to neo-Aristotelianism, to neo-Platonism, to Kantianism, and even into modern forms of rationalism. But the basic type of faith, rooted in the systematic effort of the mind, persevered.

The development of the Jewish mystical tradition brought another dimension of meaning to the Hebrew word *emuna,* the dimension of the explicitly experiential. As Jews had begun to think about how they knew what they knew, they also began to think about what they felt and how and why. Here, then, a whole range of religious experience achieved articulation, from the deeply personalist sense of God as Father and Friend to the totally formless sense of God as the absolute Nothing or the wholly Other. There developed, too, a range of intensity to this dimension of Jewish religious experience, from the intensity of mystical annihilation to the passivity of peripheral awareness. *Emuna,* in this aspect of the tradition, then, came to mean faith in the God of one's personal experience.

The final term of Jewish faith language is *bittahon,* and in its various roots it means "trust." Human trust, which is the closest analogy, develops slowly through interaction, testing, evaluation, escalation of commitment, more interaction, and so on. It is a developmental process. So, too, with God: one feels, one acts, one is responded to, one evaluates, one commits, and then one begins the cycle again—all with minimal recourse to intellectual, or mystical, or historical categories. In this mode, having faith came to mean "being faithful." It came to mean trusting in God and being loyal to him, as he has been loyal to us.

"Theology" refers to two processes: first, the articulation and explication of modes of faith and religious existence and, second, the attempt to put the ideas of faith into a rationally coherent order. Theology is, thus, a second level effort within the religious life. Theology in the sense of the rational ordering of ideas is not part of several of the types of faith listed above.

David Blumenthal

CHRISTIAN VIEW:

Faith is personal relationship with God. The conscious reflection on the meaning of that relationship is called "theology." The relationship of faith is manifest in a complex of beliefs, emotions, cult, ethics, and community structures that is called "religion."

Christian faith is personal relationship with God who reveals himself in Jesus. It is free gift of God and it implies trust, recognition, surrender. Believers reflect on their experience of faith and seek to understand it in theology. They express it in the rituals, beliefs, ethics, and structures of religion. Because those forms reflect the human response, they need continually to be renewed.

Christian thought is dependent on the Hebrew Scriptures and the Jewish tradition for its understanding of faith as a personal relationship of trust and fidelity with the God of the covenants. In the specifically Christian context, "faith" refers to personal relationship with God who is revealed in Jesus Christ. The New Testament writers reflect the various aspects of that relationship in their use of *pistis* (faith) and its cognates. Faith implies trust in God's loving care (Mt 6:25–33). It is the recognition of God's power at work in Jesus (Mk 5:34). It is acceptance of the Gospel (Acts 8:13–14). The object of faith is Jesus Christ, raised from the dead (Rom 10:9). The relationship of faith is the free gift of God, and it requires not only surrender but identification with Jesus (Gal 5:20–22).

John's Gospel, particularly, manifests the cognitive element in faith. The faith relationship means that the Christian recognizes that Jesus comes from God (16:30). The Christian knows Jesus as the Holy One of God (6:69) and Messiah (11:27). Belief in Jesus is belief in the Father who has sent him. Belief is the key to life (5:24), and unbelief is the way to condemnation (3:18–20).

Faith in Jesus and acceptance of the Gospel leads to repentance, to a change of heart and life (Acts 2:38). Faith is communal; thus, it is inseparable from love of neighbor (Jas 2:1–7). Because faith is communal, it is received through preaching (Rom 10:14–17) and the witness of the believing community (Acts 2:43–47).

The second century Church Fathers Justin and Irenaeus developed the consideration of the cognitive aspect of faith. They identified faith with assent to truths. The later Fathers, as well as the medieval theologians, continued to consider the cognitive and intellectual elements of the faith relationship. It is true that certain thinkers such as Augustine and Thomas Aquinas, as well as Church Councils, emphasized the fact that faith is the free gift of God. However, it was all too easy to lose sight of the gratuitous, relational quality of faith. The Reformers, as well as the Council of Trent, provided a corrective in their emphasis on the gratuitousness of faith.

Christian faith is personal relationship to God who is revealed in Jesus Christ. It is relationship to Jesus and communion in his Spirit. It is both the free gift of God who initiates the relationship, and the response of the person who receives the gift. There is a circular dynamic in faith; that is, faith means that the person receives God's word of revelation and responds in surrender to God. And yet, one receives that word only in relationship to a self-revealing.

Authentic faith is not irrational. It does not run counter to the dynamic of human understanding, growth, and development. It is, however, a relationship with the transcendent God. Thus, it is supra-rational; it is not confined to the limits of logical reasoning, because logical reasoning alone falls short of the relational as well as the transcendent.

Because faith is a relationship, it must be renewed in prayer, in daily conduct, and in worship with the believing community. It must also be renewed in the effort to integrate faith with the concrete realities of life. Faith has an objectifiable content: God's self-communication in Jesus Christ, the saving power of the Cross and Resurrection, the presence of the Spirit in the Church. This does not mean that faith provides facile answers to the troubling questions of existence. Rather, Christians struggle with those questions while being in relationship to God in Christ.

Faith is articulated and understood in theology, which is "faith seeking understanding" (Anselm of Canterbury). Theology is the activity of every responsible believer, for the word of God engages the whole person, including his intellect. Christians not only experience a relationship with God in Christ, but seek to understand the meaning of that experience and its implications for their lives, the relationship of their experience to that of the believing community, and the ramifications of faith in terms of responsibility in the broader society.

Theology is not simply the attempt to understand faith. Rather, it is the activity of believers who attempt to understand their faith. Theology begins with faith, and speaks from the standpoint of faith. It implies participation in the believing community which transmits and fosters that faith.

Although theology requires involvement, it is also critical. It measures a given articulation of faith against established criteria. All Christians would agree that such an expression must be consistent with, or at the very least not contradictory to, the Bible. Orthodox Christians and Catholics also look to the Fathers of the Church, Church Councils, and other official teaching, as well as to the commonly held belief of the body of the Church.

Theology changes constantly. Believers seek to understand their faith, their relationship to God in Christ. They measure their beliefs against certain criteria. But this activity is colored by the life experience of the persons engaging in the theological process. Furthermore, theological activity takes place in the context of the developments of history, society, and culture. Those developments bring new questions, such as those raised by the Holocaust, by the possibility of nuclear war, or by the heightened awareness of social and political injustice. Furthermore, cultural developments allow new possibilities for the articulation of faith. Thus, twentieth century philosophy has allowed theologians to express in new and more adequate ways, the personal challenge of the word of God.

Faith is expressed in theology. It is also expressed in a complex of convictions, rituals, institutions, and ethics which we call "religion." One perceives a certain unity in the diversity of various religions. All arise from an experience of the Holy, and are characterized by a sense of awe and mystery. All manifest the elements of divine initiative and human response. The element of human response results in beliefs, cult, ethics, and a community with a minimal structure at the least. These phenomena are also observable in Christianity.

Religion is the expression of faith, which is both free gift of God and human response. Under the quality of human response, religion is subject to the ambiguity of human existence. Ideally religion both expresses and fosters faith. It is meant to provide a context within which the human person can open himself even more to the transcendent God. And yet, one can identify religion with the divine, and thus fall prey to the temptation to attempt to control the divine with human means.

The ambiguity of religion emerges in its relationship to culture and politics. Religion gives rise to and is influenced by culture. Thus, religion can be confused with a particular cultural form; for example, some Catholics identified theology with neo-Scholasticism. Religion legitimizes social order; it can be misused to authorize injustice.

Celia Deutsch

Gnosticism

JEWISH VIEW:

Gnosticism—by its very etymology the study of saving knowledge—does not yield to direct attempts to know it; rather it becomes more and more enigmatic and mysterious as it is further plumbed. It was first identified in the works of the second and third century Christian Church Fathers, the heresiologists who took it upon themselves to explain and refute the many heresies growing up in Christianity. The earliest extant work is the heresiology of Irenaeus, but his study may be, in turn, dependent on the work of Justin Martyr before him.

Irenaeus styles his work as a defense against the heresy of gnosticism, "falsely so-called." By this he means that although the practitioners of heresy believe that they have a special knowledge or *gnosis* (γνωσις they are actually misled. The Church Fathers objected to the gnostics on the basis of their doctrine of special knowledge, which could be either a revelation or an insight. In either event, the gnostics posited that a special knowledge was the necessary factor for salvation. This claim was dangerous to the Church because it tended to devalue the Christian notion of faith in the resurrection of Jesus, the crucified Messiah.

It is hard to appreciate why so much Christian energy was devoted to dismissing gnostics if this change of focus were their only mistake. But there were several more dangerous allegations. This gnosis, the Church Fathers maintained, was the source of an enormous intellectual elitism and an artificial distinction between various varieties of Christians, based on their closeness to the special knowledge. They also appear to devalue flesh entirely, suggesting that Christ's resurrection was not in the flesh at all. They sometimes denigrated the prophecies in the Old Testament, which the Church used as the preparation for the coming of Christ, as being an imperfect record of an ignorant God, who was not the same as the God of salvation. They regularly spun out fantastic cosmologies, which were not at all present in the Hebrew Bible. They also were eventually accused of libertinism—using bizarre sexual practices in their religious rituals and even in practicing group sex and communal marriage.

It would have been difficult for moderns to have treated these claims with any degree of credibility had not a few gnostic documents come down to us, first quoted in the writings of the Church Fathers themselves but also independently found in ancient manuscripts like the *Pistis Sophia*. Even more unlikely would have been any relationship between this movement and Judaism. Since the gnostics were reported to have called the God of the Old Testament an evil demiurge (δεμιυπγος or artisan creator) and have denigrated the reports of the Old Testament, an antagonistic relationship with Judaism was assumed. Yet, scholars like Moritz Friedländer noticed that many of the cosmological speculations of the gnostics seemed to have an eerie correspondence with some of the classics of Jewish mysticism—merkabah and especially Kabalistic writings. There were also a number of formal relationships between gnostic materials and a body of spirituality known in the West as the *Corpus Hermeticum*, the writings of "the thrice-great Hermes." These works, which had been known since the Renaissance at least, were spiritual exercises purporting to have come from the Greek god Hermes or his Egyptian manifestation as Thoth. But several of the tractates also showed some familiarity with biblical works, especially the creation story in Genesis, though the relationship would have had to be fairly subtle.

Friedländer postulated that there was an intimate relationship between the earliest gnostic writings, which he identified as the *Corpus Hermeticum* and Judaism, suggesting that perhaps *gnosis* had already arisen among the deracinated and upper-class Jews of Alexandria in their search for social acceptance. These ideas were, in turn, blended by a syncretistic aristocratic class including Jews and Gentiles into the various bastardized forms of Christianity noticed by the Church Fathers.

But other discoveries were to make more popular the theory that gnosticism was actually an Indo-European mythological structure that had in turn affected the rise of Christianity. Many different discoveries fed into this theory. First, the sacred texts of the East were being translated into English—including the Indian texts but even more notably the classical texts of the Persian religion of Zoroastrianism, which had been such an important religious intuition of late antique times, only to be supplanted by Islam. And the texts seemed to be related to what was known of the religion of Manichaenism. Furthermore, Westerners had come into contact with a group of surviving gnostics, the Mandaeans (*Manda* is an Aramaic word for truth, related to the Hebrew word Da 'at or knowledge). Later on, Manichaean texts were also found. The scholars who synthesized all these new discoveries into a consistent theory can be described as the *religionsgeschichtliche Schule* or, in English, as "The History of Religions School." The term has the connotation of comparative religion in German, and comparative study has been the cornerstone of their approach.

Principal among those New Testament scholars who represented the History of Religions School—that is, who synthesized our growing archeological and antiquarian knowledge of the ancient peoples of Asia with the New Testament account of Christianity, was Rudolf Bultmann. A superb exegete of the New Testament and an accomplished theologian, he synthesized the discoveries into a new theory. According to his view, gnosticism was an Indian and Persian religious phenomenon which had been brought to the Near East by the Persian domination of the area. In particular he posited a gnostic myth of a redeemed redeemer—a savior who would be the same as the original man, who would bring the saving knowledge of the savior God to earth even as he saved himself. This overlay of myth onto the life of Jesus, Bultmann suggested, was the basis of Christianity. The pre-Christian gnostic salvation myth was actually fit into the events of the life of Jesus, and the resulting formulation was a myth of redemption most clearly seen in the Gospel of John. Since the Mandaeans revere John the Baptist but view Jesus as an opposer to their truth, Bultmann felt that the Mandaeans are the survivors of the gnostic groups preceding Christianity, who brought gnostic truth into the religion along with the ritual of baptism. The followers of John the Baptist continued in their own baptismal ways afterward, founding the independent gnostic movements like the Mandaeans, even the Manichaeans, when newly discovered Manichaean texts clarified that Mani himself came from a third-century baptizing Syrian Christian sect, and eventually, when the Essenes documents were found at Qumran in 1947, the Dead Sea Scroll community. According to this theory, the syncretistic blending of Indo-European thought and Hebrew Scriptures took place among a group of baptizing sects of the first century and was responsible for gnosticism first (of which the Mandaeans are only the last small survivors), then Christianity as a specific kind of gnostic movement, and finally Manichaeanism, which was a systematic gnosticism that grew out of a Christian context.

Following on these suggestions several Jewish scholars noted the very opposing natures of Judaism and gnosticism. Both Martin Buber and Hans Jonas suggested that gnosticism was the polar opposite of Judaism: Judaism praised the creation as good; gnosticism devalued and hated the world.

Judaism believed in resurrection of the body; gnosticism found the body impure. Judaism had a positive image of the God of creation; gnosticism found the God of the Jews to be ignorant and imperfect. Thus, Christianity could be seen as part of the opposition to Judaism. Furthermore, the climate of the Second World War was also heavily influencing scholarly opinion. Indo-European and semitic stereotypes seemed deeply opposed in the minds of both Jewish and German scholars, even among those Germans who opposed Nazism. After the war, Nazism itself, with its spurious racial theories, provided the proof that gnosticism and Judaism were unalterable enemies.

The study of gnosticism took a momentous step forward with the discovery of thirteen gnostic codices (books rather than scrolls) at Nag Hammadi in Egypt. The story of the discovery is almost as intrigue-filled as that of the Dead Sea Scrolls. However, in spite of the fact that most of the writings were in a little known or studied language called Coptic (the last phase of the native Egyptian religion which was still being spoken among the masses in Egypt in Roman times), the entire corpus was published by the middle 1970's, whereas we are still waiting anxiously for a few of the remaining Dead Sea Scrolls. To publish the material meant that a small army of graduate students learned Coptic and began a common task of translating the texts together. In the case of the Dead Sea Scrolls, the Hebrew and Aramaic texts of interest to Bible criticism and especially the New Testament were translated soon. It turns out, however, that the most important issues in the Qumran texts may be halakhic, relating to Jewish law. Scholars who can adequately understand these texts need legal training in Judaism, and that team is just now finishing its work.

The Nag Hammadi Corpus, as it is now known, is a much more circumscribed group of documents, has recently been entirely published in English, and has increased our knowledge of ancient gnosticism by leaps and bounds. It now appears that the codices were in the library of the monastery founded by Pachomius, the father of Egyptian monasticism. Evidently the Christian monks of Egypt had a wider selection of books available to them than the Orthodox Church would have thought appropriate! There is no evidence in the codices for a pre-Christian gnosticism, though there is certain evidence for the existence of non-Christian gnosticism. Of course, non-Christian gnosticism was already known from the testimony of the famous pagan philosopher, Plotinus.

In the meantime, however, it was clear that Bultmann's synthesis would not hold. The pre-Christian gnostic salvation myth demanded a group of evidence which has not yet surfaced. There was no evidence of pre-Christian gnosticism; the Indic creator and savior were not the same person; nor did the full form of the myth appear anywhere before Christianity. It may be that the unified myth was achieved only during Christian times, which leaves open the possibility that it was Christianity itself which served as the matrix or catalyst out of which gnosticism arose.

Several conferences chart the scholarly history of the problem. The first famous conference, the Conference of Messina in Sicily in 1966, summarized the issue of terminology. It decided to use the term gnosticism to refer only to the full-blown, anti-cosmic religion that we see often in the Nag Hammadi writings and opposed by the Church Fathers. It decided to use the term *gnosis* to describe any of the characteristics of gnosticism that existed before that. Since so many different scholars from various perspectives attended, it was not possible to come to any conclusion on the crucial issue of whether Christianity preceded *gnosis* or vice versa. The issue was framed in these terms: was *gnosis* pre-gnosticism only or was it proto-gnosticism—that is, already essentially gnosticism? No consensus was possible. Furthermore, scholars continued to use the word *gnostic* to refer to either *gnosis* or gnosticism, thus reinstating in adjectives the confusion that was removed in the nouns by the final statements of the conference.

There are few strict adherents to Bultmann's hypothesis left. Furthermore, from the point of view of the rabbinic witness to the heresies of Christianity and gnosticism, it appears as though Christianity was earlier. That is to say, the rabbis seemingly polemicize against systems like Christianity where "two powers" are aligned in complementary, helping fashion well before they begin to polemicize against any system in which the "two powers" are opposing. They also seem to be able to distinguish all of this from any criticism of Zoroastrian dualism. While this is not a conclusive evidence, it does support the notion of the Church Fathers to an extent— namely that gnosticism appears to be later than Christianity and often grows out of it in some way.

With the door shut in so many important ways on Bultmann's theories, the issue of the relationship between Judaism and gnosticism could be reopened. The problem of the opposition still remained: How could a movement which was so anti-scriptural and even anti-Jewish have found its roots with Judaism? The answer seems to have something to do with the social location of the various groups. Indeed, the same question could be asked about Christianity itself, since it too contains many anti-Jewish statements. In the latter case, scholars are coming to see that a great many of the anti-Jewish statements of the New Testament ought to be seen as the results of an unfortunate polemic between the nascent religion and developing rabbinic

Judaism. Just as the social opposition of Jews was countered by anti-Jewish statements in the New Testament, so too the opposition of Jews can be seen in the development of gnosticism as well. It appears as though gnosticism is partly a further step in the polemic. Judaism seems to have objected to a variety of Christian notions with the criticism that it was a violation of monotheism to think that there was a father and a son. Gnosticism seems intent on changing that bifurcation into an opposition. It is as if gnostics responded to Jewish criticism with a mythological argument: Your God, in whose name we have been ostracized from the synagogue, is an ignorant God, because he does not know of the God of salvation. This would also explain how there are so many Jewish names in gnostic speculation yet so much of it is terribly anti-Jewish. Somewhere in gnosticism there must have been some Jewish influence. But it is not clear that it is contemporary with the polemic. No actual Jews need to have been involved in the polemic after the first generation or so. This is because the polemic continues amongst various groups of Christians, with the Hebrew Bible serving as symbol of the issues dividing the groups. I have already noted how deeply the Orthodox Church resented gnostics and how strongly it fought against it. The Orthodox Church criticized the gnostics for denigrating the God of the Old Testament and the gnostics appear to have responded by saying that the God of the Old Testament, in whose name they were expelled from the Church, was not worthy of their respect or worship.

A second conference on gnosticism, this time held at New Haven in 1978, was able to distinguish between two different kinds of gnostic sects in the Nag Hammadi corpus: Sethian and Valentinian. Valentinian texts were closely associated with the variety of Christianity founded by Valentinus, which was designed to be Christianity proper and was gradually isolated into sectarian status by the Church Fathers. This is quite different from the Sethian material, which has considerably more Jewish tradition in it but is far less unified and probably not the result of a single teacher. There is little agreement about the sources of this material but there is within it clearly a very significant amount of Jewish tradition, mostly used polemically.

Furthermore, there seems to be a great affinity between some early gnostic systems and the speculations of Kabbalism. This may have been a continuous tradition within popular and underground Judaism. Equally prominent as a possible chain of tradition is to follow the gnostic strain into Christianity, Mandaeanism, Manichaeanism, and into Islam where it becomes part of the early Extreme Shia'. From here it influences Jews, who in turn bring it back into medieval Jewish Kabbalah. These relationships have not yet been fully explored by scholars because of the immense language difficulties involved in tracing the thought through Greek, Coptic, Aramaic, Persian, Arabic, Hebrew and many other languages. So there are many interesting and complicated relationships between gnosticism and Judaism which have yet to be adequately understood in the gnostic material.

Besides the historical relationships there is another strand of scholarly work on gnosticism which impinges on Judaism. Gnosticism may be studied ahistorically as a category of religion itself. Many people tend to use the term as if it is a building block of religion—like ritual, prayer, mysticism, or sacrifice. As an analytic category which may appear in any religion under specific periods of time, it may also appear in Judaism. Certainly any phenomenon in Jewish mysticism—merkabah, early Kabbalah, Lurianic Kabbalah, Hasidism—may evince gnostic tendencies. Hans Jonas wrote a classic work, *The Gnostic Religion,* in which he combines historical study of ancient gnosticism with an analysis of the relationship between gnosticism and modern existentialism. Gilles Quispel, who also studied the Jewish background to gnosticism, wrote a classic work called *Gnosis als Weltreligion* (*Gnosis as a World Religion,* but it has unfortunately never been translated into English) in which he shows the relationship between gnosticism and psychoanalysis, especially Jungianism. Indeed C.G. Jung was fascinated with gnosticism as an early attempt to balance the internal forces of the psyche in the same way that psychoanalysis does in the modern period. Jung wrote a great deal more about alchemy because more was known about it while he was writing. His somewhat more enigmatic references to gnosticism attest to the fascination which it had on him. In the end, however, he saw both gnosticism and alchemy as imperfect vehicles for real-realization or individuation because both identify too fully with the unconscious, symbolized by the unknown God beyond the gods acknowledged by any culture. Jung found that the gnostic myths were particularly potent for people who were going through what would today be known as a mid-life crisis.

No matter how great the bridge separating Judaism and gnosticism, it is clear that Judaism and Christianity are both essential parts of the development of gnosticism and that modern intellectual formulations of the issue of gnosticism were also deeply involved in modern agendas that concerned Judaism deeply. Yet, in the end, the antagonism that was found in second through fourth century gnosticism seems to be the result of the previously fought battle between Judaism and Christianity rather than the result of specifically Jewish impetus to assimilate into the Hellenistic world.

Alan F. Segal

CHRISTIAN VIEW:

The term "gnosticism" is a modern generic designation for a number of second and third century groups which claimed to possess the revealed knowledge (Gk. *gnosis)* necessary for the human soul to return to its origins in the heavenly light realm. Various mythological accounts of the origins of the heavenly and the material worlds provided the explanation for the soul's plight. Typically, the heavenly realm, often referred to by the Greek word for "fullness," *pleroma,* consists of a series of beings that emanated from the transcendent, unknowable God. The youngest or weakest, in many variants she is Wisdom (Gk. *Sophia),* unstable in her contemplation of God or her adherence to her male partner. This instability gives birth to a misshapen creature which must be excluded from the Pleroma. The divine side of her offspring expresses itself in the emanation of demonic angels and the creation of the lower, material world. However, the elements of the light-world which are now trapped in darkness must be restored to the Pleroma. Often a revelation of the heavenly Adam warns the creator that he is not the only god, a boast elicited when he looks on his creation, and inspires his minions to create the earthly pair Adam/Eve. The tree of knowledge represents the efforts of a heavenly Wisdom figure to awaken Adam/Eve to their heavenly nature. Their creator retaliates by trapping them in the darkness of the material world—often through the passions associated with the body. Consequently, gnostic enlightenment does not come to humanity until the descent of Wisdom, or the heavenly male revealer (Seth; Christ). The revealer's call awakens the spiritual seed to its true divine nature. Rituals such as baptismal washings, anointings, and prayers for the ascent of the soul were designed to guarantee its return home to the Pleroma.

At the end of the nineteenth century, German scholars suggested that ancient gnosticism had its roots in a heterodox form of Judaism which had become disillusioned with Israel's God. The creation myths have used and interpreted stories from Genesis and from apocryphal Enoch traditions about the fallen angels. Heterodox, Jewish exegetical traditions played an important role in formulating the story about the origins of the world and the creation of humankind that appear in a sub-class of gnostic writings that modern scholars refer to as Sethian. These myths claim that the divine seed originally implanted in Adam and Eve had been preserved by Seth and transmitted to his gnostic descendants. The Christian version of these traditions identified the Christ with the heavenly Seth.

Some modern scholars think that the ancient Christian view which held that the origins of gnosticism are to be found in Samaritan sectarianism was essentially correct. The Act of the Apostles (Acts 8:9–24) describe a Samaritan magician, Simon Magus, who attempted to purchase the power of the Holy Spirit from Peter. By the second century, a distinctive gnostic religious sect had formed around a prophet called Simon and his female consort, an ex-prostitute, who was said to embody the fate of the soul fallen into a world of demonic passions until rescued by saving knowledge (*gnosis*). Second century Christian authors describe Simon as the originator of the many-headed monster that constituted the gnostic sects of their time (Irenaeus, *Against Heresies* I, 23.2–4). Orthodox Christian writers did not consider Judaism itself to be responsible for the gnostic groups. They would have been more inclined to agree with the Church historian, Adolf von Harnack, at the beginning of the twentieth century, who described gnosticism as the "acute Hellenization of Christianity." The third century Roman presbyter, Hippolytus, sought to show that all the heretical forms of Christianity were the result of excessive adaptations of Greek philosophy (Hippolytus, *Refutation of all Heresies* 35–51). However, he acknowledged that gnostics used apocryphal traditions ascribed to Adam, Moses and Isaiah (*Refutation* 26.1-8; 39.5; 40.2).

The contributions of popular stoic and platonic ideas to the formulation of gnostic speculation in the second and third centuries have been amply demonstrated by the collection of original writings found near Nag Hammadi in Egypt (ca. 1945). Discussions of the transcendence and unknowability of the highest God found in these texts have parallels in second century Platonism. The third century, neo-platonic philosopher, Plotinus, wrote against gnostic ideas that influenced students in Rome. Some of the gnostic writings mentioned in Plotinus' biography have been found at Nag Hammadi (cf. *Allogenes, 3 Steles of Seth*). These writings appear to emphasize the mystic ascent of the soul to a vision of the transcendent Father as the goal of gnostic enlightment. They reject the mediation of a Christ figure that is typical of Christian gnostic systems (cf. *Zostrianos*). Therefore some interpreters suggest that some third century gnostic teachers turned away from Christianity to religious forms of Platonism.

Orthodox Christian writers understood gnosticism to be a chaotic heretical movement which perverted the truth of the Gospel because its teachers refused to accept the authority of the Church's rule of faith or her understanding of Scripture. This refusal was reflected in the gnostic insistence that the God of the Hebrew Scriptures was a malevolent creator, not the Father of the Savior, Jesus Christ. The second century gnostic teachers who are best know to us, Valentinus, Ptolemy, Heracleon, Basilides and Isidore, all claimed to be Christian teachers. They wrote sermons, hymns, treatises and commentaries on Christian Scriptures. Most of the works attributed to them have not survived. Though scholars had hoped that some of the Valentinian theological treatises in the Nag Hammadi collection might be attributed to Valentinus, himself (e.g., *Treatise on the Resurrection; Gospel of Truth*), most interpreters now think that these texts were composed by later writers of the Valentinian school. These texts show that Gnostics intended to demonstrate that traditional Christian doctrines, images and texts should be reinterpreted in light of gnostic myths of redemption. The key to saving knowledge (*gnosis*) is recognition of the internal divine spark that is awakened by revelation. The soul's unity with its heavenly, angelic counterpart was enacted by rituals that often paralleled the orthodox Christian rites of baptism, eucharist and anointing. However, gnostic writers argued that orthodox Christians were deceived by the evil creator into thinking that salvation could be attained through what belonged to the material world. Salvation, they insisted, required that the individual soul be transformed. Gnostics held that the spiritual Christ did not die on the cross. Therefore they rejected the orthodox Christian view that the physical death of Jesus on the cross atoned for the sins of humanity. Gnostics also rejected the concept of a resurrection of the physical body.

This gnostic view of the material world follows from the creation myths which treat the creation of the world as the work of an ignorant demiurge who was trying to imprison the light which belonged to the heavenly realm. Sethian mythology interpreted the "us" in Genesis 1:26–27 as a reference to the demons who assisted the ignorant creator. Orthodox Christians insisted that such interpretations of Genesis were contrary to divine revelation. The God who is "father" of Jesus is the same God who created the world, gave the Law to Moses, and inspired the prophets. When second century gnostic writers attack the Creator and the Law, they have such orthodox Christians in mind. There is no evidence that these authors had any knowledge of Jewish traditions aside from those embodied in the originating gnostic myths of Sethianism and in the heritage of orthodox Christianity.

A letter from the second century gnostic teacher, Ptolemy, to a wealthy patroness, Flora, exhibits the way in which Valentinian writers explained the Old Testament. Since elements of gnostic truth are found in the Old Testament, it cannot all be the work of the ignorant creator. Ptolemy appealed to Jesus' sayings about divorce (Mt 19:8) and his critique of Pharisaic traditions (Mt 15:4–9) to show that the Law contained different levels of revelation. The pure divine legislation was fulfilled by the coming of the Savior (e.g., the Decalogue). Law mixed with evil, he destroyed. Law which was intended to be symbolic of heavenly realities was abolished in its literal sense but maintained in the spiritual sense (e.g., ritual ordinances). After describing the divisions in the Law, Ptolemy turns to their origin (*Letter to Flora* 7). Neither the transcendent God, who is also the Good, nor the Devil can be said to be responsible for the Law. Therefore, Ptolemy argued, the Law must have been given by the artificer, the Demiurge who fashioned the universe. Ptolemy closes with a promise to reveal to the addressee how the universe of indeterminate and corruptible beings originated from the transcendent at a later time (*Letter* 8–9). It is this tradition, presumably a variant of the Valentinian cosmological myth, that Ptolemy refers to as "apostolic tradition" (*Letter* 9).

Many scholars today question the use of the generic term "gnosticism" to describe the diverse sects found in the catalogues of heresiologist. Those who taught this form of spiritual wisdom in Christian circles considered themselves to be the true Christians. Treatises found in the codices from Nag Hammadi allegedly contain secret traditions that the risen Jesus had given to various disciples. Outsiders, like the anti-Christian polemicist, Celsus (flor. ca. 178), could not distinguish gnostics from other Christians. Even though heterodox Jewish traditions were used in the initial formulation of gnostic mythological material, the real growth of various sectarian groups that are referred to as "gnosticism" occurred within the context of second and third century Christianity. Unlike the religious sect, Manichaeism, which shares a gnostic mythology, and was founded by the prophet Mani in the mid-third century C.E., most of the groups which come under the general designation "gnosticism" did not set out to be an independent religion. Instead, they claim to represent the true wisdom hidden in Christianity and unknown to most believers. Some of the treatises from Nag Hammadi (especially, *The Apocalypse of Peter*) suggest that the author and his readers are still under the authority of Orthodox Church leaders. As sociologically identifiable entities in the second and third centuries, Gnostic groups appear to be particular "schools" or cult associations within the broad spectrum of Christianity.

Pheme Perkins

God

JEWISH VIEW:

The central concept in Jewish theology is monotheism. Affirming God's unity and oneness is more than a numerical claim. Monotheism claims that God is unique, that the divine transcends all experienced pluralities. Jewish monotheism affirms that God creates good and bad, light and darkness, uniting all polar opposites in one Being. The suggestive question "Is God a divinity near by and not far off as well?" (cf. Jer 23:3) finds a response in the poetry of Judah Halevi (twelfth century) which wonders at the omnipresence of that deity who is both immanent and transcendent, unique and yet intimately connected with all other beings, distant from creation and yet close to all creatures.

Jewish monotheism is complex, proclaiming equally the variety of all divine manifestations and the unity lying incomprehensibly behind them. Jewish philosophers point out that the attributes of God, the divine qualities of mercy, justice, power, wisdom, and the like, are *active;* they are divine effects, not the divine essence. That essence is hidden and unfathomable, just as is the uniqueness of the deity. Even God's essential name is hidden; it is ineffable, unpronounced. Jewish mystics point to God's personal reality as *Ein Sof,* the infinite, which is shrouded in mystery. Human beings perceive God as YHVH, the active divine force in history, and as ELOHIM, the divine presence immanent in the natural order. God is thus both becoming and being but also a reality beyond either.

Being and becoming are each composed of various distinct elements. The mystics developed an elaborate scheme which points to the divine aspect of each of these elements. This scheme of *sefirot* or divine manifestations focuses on the infinite variety of God's involvement in this created world. The Jew has no need for a particular human being to represent God's immanence. Every human being and every creature is a divine image. That image as represented in the system of *sefirot* becomes a channel by which each Jew can develop an intimate relationship with deity. At the same time, however, these *sefirot* are merely active expressions of God; they are attributes of action creating pathways to an unfathomable deity. The great heresy feared by the mystics—one attributed to the talmudic heretic Elisha ben Abuya—is "cutting off the roots," separating these attributes from the hidden divine source and giving them an independent status. Their divine aspect lies in their identification with God's secret unity, not in their clear distinctive and individual manifestation.

The variety of these individual manifestations can be grouped in three categories—creation, redemption, and sustenance. God, understood from the perspective of human experience, is Creator, Redeemer, and Sustainer. These three attributes are distinct in themselves but are also expressions of the divine unity. God's personality is not divided; human experience is necessarily fragmentary and these divisions reflect that necessity. The three divisions are creations of human experience.

Recognition of God as Creator is traditionally attributed to Abraham (Genesis *Rabbah*). Abraham, Jewish tradition relates, observed the created world and saw that it was like a house on fire. Surely there must be an owner of the house, he thought. At that time he reached the intuition of God as the concerned Creator of a world in crisis. The Jewish view of God as Creator is not merely the philosophical assertion that every effect must have its cause. Creation was not merely a once and only event. God's creative power is a continual reality of human experience. The Jew celebrates that creative power in the Sabbath. Sabbath observance symbolizes the Jew's trust that God as Creator has established order, meaning, and purpose in the world. Human interference in creation is not essential for its continuation. By refraining from any active interruption in the natural order the Jew affirms that God's own creative skills are sufficient for life to go on.

The Sabbath is not only a celebration of creation. The holiday is also a remembrance of the Exodus from Egypt. God acts as a Redeemer in world history. The Jewish story of redemption takes as its model God's liberation of the Hebrew slaves. Three elements are combined in that liberation—freedom from actual bondage, revelation of Torah, and entrance into the Promised Land. These three elements make up the basis of the Jewish view of God as Redeemer. Redemption begins when people are given the opportunity to make choices. God's redemptive action is, first, that of allowing individuals moral freedom. The slave who rejects freedom has according to biblical law rejected a divine gift. Freedom, as the opportunity to choose, can be misused.

Arbitrary forces often shape human decisions. A decision made on the basis of desire, momentary impulse, or coercive needs is not free. God's redemptive power is also present in the moral law given to people. The rabbis said that freedom was inscribed on the tablets at Sinai. God liberates human beings from their passions by providing the antidote of religious instruction. Finally merely academic decisions are hardly liberating. God also provides concrete opportunities for putting those decisions into practice. The social and political challenges of an independent community, symbolized by Israel's life in the land of Canaan, are also God's gift. God redeems by offering people the liberty to make choices, the moral instruction to be free of internal coercion, and the concrete tools for realizing ideals in the real context of social and political life.

While the symbol of this redemptive power is Israel's liberation from Egypt it is universal rather than particular in significance. The story of Noah and God's covenant with Noah provides a paradigm of redemption for the non-Jew. Here too God preserves the ability to choose, presents humanity with a redeeming moral code, and creates the context for social and political creativity. The Jewish messianic expectation is not merely parochial but sees all humanity as participating in an event which is characterized by political liberation, reaffirmation of Torah law, and a new social order.

God's involvement with human beings is, as both creation and redemption suggest, a caring one. The messianic hope is predicated on such care. God's continued sustenance of creation and presence within it form the basis of Jewish affirmation of divine concern. God's indwelling presence—technically called *Shekhina*—is said to dwell with Israel among the nations and to suffer with the Jewish people. God, in the form of the *Shekhina*, laments at the destruction of the Temple; in the form of a weeping woman she can be found wandering the ruins of Jerusalem. The *Shekhina* suffers pain wherever any Jew suffers pain. When Jews are persecuted, then God as *Shekhina* is persecuted as well.

As *Shekhina* God's presence pervades Jewish experience. Wherever three are engaged in studying Torah, there the *Shekhina* is found. In an assembly reciting the grace after meals—there too is the *Shekhina*. God's indwelling presence appears when the sick are visited, when the naked are clothed, when the dead are buried. The *Shekhina* stands symbolically as an image of God's involvement in daily crises of human life. The Jew is aware of God's continuing concern and care for humanity by sensing the *Shekhina* wherever ethical or moral actions are being performed.

Awareness and sensitivity of God's indwelling presence leads to certain consequences. The Jew is not to take personal pain and suffering as a private matter. God's *Shekhina* is involved. When a Jew prays it should not be, "Oh how my head hurts; heal me, O Lord," but rather, "Oh how the *Shekhina* is in pain; heal me, O Lord, for thy own sake!" The Jew is immersed in God and God in the Jew. The closeness of the divine presence and its healing, comforting power are daily Jewish experiences.

The duality of Jewish theology—its affirmation of God's immanent connection with the world as its Sustainer and its recognition of the philosophical and theological dimensions of the divine—is the natural result of its monotheism. A Jewish-Christian dialogue should take this diversity which grows from a monotheistic insight very seriously. Historically Jews and Christians have been divided on their understanding of God's attributes. Jews, emphasizing the paradox of monotheism, have refused to give independent status to God's attributes of Creator, Redeemer, and Sustainer. They find in Christian claims of a Trinity just the "cutting off of the roots" which Judaism defines as heresy. Christians, on the other hand, often fail to realize that Jews do have access to a close, intimate relationship with God. Redemption is as much a divine reality for Jews as for Christians. God's indwelling presence is a fact of Jewish experience no less than of Christian religious life. A monotheistic view of God should not preclude the existence of various paths to the hidden unity of divinity. Jews and Christians may well agree that God's essential nature is unity. They may also allow each other the privilege of diverging ways of symbolizing that unity in a world of diverse and varied experiences of divinity.

S. Daniel Breslauer

CHRISTIAN VIEW:

"God" is the term which designates the Supreme Being and Source of life. The Christian tradition, rooted in the experience of the Hebrew Scriptures, experiences God as personal. That is, God is known as free, knowing, loving, and self-communicating. While utterly distinct from the world, God is yet the source of creation, life and growth.

The biblical tradition also describes God as Lord of history. While leaving people free, God acts in such a way that events of social and personal history become the arena of divine self-revelation where human beings are brought to the fullness of their potential. In God's self-revelation in history, humans know the Divine to be merciful and compassionate. And yet, that self-revelation also discloses God as the Absolute, who is beyond the grasp of human understanding.

God is thus mystery. The Divine is immanent, near to human beings, offering divine self-revelation to them and acting on their behalf. God is encountered in creation and history. Yet he is also transcendent, always beyond the limits of the human horizon of experience and understanding. Throughout the development of the Christian tradition there have been theologians and mystics who have said that one can speak of God only through a *via negativa* (negative way). Such writers tell us that the only thing meaningful we can say about God is what God is not: God is not material, not changing, not limited. According to these writers, any description of God is analogical.

The mystery of God is not a negative statement. If we use the image of light and darkness, we can say that it is a darkness caused by an excess of light, rather than by an absence of light. The experience of the mystery of God is like that of trying to look directly at the sun and finding that one cannot see. Furthermore, the mystery of God is analogous to the human experience of the mystery of self, of other, and of life itself. Even as we grow in self-awareness, in understanding of others, in insight into the meaning of life, we discover that what is actually being disclosed is that which lies beyond our grasp.

The witness of the Christian Scriptures, of liturgy and piety, as well as theological reflection, shows us that the distinctively Christian experience of God is God as Trinity, that is, that the one God exists and communicates the divine self-revelation in three distinct manners of being, each of which is truly God. We thus attribute one divinity to three "persons": Father, Son and Spirit.

As does the Jewish tradition, Christian tradition describes God as Father. God is the eternal and unoriginated source of all being and life. In the specifically Christian experience, God's Fatherhood is reflected in the description of Jesus in the New Testament. Jesus addresses God with the diminutive *Abba*. Jesus is shown as the obedient Son, chosen by the Father. He announces in word and deed the good news of the Kingdom of God. He does the Father's will in all things, even in the face of an opposition which will take him to a shameful death. God's Fatherhood is most fully apparent in the resurrection of Jesus the Son. In raising Jesus, the Father reveals that his faithfulness extends beyond the barriers of death. Speaking of God as Father and of his Fatherhood in reference to the Sonship of Jesus is not contradictory or evasive. Rather, it indicates that the experience of God as Trinity is an experience of relations. God, the unoriginated source of being, is Father precisely in relationship to the Son.

The Son is the Father's eternal Word of knowledge and self-communication, the Logos. That is, God speaks his knowledge and love so completely that the Word is itself divine, the Son. In the person of Jesus, God communicates himself totally so that we say that Jesus is the Word incarnate. Jesus is thus God's self-communication in history. He shows us the Father in his person and life, his death and resurrection. In Jesus the Father shows us who he is: loving, faithful and true.

The Father knows and loves. He speaks a Word in which he communicates himself fully—the Son. The Son's response of love, and the Father's love for the Son, is the Spirit. We can call Jesus the Word incarnate because he is the one upon whom the Spirit of God is poured out. He is conceived by the power of the Spirit; he is anointed by the Spirit at baptism and works through the power of the Spirit. Jesus is led, impelled, by the Spirit who is the force of God's life and love during his lifetime, and he is raised by the power of that same Spirit after his death.

The Son is the Father's Word of self-communication. The Spirit is the love of Father and Son. He is the life-force of God, acting in the formation of a world out of chaos. He is the source of human wisdom and dynamism, and through his presence human beings perceive, however obscurely, the meaning of life and history. It is thus the Spirit who acts in the hearts of people to bring about the acceptance of God's self-communication, whether that acceptance be explicitly Christian, or take place in another religious tradition, or consist in the sincere struggle to live an authentic human life.

In the explicitly Christian experience, the Spirit is sent forth on humankind through the risen Jesus. The Spirit bears witness to Jesus as Christ. Thus, it is through the Spirit that a person acknowledges Jesus as Lord and calls God *Abba*. Furthermore, the Spirit bonds and unites the community. As the Spirit is the love between Father and Son, so too does he bind the members of a community one to another in mutual concern and service.

The distinctively Christian experience of God is that God is Trinity. Just as we found an analogy for the mystery of God in human self-understanding, so too with the doctrine of the Trinity. Human persons know and understand themselves, and yet they do not know; they remain a mystery to themselves. They enlarge the horizon of knowledge through questioning the meaning of life and existence. Yet, even as the horizon widens, the awareness of mystery deepens, for human beings are open to the infinite. The experience of the finite human spirit which knows itself and is yet open to the infinite is an analogy of God's knowledge and self-communication in the Son.

The human's consciousness of self and openness to what is always beyond is realized most fully in love. The encounter of love allows persons to give and to receive themselves. Yet here, too, there is mystery, for the other is never grasped in love. The experience of the mutual giving and receiving that we call love is, again, analogous to the love between Father and Son, which we call the Spirit.

Although we find an analogy of the Trinity within human experience, the doctrine of the Trinity is not merely an anthropomorphic image. Rather, as the creation account tells us, the human person is theomorphic, made in the image and likeness of God. Thus, the human person is knowing and loving because God is knowing and loving. The human person is truly human only in relation and communion with others because God is relational and communal.

We have used the masculine nouns "Father" and "Son" to describe the Trinitarian relationships of generation and begottenness because Christian theology has traditionally used those categories. God, however, is neither masculine nor feminine. Rather, the divine includes both masculine and feminine qualities while exceeding both, a reality explored by certain Christian mystics, as well as by contemporary theologians.

The Christian doctrine of God as Trinity can cause misunderstanding in Jewish-Christian dialogue because it can appear as tri-theism. Indeed, Christians are sometimes tempted to perceive Son and Spirit as distinct from their relationship to the Father in one divinity. The Jewish-Christian dialogue can actually provide an occasion for Christians to reflect on, and, when necessary, to correct their understanding and thus to appropriate more adequately their experience of God as Three-in-One.

Celia Deutsch

Holiness

JEWISH VIEW:

The experience of the Holy is of two sorts —one designated by the Hebrew term *kadosh* (sanctity) and the other by the term *kavod* (glory). The former is characterized by awe, terror, transcendence; the latter by immanence, divine nearness, personal transformation. The prophet Isaiah's vision of a heavenly deity who fills the Jerusalem temple with just his shirt tails (6:1) illustrates *kadosh*. The vision stresses the distance between the divine and the human, the need for angelic intermediaries between heaven and earth, the terror of God's presence in the midst of the people. The promise that Israel will be a "kingdom of priests and a holy people" (Ex 19:6) illustrates *kavod*. God's indwelling place among Israel transforms the nation itself. Because God is among them Israel has a special task, takes on an aura of responsibility, and becomes an agent for divine action in the family of nations.

Both *kadosh* and *kavod* are divine attributes which human beings seek to emulate. Jews are told to become holy as God is holy (Lev 19:2). That holiness is understood in two ways. The Jew is to be separate from corruption and evil. Just as God is distinct from creation, so the Jew is distinct from other nations. One aspect of Jewish life and practice is its ability to keep the Jew distinctive and separate. Holiness in this sense is the experience of *kadosh*. Through obedience to *halakha* a Jew meets with God and actualizes the divine purpose. This ability to realize the divine plan and to share the divine task points to holiness as *kavod*.

The Jewish experience of holiness is found by sanctifying space, time, and personality (cf. Israel). In each of these spheres holiness is first a divine property and then, by extension, a human one.

God's presence sanctifies space. The Ark of the Covenant, the *Aron*

Kodesh, emanates a holiness that sanctifies the land and people of Israel. Because God's presence pervades Beth El, Jacob experiences its holiness. The Jerusalem Temple is the mysterious locus of divine power. While God fills the world, the Temple represents a special concentration of that force.

Because God's presence sanctifies space Jews can create holy space by preparing a place for the divine presence. When Jews are engaged in holy deeds—studying Torah, prayer, ethical actions—a place is sanctified. A meal at which words of Torah are spoken becomes holy; the table takes on the sanctity of the sacrificial altar.

The *minyan,* or prayer quorum, expresses this same sense of human sanctification of space. Where ten male Jews gather, God's presence dwells. A Jewish community creates holy space by its religious activity. Stories tell how the patriarchs—Abraham, Elijah, David—are compelled by the holiness of this activity to make earthly visitations to complete a *minyan.* Other stories tell how the holiness of a *minyan* mysteriously heals someone suffering from a deadly illness. Miracles occur because Jews have hallowed space through their engagement in religious Commandments.

The association of holiness and the Commandments is particularly clear in regard to the sanctification of time. Sabbaths and festivals are God's gift to the Jew. God has created hills and valleys in time no less than space. The sacred calendar discloses those times when God is most near, when divine holiness is most accessible. There is, however, a reciprocal element in festival celebrations. God sanctifies the day by creative fiat; the Jew sanctifies it by temporal action. Both types of hallowing are necessary. Heavenly holiness and earthly sanctity are interdependent and intrinsically connected to each other.

Each holiday begins by the recitation of *kiddush*, a prayer by which the Jew celebrates the holiness of the day. This prayer makes reference to God's act of sanctifying Israel, of making the Jew holy through Commandments. At the same time holidays are opportunities for the Jew to sanctify life and time. During the holiday the Jew is not merely a passive object, but an acting subject. The day is *made holy* by the acts which Jews perform. The time is holy because it is shared with God. The holiness of Sabbath and holidays is not static but dynamic—it depends on the meeting between the divine and the human.

Commandments as such are opportunities for this meeting of the divine and human. The entire life pattern of Jewish observance is devoted to actualizing the "divine image" in human beings. This image is awakened through acts which God and human beings share in common. God sees Israel's holiness as dependent upon performance of Commandments: "If you fulfill my Commandments you are sanctified, but if you neglect them you will become profaned" (Exodus *Rabbah* 15:24). As a means of attaining transcendent holiness the Commandments surpass human understanding. The ashes of the red heifer purify, but they defile the priests who prepare them. The source of the holiness in the Commandments is divine and transcendent, defying rational explanation or reasoned argument.

The power of these Commandments is that they enable the Jew to share that transcendence which makes God holy. They separate the Jew from uncleanness, stimulate the desire for self-perfection, and create self-awareness. Rabbinic Judaism states: "He who fulfills the words of the sages is holy" (TB *Yebamoth* 20A). Obedience to divine injunctions, even when they cannot be understood, transforms human life. The human being who partakes in Jewish observance activates potentials untapped by other means.

These Commandments should not be thought of as extraordinary, burdensome, or demanding superhuman strength. While derived from an incomprehensible divine source they are experienced as immediate and part of human life. The mystics explain the purpose of the Commandments as that of *devekut,* cleaving to God in the midst of everyday life. The performance of Commandments unites the Jew with God in the most routine and common actions of existence. The Jew is immersed in the divine through the Commandments when going about ordinary business, when conversing in the marketplace, when eating, going to sleep, working, or resting. Life is sanctified because the *person* is made holy.

The key to the Jewish conception of holiness is that just as God's holiness is both near and far, both transcendent and immanent, so too every human being can be holy. The Jew is holy through self-separation from profane time and profane places. But holiness also comes through involvement in daily affairs, through transforming personal life in all its variety and in every sphere of living.

Christians in dialogue with Jews need greater awareness of the complexity of the Jewish understanding of holiness. Jewish life is an orchestrated balance between the inner experience of awe and trembling and the external activity born of the responsibility for immanent holiness. Jewish liturgy and prayer is more than mere empty form. The Jewish expectation of holiness is not as a reward for earned salvation, but rather as an unexpected gift of grace. Holiness is hardly just a human achievement—it is a response to God's explicit command.

The nature of holiness as a command is central for Jewish life. A Christian will misunderstand Jewish thinking about holy space, time, or personality unless the command to be holy is taken seriously. This command bridges the gap between transcendence and immanence. Because space which a Jew sanctifies—whether the Jerusalem Temple, a synagogue, or the home—is a response to the divine presence it is not mere place, the Jew does not need a "heavenly Jerusalem" in which there is no Temple because it is "all holy." Commandment enables the Jew to make *any* place "all holy." The Jew does not need to be told to pray simply, to avoid ostentatious holiday observances. Holidays are as much challenges to human humility and human response as occasions for specific rituals. The submission to God which is essential in prayer is part of the Jewish approach to holiness in time, as is the equally essential sense of responsibility for keeping holy that which God has sanctified. The Jew experiences the danger of hypocrisy and responds to it by seeing all of life as the arena for sanctification. No place is too profane to become holy. Jewish practices escape mere formality and external show by being integrated in daily experience. The command to make life itself holy prevents Judaism from allowing a ritualistic self-satisfaction to undermine genuine religious appreciation of the Holy.

S. Daniel Breslauer

CHRISTIAN VIEW:

Holiness is the effect of justification by grace. Strictly speaking, only God is holy, that is, set apart. But through grace, which is God's self-communication, the human person is drawn into the very holiness of God because he is drawn into communion with him. Human holiness is both divine gift and human surrender to the God who gives himself in grace. In terms of Christian self-understanding, the holiness of a Christian is the effect of being justified by God who gives himself in Jesus, and the response to that gift.

The Synoptic Gospels do not use the word "holiness." The response of surrender to God's gift of himself is described in terms of discipleship. Discipleship means responding to the call of Jesus to follow him (Mk 1:17–20). Jesus' call requires radical decision; it has priority over the demands of all other relationships and claims (Lk 9:57–62; 14:26). The call of discipleship means that one assumes the pattern of Jesus' life and ministry. Thus, disciples are called to love others, even their enemies (Mt 5:44–48). They are sent out by Jesus to preach the Kingdom of God, to heal and to exorcise (Mt 10:1–8). Furthermore, because Jesus has suffered persecution and death so, too, disciples will know a similar fate. (Mt 10:24–25).

John, too, speaks of Jesus' call to follow him (1:35–51). He describes discipleship in terms of rebirth (3:3–7), of eternal life (4:14). Discipleship is the Father's gift (6:37). It implies recognition of Jesus' identity and belief in him (6:68–69). Jesus invites his disciples to love and to remain in him. The disciples respond by observing Jesus' command to love one another, to the point of laying down their life.

Although neither the Synoptics nor John's Gospel uses the term "holy" or "holiness" to describe Christian discipleship, one does find that in Acts Jesus is called holy (3:14; 4:27, 30). By extension, this term is used of his followers (9:13, 32, 26:10).

Paul frequently calls the Christians "saints," literally holy ones. He described Christian holiness in various ways. It is the action of the Father (1 Thess 5:23). The Christian is sanctified in Christ (1 Cor 1:2) and in the Holy Spirit (Rom 15:16). To be holy is to be set apart for God, and to be separated from the compulsion of sin (1 Cor 6:1, Eph 5:3). Holiness is reconciliation in the death of Jesus which has already occurred (Cor 1:22), and is directed to the goal of all Christian life, the fullness of Jesus' coming which has yet to happen (1 Thess 5:23).

Christian holiness is God's gift in the death of Jesus and the gift of the Spirit. It is already accomplished; thus Paul speaks in the indicative. Yet it must also be appropriated, and so Paul uses the imperative: "walk by the Spirit" (Gal 5:16). The Christian appropriates the gift of holiness by walking by the Spirit and bearing the fruits of the Spirit (Gal 5:16–23). The most important priority in Christian conduct is love of others, which is shown in service and consideration (Rom 12:9–13). As in the Synoptic tradition, Christian love extends even to one's enemies (Rom 12:14–21).

Various New Testament traditions thus describe Christian discipleship, or holiness, as being both gift and response to the gift. It belongs to all in the Christian community by virtue of baptism. It is appropriated in a life patterned on that of Jesus, in loving service of others with particular attention to the marginalized and deprived. Thus, Christian holiness has both individual and communal dimensions.

The fundamental reality of Christian holiness is that of grace, of discipleship. Throughout the history of the Church, people have interpreted holiness according to a variety of models or ideals. During the first two centuries, many understood martyrdom as the ideal fulfillment of baptism which incorporated the person into the death and resurrection of Jesus. The monastic life developed in the fourth century and was long regarded as the ideal of holiness. The Renaissance, with its emphasis on the individual, gave rise to humanism among Catholics. Among the Reformers, it resulted in a heightened awareness of the individual's relationship to God. Recognition of the socio-political reality of human consciousness has led contemporary religious thinkers to understand Christian holiness as including such a component.

Holiness is not the possession of a few extraordinary persons. All Christians are called to holiness by virtue of their baptism. All are called to a radical decision in discipleship which subordinates other claims to Jesus' call. Christian holiness is both personal and communal. It is personal because it is fundamentally a personal relationship with God in Jesus. It is communal because it is lived in the believing community which is the Church.

Christians appropriate the baptismal gift of holiness and renew their response to the call to discipleship in prayer and in the generous service of others. They enhance that gift in attentiveness to the Spirit of Jesus who moves them to make concrete decisions which reflect their option to follow the Lord.

Christian holiness is this-worldly. It leads Christians not only to a growing union with God in Christ, but to involvement with their neighbors. By extension, the call to discipleship leads Christians to political decisions which are coherent with the Gospel, which respect the sacredness of life and concern for people, particularly the marginalized and the deprived.

Christian holiness is also eschatological. Christians hold earthly goods with open hands, receiving them as gifts of the Creator, while aware that all things are passing and that the fullness of the Kingdom has not yet come. While making political decisions coherent with Gospel values, they are aware that neither Gospel nor Kingdom of God can be identified with any political choice, event, or movement.

Christian holiness is lived according to the personality, gifts, and limitations of each person. Thus, while fundamentally the same, the response to God in Christ, the surrender of faith takes on a variety of forms which manifests the richness of grace itself.

Christian holiness is never fully accomplished because human life, while graced, is also stamped with the ambiguity of sin (q.v.). Although the person responds as generously as possible to God's gift of himself in Christ, there is always within the person that which is not yet fully open to God's grace. Some measure of selfishness remains. Awareness of this reality, however, is not cause for discouragement. Rather, it is a reminder that holiness, as life itself, is a process of growth, and that Christians can walk confident in the mercy of the God who calls.

Christian holiness is a share in the holiness of God through the surrender of faith. It is the following of Jesus in living the Gospel and is manifest most clearly in loving service of others. Christian holiness is lived in countless ways, according to particular situations, by human beings who are still touched by selfishness, yet grow in response to the call of God in Christ.

Celia Deutsch

Ideology

JEWISH VIEW:

Ideology, many thinkers argue, is a peculiarly modern phenomenon. Rabbi Jacob Agus, e.g., comments that "when theology ceased to dominate the minds of men, the age of ideologies was begun" (*Jewish Identity in an Age of Ideology*). According to this view, ideology is a replacement for traditional belief. When God and divine instruction are no longer central, then secular ideas become the focal point for social and cultural movements. The age of ideology spells the end of the age of religion.

Ideology, however, may be understood more broadly. L.B. Brown suggests that ideology is "an integrated set of propositions about some important social area or domain" (*Ideology*). To this definition one additional feature must be joined: motivation. An ideology is a set of integrated propositions implying behavioral consequences. With this in mind even classical Jewish thought can be understood as ideological. Jewish religion was focused on ideas that mobilized action even before the modern period. Tradition recalls that God declares, "If only Israel had forsaken me and kept my Torah" (*Pesikta d'Rav Kahana*). Jewish theology is not directed to metaphysical speculation but uses ideas to motivate correct behavior.

Judaism, then, even in its pre-modern period was distinctly ideological. While theology was often diverse, practice was unified and central. In rabbinical discussion the primacy of action over theory was stressed again and again. Judaism was ideological because it provided an integrated worldview which advocated a specific course of action. Agus, however, is right in noting a difference between pre-modern and contemporary Judaism. In its pre-modern form Judaism was a theological ideology; in its contemporary expression Judaism comprises a variety of religious and non-religious ideologies. Jewish theologian Mordecai Kaplan explains the difference this way.

While previously "one ideology, uniform and unchanging, came to be regarded as indispensable to salvation (now) there is the alternative of permitting different ideologies to be developed" (*Judaism without Supernaturalism*).

Judaism, then, began as an ideology of Torah rather than a theology of religion and has become a collection of practices and cultural expressions that is supported by various ideologies. The purpose of these modern ideologies is to legitimate a modern continuation of a civilization inherited from the past. There are two basic ideological moves that can be made. The first is to see Jewish culture as the necessary vehicle for Jewish religion. That ideology insists that only by continuing the traditional culture of the Jewish heritage can the ideals of Jewish religion be preserved. Martin Buber expressed this view clearly. He insisted that Jewish revelation, "in distinction to the revelations of all other religions, presents itself as an incident in history (*Israel and the World*). This means that only an historical expression of Jewish culture can fulfill the meaning of that history. Judaism is supported by various ideologies of cultural identity, historical purpose, and political significance because without these ideologies Jewish religious values would be lost. Ideology is not a negative term denoting a reversal of traditional Jewish values. It is rather a traditional Jewish approach which recognizes that without concrete historical realization Judaic ideals are meaningless.

A second approach is the reverse of the first one. For Zionists Jewish religion is often the vehicle for Jewish nationalism. From this standpoint religion is the ideology by which national identity is preserved. Ahad Ha-Am (pen name of Asher Ginsberg, 1856–1927) argued: "Our religion is national—that is to say, it is a product of our national spirit—but the reverse is not true" (*Selected Essays of Ahad Ha-Am*). Judaism according to this view is essentially a national culture which incidentally has a religious ideology mobilizing support and adherence.

This second approach is not only used by Zionists. Secular Jews agree in seeing Judaism as primarily cultural with religion as an ideology motivating certain behavioral patterns. Horace M. Kallen reflected on the ideological roots of Judaism. He notes that there are a number of distinctly different Jewish "views of life" and argues that modern Jews select elements from the tradition "to rationalize their own ends and to justify their own struggles" (*The Religion of Secular Jews*). Judaism on this account is a reservoir of ideologies some of which can be used to support one idea and others to support an opposite point of view. In Kallen's standpoint, as in the Zionist approach, the concrete program advocated comes first and the ideology is only a secondary addition.

There is no need, in the opinion of both groups, to remove ideology from Jewish religion. Judaism is intrinsically ideological. Perhaps this characteristic of Judaism marks it off from Christianity. Arthur A. Cohen has suggested that the confrontation between Jewish and Christian religion is not that between one theology and another but between two religious communities. The Jewish concern is the practical result of belief, that is to say, the way that religion functions ideologically. Cohen declares that "there is no polarity of Synagogue and Church, only the polarity of two communities, the people of Israel and the ecclesia" (*The Myth of the Judeo-Christian Tradition*). Politics rather than religion, ideology rather than theology separate the Jew from the Christian.

From this perspective it is essential that dialogue between Jew and Christian include a discussion of ideology. If Judaism has entered the age of ideologies rather than ideology, then fruitful discussion between Jews and Christians may be possible in a way never before feasible. The variety of Jewish ideologies may include advocating ecumenical exchange, cultural pluralism, and coordinated action between Jew and non-Jew. The Jew may be able to admit that Christianity, no less than Judaism, can be represented by a plurality of ideologies, of which antisemitism was only one. Christians may be led to a more open dialogue by recognizing the variety of options within Jewish religious life and thus begin to overcome some ancient stereotypes.

Another importance for dialogue found in a discussion of ideology is the difference between Jewish and Christian evaluations of the role of ideology in religion. Jews need to recognize the Christian's indifference to ideology as a *religious* expression. When Jews learn that Christians see themselves in terms of belief rather than action, abstract thought rather than practical motivations, they can better understand some actions in the past which have been, all too often, attributed to deep-seated Christian religiosity. Once persecutions and prejudice are relegated to a secondary role as actions rather than beliefs, the Jew can understand why Christians do not associate the atrocities of Christian history with Christian religion. On the other hand Christians need to recognize that Jews *do* take ideology seriously as an essential element in religion. Judaism is a culture focused on action and community. Belief takes its meaning only from the deeds it inspires; religious ideals find their fulfillment only in concrete history. The Jew is committed not only to certain beliefs but to the ideological implications of those beliefs. Indeed a central Jewish concern is that of deriving ideological consequences from apparently abstract religious statements. Christians will seriously misconstrue Judaism if they negate the importance and centrality of religious ideology. To speak of Judaism without speaking of either traditional ideology or of modern ideological options is not to speak of Judaism at all.

S. Daniel Breslauer

CHRISTIAN VIEW:

Ideology is a rather abused term. It is sometimes said that an ideology is what you call someone else's system of ideas if you don't like it, especially if you think he is trying to foist that system on others. Attitudes associated with such a definition of ideology include intractability and a vested interest in maintaining certain social relationships.

The term itself has a long history, going back to Francis Bacon and associated with such people as Napoleon, Condillac, and de Tracy. The word ideology is often invoked amid an anti-religious critique of the way religious institutions maintain certain worldviews which guarantee their continued hegemony. This view of religions was employed by Ludwig Feuerbach and then refined by Karl Marx, for whom ideology was "a false concept of reality, the separation of theory and practice."

Ideology in contradistinction to utopia was the centerpiece of the sociology of knowledge explored and described by Karl Mannheim. Mannheim pointed out how one's environment—social, economic, and religious—affects one's knowledge and worldview. In such an analysis, the determination of value could be as easily assigned to one's social standing or eduction as it could be to any "objective" source. Such a critique carried with it the danger of relativism; applied to religion or knowledge it is related to scientism in which something is of value insofar as it can be subjected to the same sort of analysis as physical objects of the universe.

Ideology can also be a neutral term; as it is used today, however, it usually has a pejorative meaning, as in the phrase, "Christianity is an ideology." If used among missionary countries, such a phrase usually means that a foreigner is foisting a strange way of believing or a strange set of beliefs on an unsuspecting native population. If said of a mainly Christian population, it means that the population are victims of Christianity's worldview and that they are impervious to other ways of viewing things. But as a neutral term it can be "simply a symbol system, a set of templates with high emotional charge and strong emotional investment that provides a chart by which a person can find his way through a complex, confused, and organized social reality" (Andrew Greeley).

One hears, most often in scholarly circles, of an "ideological critique of religion"; this means an investigation of the phenomenon of religion that is sensitive to the context—historical, economic, class—from which a statement, idea or doctrine should emerge. In such a critique, one asks: Whose interests are served? Who profits? What structures are threatened? Who is the dominant class? As a Christian, influenced by the God of the Hebrew Scriptures, one begins to see things from the viewpoint of the poor, the oppressed.

The importance of ideology, and, more specifically, of the ideological critique of religion, is that it has had tremendous influence among one of the major Christian trends of the last twenty years: "liberation theology." Liberation theology is a method of doing theology not so much from a supposed objective viewpoint, but from the posture of commitment: commitment to the poor and working for their advancement in the world. The test of the doctrine/worldview/theology is not only what kind of worldview this fosters, but also what kind of action and attitudes it spawns.

Liberation theology seeks a new meeting ground between theology and sociology, and it is in sociology that ideology has its proper definition. Indeed, Juan Luis Segundo, as one typical liberation theologian, considers that one of the Christian theologian's task is to rid religious dogma of "ideological distortion." He speaks of "*disideologizing* the oppressed mind from the ideology of the oppressors." Theology needs to be self-critical. Indeed, "disideologizing" is one of the tasks of the Christian theologian in the Jewish-Christian dialogue (*The Liberation of Theology*).

The ideological critique of Christianity in the Jewish-Christian dialogue has only lately become a topic of some Christian theologians. In such a critique, a Christian theologian would start from the *experience* of the Holocaust and ask: Is there anything in the Christian faith life or credal statements which might have contributed to an atmosphere within which anti-semitism could have flourished? Has the language which Christians used to express their belief left theological room for the ongoing religious significance and validity of Judaism or has it excluded Judaism after Jesus from the religious map?

By looking at the consequences of the theological enterprise, the Christian in the Jewish-Christian dialogue may come up with some startling and uncomfortable suggestions. Many Christian theologians in our history, innocent of an ideological critique of religion, have pursued theology in a different way. They have looked simply to biblical texts (usually removed from their historical contexts) and to Church tradition to formulate doctrine. Yet if one simply begins with an array of inspired texts, applying them to the current historical situation, one seldom moves from merely interpreting reality toward changing it, or, worse, one's thinking begins to legitimate the way things are for the dominant class. On the other hand, if, as some contemporary theologians are doing, one views the consequences of theology in a particular way, one may be in a better, albeit historically different, place to view it critically. An ideological critique calls into question the conscious and unconscious presuppositions of any position. One of the most startling but also predictable dimensions of the Christian-Jewish dialogue is the way that one's presuppositions and unexamined ways of viewing things are challenged, stretched, and threatened. At the same time, believing in a God who enters into relationship, Jews and Christians can do no less than to enter into relationship where both have something to offer and both have something to learn.

Ideology itself need not be on the agenda of the Christian-Jewish dialogue, but sensitivity to the kind of questions which thinkers such as Karl Mannheim and Juan Luis Segundo have raised will free both Christians and Jews from a rigidity which does not allow a new idea to penetrate and affect what they have believed all their lives. Ideological critique is a tool of analysis; it is not the object of analysis. But in the Jewish-Christian dialogue, it can be an essential tool.

Michael McGarry

Israel

JEWISH VIEW:

The term Israel, properly pronounced *Yisra'el,* contains within it three ideas which can be conveniently signaled by three Hebrew words: *am, eretz,* and *medina* (people, land, state).

Am Yisrael means the people of Israel and refers to the Jewish people. The roots of this people are traced back to Abraham-Sarah and, through them, to Noah and Adam-Eve. Many think this is mere mythology, but already in the early Middle Ages Jews realized that the evidence for this chain of descendants is what they called "the true tradition," that is: my father told me I was a Jew, his father told him, his father told him, and so on. No one made it up. It is simply that each generation has been integrated into the chain, even if written documentation no longer exists to "prove" the validity of the chain itself. Membership in the Jewish people, then, is a matter of lineage. One can also join the Jewish people by conversion, in which case one is integrated into the line of descent.

Am Yisrael received two formative calls: the first is the promise of seed to Abraham through Isaac (Gen 21:12) and the second is the covenant (q.v.) made at Sinai between God and the Jewish people (Ex 19:5; Dt 7:6–8). These crucial moments established for all time the substance and continuity of the Jewish people. The two concepts taken together establish Jewish identity as a combination of biology and culture, of lineage and calling.

Jews express the concept of *Am Yisrael* theologically in the doctrine of the Chosen People (q.v.). The Bible states that God chose the Jews, and the rabbis have embodied that idea in many places in the liturgy. Some Jews in the modern period are intellectually unhappy with the idea of the Chosen People and they reject it as a theological doctrine, with one group, namely Reconstructionist, even eliminating it from the liturgy. However, even these

Jews retain the value of the specialness of the Jewish people and its tradition. Similarly, secular Jews (for whom religion is only a minor part of their Jewish identity), while rejecting the theological formulation, usually preserve a sense of the specialness of Jewish life and culture. Thus there are to be found books on "the contribution of the Jews to civilization," "the uniqueness of Jewish history and destiny," and so on (cf. Ideology). Thus, too, people who visited the Jews of the former Soviet Union where Jewish education was forbidden sometimes found notes surreptitiously slipped into their pockets which read, "*Am Yisrael Chai*—the Jewish people lives."

Eretz Yisrael means the Land of Israel and refers to what Christians call the Holy Land. The roots of this idea, too, are traced back to Abraham-Sarah and, through them, to the moment of creation. The whole universe is God's, no one else's, and he can do with it whatever he pleases. He promised a special piece of it to Abraham and his seed, and it remains theirs for all eternity. No one, no regime, can deprive them of it. No accident of history can change the promise of the Creator.

Eretz Yisrael had several formative moments. The first is the original promise of the Land to Abraham and his seed through Isaac (Gen 17:7–8). The second is the promise of the Land to the Jewish people as a whole (Dt 30:3–5). The third is the conquest of the Holy Land by Joshua; then, the conquests by King David; finally, the resettlement of the Land after the first Exile under Ezra. It is important to note that, while the promise is eternal, the actual boundaries have varied through history.

Eretz Yisrael, too, is expressed in theological and in secular terms. Theologically, the Land is as much a part of the covenant as the people. Both are given freely by God. Both are binding forever. Neither can be removed from the concreteness of its existence. In secular terms, the attachment to the Land is rooted not in God's word, but in history and culture. The Land is the ancient homeland of the people. It is the crucible of its civilization. There, the great works were produced. There, the original language was spoken. And Jews have always maintained a presence there, even in the worst of times. In both modes of thought, the Land is said to receive and respond to its children while rejecting strangers. The Land is even said to reject its children when they profane it. There can be no true national existence, however, without it.

Medina(t) Yisrael means the State of Israel and it refers to the political form of Jewish civilization in the Land at a given period. There have been three Jewish commonwealths: the first under Joshua, the Judges, and the Kings; the second under Ezra, the Maccabees, and the Herodians; the third under the democratically elected leadership of the people. The last-

mentioned is the current State of Israel. Each state has had different boundaries. Each has had a different political order. And each has administered its
responsibilities with greater or lesser care.

Political sovereignty for the Jewish people in its Land implies two
important ideas. First, Jewish religion has always regarded the state as subject to the will of God. Second, the ideal Jewish state, theologically, is one
which is headed by a righteous descendant of the line of King David. This
person, the Messiah or anointed (king), will rule in justice as God rules the
world (Is 11). Davidic kingship-messiahship is thus also a moment within the
covenant between God and the Jewish people. It, too, is a promise, given
freely by God and valid eternally. Interestingly, Jews have reserved judgment
on whether the current State of Israel is messianic in import. The contemporary liturgy refers to the State only as "the beginning of the growth of our
Redemption." Many secular Jews reject the messiahship motif but they preserve the idea of the right of the Jewish people not only to have its own
Land, but also to govern itself as a free people, to protect its citizens, to tax
them, to educate them—in short, to serve the people in all the ways in which
a modern state serves its people.

This movement for national revival, whether it be in its religious or in
its secular form, is called "Zionism." Zionism implies the theological and/or
historic right to the Land and to a State, with all the rights and privileges pertaining thereto. Zionism is thus a movement for the revitalization of Jewish
civilization, in the homeland, under the aegis of a Jewish state. It is a movement of Return (q.v.).

These three concepts—People, Land, and State—are very difficult for
Christians to grasp. Christianity has no concept of bio-ethnic identity; there
is no "Christian people" which is bound by ancestry. Christianity also has no
concept of Land; there is no "Christian homeland." The connections between
spirituality and bodies, and between religion and geography, have no easy
parallels in Christianity. Yet, these ideas are core and central to Jewish identity, religious and secular, especially in the aftermath of the Holocaust. No dialogue can begin without acknowledging these realities. Jews must state
clearly their positions and Christians must reconsider the meaning and extent
of covenant.

The problem of the State of Israel is even more difficult because of the
political situation in the Middle East. There are Christians who tend to have
sympathy for the Palestinians and to construe the problem of the State in that
light. Christians also have considerable missions in the Middle East and
hence are exposed to views of the situation that need to be discussed. Yet dia-

logue that does not deal with these issues is no dialogue; it is avoidance of issues.

David Blumenthal

CHRISTIAN VIEW:

When a Christian hears the word, "Israel," he or she thinks either of the people Israel of Old Testament times or the land, the nation of Israel of modern times.

For many Christians, "Israel" is a synonym for "Jews," the Jewish people, the historical people at the time of Jesus. Originally meaning "God struggles," or "God is strong," Israel emerged as a name with the incident of Jacob struggling with God (Gen 32:29); later it came to be a tribal name and a sacred name. The tribes were named after the twelve sons of Jacob, and they had a strong sense of a covenantal relationship with God. Some of the synonyms for the people Israel in the Hebrew Scriptures were "people of Yahweh" (Is 1:3), God's servant (Is 44:21), God's chosen one (Is 45:4), God's flock (Ps 95:7), God's vineyard (Is 5:7), and God's spouse (Hos 2:4). The rise of Judah in the south saw a parallel use of "Judaism" as the name given to the Jews by the Gentiles; still "Israelite" was used as the sacred name in prayer. It became the focus of Jeremiah's prophecies about a restored Israel (30:10, 31:2, 31, etc.).

At the time of Jesus, Israel was identified with the occupied Jewish nation. Christians understood Jesus as God's gift to Israel, the glory of Israel (Lk 2:32), the king of Israel (Mt 27:42), the Savior of Israel (Acts 13:23f). The sacredness of Israel as a name for the Jewish people is maintained in parts of the New Testament (e.g., Rom 9:6f), but Christians soon understood Jeremiah's prophecies of a renewed Israel as applying to them since the twelve apostles were the obvious parallels of the twelve sons of Jacob. Attendant therefore to Israel as a designation for the Jewish people up to the time of Jesus was the early Church's penchant to identify itself as the "New Israel," the new sacred nation. Such a designation smacks of Christian supersessionism, the theory by which Christians appropriate for themselves the sacred designation for Israel as the "new people of God," the "new Israel," and the true object of God's love, etc.

In modern times, the designation of the Jewish nation state as Israel brings to the fore the link between the people and the land. For many Christians, it is something of an enigma why Jews should hold land so closely linked to their self-identity. Christianity understands itself as a universal religion which is not identified with any particular geography. Thus the intimate relation between land and peoplehood makes the State of Israel one of the prime areas for Christians to learn from their Jewish brothers and sisters about their land tradition.

Not only do Christians need to hear why Jews are so tied to the land, but they also need to know some of their own history which divorced the Jewish people from their land. According to some Christian explanations, after the death of Jesus, exile from Palestine was the Jews' punishment for complicity in the death of Jesus. Christians for centuries forbade Jews to own land and this functioned as the necessary historical backdrop to the myth of the wandering Jew. There was not much Christian support for Zionism in the late nineteenth and early twentieth centuries. For example, in response to Theodor Herzl's plea for Vatican support for the Jews' return to Israel, Pope Pius X remarked that, since the Jewish people had not recognized the visitation of the Lord, the Vatican could not recognize the Jewish people, much less their claim to land.

Many Christians today support the Jewish claim to the land of Israel. Although they often refer to it as the "Holy Land," because it was the home of Jesus, these Christians trust that the Jews will maintain accessibility to the holy places for pilgrimage and freedom of worship for Christians who live in Israel. Formerly, the Vatican maintained a staunch neutrality over the State of Israel. But in December 1993 and January 1994, Pope John Paul II initiated a series of moves that led to recognition of the State of Israel by the Vatican. Although they had long withheld this recognition because of the continuing dispute over borders, and the fear that Arabs would mete out reprisals on Christians if the Vatican did recognize Israel, they changed because of the clear progress made toward solving these problem in the "Peace Process" that had been going on for several years among Israel, Jordan, the Palestinians and the Palestine Liberation Organization.

In a statement issued in 1982, the World Council of Churches noted that the State of Israel, for Jews, "constitutes part of the long search for that survival which has always been central to Judaism, throughout the ages."

In the United States, support for Israel finds different bases. Some, especially evangelicals and fundamentalists, view the Jewish return to Israel as partial fulfillment of the prophecies of the end time. Others see the rise of the State of Israel as a just world response to what happened to the Jews in the Holocaust. Still others, beginning to see the centrality of land in the life of the Jews, support it as a faith and political commitment to their belief in a God who does not renege on his promises.

The U.S. National Conference of Catholic Bishops in a statement of 1975 said: "Whatever difficulties Christians may experience...they should strive to understand this link between land and people which Jews have expressed in their writings and worship throughout millennia as a longing for the homeland, holy Zion. Appreciation of this link is not to give assent to any particular religious interpretation of the bond. Nor is this affirmation meant to deny the legitimate rights of other parties in the region, or to adopt any political stance in the controversies over the Middle East, which lie beyond the purview of this statement."

Thus, among Christians, one notes a mixture of theological, political, moral and cultural grounds for supporting the State of Israel. Some Christians balk at full support of Israel because they think support is co-extensive with a support for specific Israeli policies and/or civil governments. Many Christians (without sufficient historical knowledge) are confused by the Palestinian claim to the same land, particularly when that claim is cloaked in language of liberation.

The importance of Israel in the Jewish-Christian dialogue can hardly be exaggerated. Therein Christians, allowing Jews to define themselves in their own terms, will learn something about the link between peoplehood and a land to call their own. The land is closely linked with the will to survival. Indeed, Christians who have long traveled the road of inter-religious dialogue suggest that the retrieval of a theology of land might be the most precious outcome of the Jewish-Christian dialogue.

Finally, Israel is important for the Jewish-Christian dialogue for what it may implicate with regard to antisemitism. The connection between anti-Zionism and antisemitism is complex and multivalent; one can be one without being the other. But suspicions of antisemitism among anti-Zionists is very great. This can only be sorted out in the dialogue. As Edward Flannery has said, "The difficulty resides in the unconsciousness of present-day anti-Semitism. Since it is unconscious, it is necessarily denied, even by the anti-Zionist, who generally shows more of its characteristics than does the run-of-the-mill anti-Semite."

Michael McGarry

Jewish-Christian Dialogue

JEWISH VIEW:

Christians and Jews live in the same world, under the same skies. For the last two millennia they have shared a history, at once with each other and alienated from one another. For a long time, the Jewish-Christian relationship was one of confrontation and theological warfare, with sad consequences for the Jewish people. The relationship was not dialogical but an interchange of monologues.

In the beginning of the Christian era, Jews and Christians were brothers, separated but within one family, discussing points of religious commitment: the missionship of Jesus, his divine vocation, the concept of the Messiah, the Christ. The separation later on progressed in a number of stages. The first one was a theological misunderstanding, that is, Paul's one-sided view of Israel, developed and restated by Church Fathers and medieval thinkers. Israel was denied a role in God's design; Christianity was the *new* Israel, the fulfillment of hope. This denial was based on a theology, the "teaching of contempt" (Jules Isaac, in a book of that title), which negated Israel's mission, a view which led to violence and the separation of the Jewish community from society at large. The teaching was a denial of the Jewish testimony, the right to be different in the witness to God.

Another aspect of separation was political, viz., the recognition and acceptance of Christianity by Constantine (fourth century), establishing Christian religious supremacy in the Western world. The fate of Jews was thereby stamped for many centuries, imposing upon them second class citizenship, alienating them from European history and condemning them to prejudice and persecution. Jesus, the liberator of Gentiles, had become the oppressor of his own people.

The Christian teaching denying Israel's vocation resulted in social isolation. Jews were obliged to live in ghettoes and to wear special badges identifying their Jewish condition; they were forbidden to work in a number of occupations or to enter trade corporations (guilds) and, in effect, were forced into servitude without practically any economic or political rights. Theological confrontations, persecution by Crusaders and others, and the burning of sacred texts became historical realities for Jews scattered throughout Europe.

Historical changes, such as the French and industrial revolutions, gave rise to a new social class, the middle class, which transformed European feudal society. It enabled society to absorb Jews and other minorities into national life, though the prejudice of centuries prevented their total integration. The Nazi onslaught of the twentieth century revealed currents of hatred against the Jewish people that had lain more or less dormant in Western culture.

After the Holocaust, our century witnessed a change in the mood of the Jewish-Christian relationship. The monologue situation has slowly been replaced by dialogue, the encounter of two equals. Christian soul-reckoning is taking place to clarify differences and remedy a past attitude of contempt. Since 1945, national and international ecclesiastical organizations, the Holy See (Vatican II documents), the World Council of Churches, European episcopal conferences, the National Council of Churches and the National Conference of Catholic Bishops in the United States have published documents on Christian-Jewish relations. The statements denounce antisemitism, some of them recognizing spiritual responsibility for the atmosphere that resulted in the Nazi genocide. They recommend specific changes for presenting Jews and Judaism in catechetical textbooks, modify liturgical expressions denigrating Judaism and urge the study of Jewish sources at the time of Jesus, in particular Pharisaic theological writings. Very few documents, however, refer directly to the State of Israel and the role of Zionism in contemporary Jewish existence and vocation.

The dialogue involves a process of meeting and recognition between two faith communities, two experiences of God: Christianity and Judaism. It is an encounter of subjects of faith, not objects of contempt, two equal testimonies to God. For each partner it means the recognition of the other as a constituent in God's design, the acceptance of a different approach to the Eternal, a different though not conflicting spirituality.

The process of dialogue implies on the Christian side the overcoming of prejudice; for Jews it means the coming to terms with the trauma of memories. The negative effects of prejudice must be overcome by education and an emphatic study of Judaism, its history and its relationship to Christianity.

The painful effects of memory are more difficult to overcome. The Jewish people have suffered centuries of persecution and contempt, leaving images if not scars difficult to erase, a feeling of disillusionment inviting self-righteousness and distrust. The Jewish dialogue partner requires signs, gestures of friendship and fraternity to erase these images. He needs to be reassured of the seriousness of Christian commitment to friendship; otherwise the dialogue will become just another form of the old threat of denial and of conversionary activity.

The end of the twentieth century finds Jewish and Christian witness stimulated by the challenge of total evil, and by the renewal of hope. Given Auschwitz and the State of Israel, both communities must examine and try to understand the renewed dimensions of exile and return in the life of Jews as well as in universal terms. Both communities are confronted with the search for meaning, God's hidden face in the midst of the Holocaust horror.

This examination implies an understanding of the Jewish-Christian relationship in all its dimensions. For Christianity it calls for an attempt to understand the Holocaust, the suffering of the people of God, an event in the midst of a Christian society, and also the centrality of the State of Israel to Jewish life. One-sided criticism of Zionism and political aspects of Israel continues, repeating in many guises and under new theological formats the teaching of contempt of times past. Judaism is thereby denied a role in history.

Judaism for its part will have to understand Christianity not as persecutor of the past but as another way to God. Judaism will have to face the meaning of Jesus, a teacher, not the Jewish Messiah, invested with a mission to the world, to bring God and humanity together.

New bonds of friendship, of covenantal friendship, are healing the alienation of centuries. Jews and Christians are coming to recognize one another beyond prejudice and memory, accepting each other as children of God. Thereby they practice, following Martin Buber's concept rooted in the Pharisaic tradition, that when two or three are truly with one another they are together in the Name of God. Dialogue is the attempt at being truly together, in and with God.

Leon Klenicki

CHRISTIAN VIEW:

Jewish-Christian dialogue, just as any inter-religious dialogue in our time, refers to a situation in which persons of different religious traditions take part as equal partners in a conversation, while each accepts the self-definition of the other.

Former Christian consideration of Judaism (as well as of other religions) encouraged proselytism. That is, Christians believed it not only legitimate but praiseworthy to exert economic, psychological, or spiritual pressure on non-Christians in order to gain new members for the Church. The dialogical position, however, is one in which the parties accept one another as mutually equal partners. Inter-religious dialogue is confessional; people speak from the experience of their own faith traditions. However, they are willing to accept the witness of people of different traditions in the framework of their own self-understanding. Such mutual witness becomes a common challenge for all parties to examine and articulate their own faith experience.

Dialogue between Jews and Christians is a recent development in a two thousand year history. Although there were always some exceptions, relations between the two communities were characterized by the animosity and mistrust bred by antisemitism (q.v.). Through dialogue many Christians have discovered Judaism in its own terms as a living faith tradition with a continuous development in the post-biblical era. The discovery of Judaism has led many Christians to correct certain misunderstandings present in the theology or in popular belief. The most obvious example is that informed Christians no longer speak of deicide, the age-old accusation that the Jews killed Jesus. (Critical scholarship has shown the role of Roman occupation officials.)

The witness of Jewish life made Christians realize that, contrary to their former understanding, God has not abandoned the covenant with the Jewish people. Attentive to Jewish experience, they realize that God continues to be faithful to the Jewish people, to guide Jews in historical events and to address them in Torah. They understand that Jews continue to live in fidelity to their tradition according to a variety of interpretations of that tradition.

Attentiveness to Jewish self-understanding has helped Christians to recognize that Torah does not imply legalistic deeds but an interiorized practice of the *mitzvot* (Commandments), in obedience to God. Furthermore, Christians involved in dialogue have discovered that, while they share with Jews a common legacy in the Hebrew Scriptures, their own reading does not exhaust the meaning of those texts (cf. Bible).

Jewish-Christian dialogue with its correlative Christian discovery of

Judaism has corrected Christian understanding of the Pharisees. Scholarly investigation has shown the portrayal of the Pharisees in the New Testament to be a caricature drawn in such a way as to convey the primitive Church's polemic with the Jewish community. Christians can thus understand better the character of the New Testament texts as well as the historical role of the Pharisees in the development of Judaism.

Jewish-Christian dialogue has led Christians to an awareness of the significance of the Holocaust in Jewish self-understanding. Correlatively, it has also resulted in a new appreciation of the rebirth of the State of Israel. Dialogue leads Christians to understand Jewish attachment to the land not simply as a twentieth-century phenomenon, but as integral to Jewish tradition and self-definition.

Christian discovery of Judaism has resulted in sensitivity to Jewish self-definition as well as an understanding of Christianity's indebtedness to Judaism. Thus, Christians realize that while it is not essential for Jews to understand Christianity in order to understand their own tradition, it is necessary for Christians to understand Judaism for an adequate understanding of Christianity. This is true not only because Christians claim the Hebrew Scriptures as integral to their Bible, but because Jesus was a Jew, as were the members of the primitive Church.

Jesus and the first Christians were nourished by the Hebrew Scriptures and by the richness of Second Temple Judaism. This is evident in the use of such concepts as Kingdom of God, resurrection of the dead, and the primacy of love of God and love of neighbor. From a literary point of view, one sees the influence of Jewish tradition in Jesus' use of parables and in the hermeneutical principles used by the early Church to interpret the Hebrew Scriptures. The legacy of Judaism was, to be sure, reinterpreted in light of the Christian experience; the concepts are used differently. Nonetheless, Christianity's roots are sunk deeply in Jewish soil.

Christian re-examination of their tradition in the light of Jewish self-understanding presents exciting new directions for Christian belief and life. This is not to say that anti-Judaism or antisemitism has been eradicated. It is to say that dialogue provides a challenge to Jews and Christians to grow in their faith commitments as they explore together the significance of their traditions for a contemporary world.

Celia Deutsch

Justice

JEWISH VIEW:

From the Jewish perspective, grace is God's relationship to the world entailing justice and mercy. An ancient Jewish tradition states that in order to create the world God was forced to bring together justice and mercy. Just as a glass will break if filled with either boiling water or ice, so the world could not stand if filled with only justice or only mercy (cf. Genesis *Rabbah* 12:15). God filled the world with an admixture of the two and thereby enabled it to stand. The mystics explain that God's first attempt at creation was a failure because the earthly vessels could not withstand the power of the divine love and were shattered. The object of the mystic is to restore balance between love and judgment, between mercy and strength in the world.

This mystic insight represents the Jewish contention that God's grace lies in being both merciful and just. A human king is loved if he is merciful and feared if he punishes; God is both loved and feared whether doing mercy or justice. Where God's power is found in the Bible, rabbinic sages comment, there too one finds divine humility (cf. TB *Rosh Hashanah* 17b). God is both King and Shepherd, loving Father and strict Judge. Psalm 145:17 explains that while God's ways are those of strict justice, his deeds are pure love.

The balance seems to tip in the direction of love. God's intimate relationship with the created world is a merciful one. Justice is required if the world is not to return to chaos. God's basic nature, however, is one of forgiveness and loving kindness. Israel prays for God to be merciful. God, according to Judaism, also prays. Divine prayers are an internal dialogue within the deity: "May my attribute of mercy overcome my attribute of justice" (TB *Berakhot* 7a). Because compassion is the characteristic divine trait, Judaism sees judgment itself as an act of mercy. God judges at the most auspicious times: Israel is judged when involved with the Commandments; the nations of the world are judged when they sleep and have no opportunity to commit sins. Whenever Israel recites the thirteen attributes of God the deity must move from the throne of justice to the throne of mercy. The sound of the *shofar*, the ram's horn, performs the same function of changing divine justice into divine compassion.

Another aspect of judgment which transforms threat into promise is the possibility of merit, of *zehut*. Far from being an earned reward, a salvation based on works, the rabbinic doctrine of merit is based on the idea of grace. God has attributed merit to individuals as a means of mitigating the inevitable judgment which awaits them. That merit is sometimes inherited. The merit of the fathers and mothers derives from the religious traditions they established. God's mercy enabled the patriarchs and matriarchs to originate ways of acting and ritual observances that transform punishment into reward. When a Jew follows those ways which were bestowed graciously on Israel's forebears, then that ancient grace becomes contemporary. Sometimes merit comes from association with others. A scholar is precious in God's sight. An ordinary Jew associating with a scholar, serving or aiding scholars, acquires merit. A leader of the community derives merit from the communal body itself. Merit by association emphasizes that God's grace extends the righteousness of the few to those who identify with them. Again the issue is not *earning* merit but rather the grace of a God whose mercy is awakened in various ways despite the rigorous demands of justice.

Merit, so far from being earned, is often merely a metaphor for God's grace. When an individual has no empirical right to *zehut,* when a person can claim no basis for divine mercy in actions, by inheritance, or from association with others, God imputes merit anyway. Exodus 33:19 is used to show that individuals apparently unworthy of God's favor still receive it. "I will show favor upon whomsoever I will," God states, thus demonstrating that God will provide the necessary *zehut* to make mercy predominate over justice for every human being.

The Jewish emphasis on God's grace makes the problem of theodicy particularly pressing. How can human suffering be reconciled with the view that God acts graciously with every creature? Some rabbis suggest that suffering in this world is a gracious act preventing worse punishment in the world to come. Others suggest that the reward of the righteous is not physical but purely spiritual—the divine light that rests on the upright is reward enough. Perhaps the most prevalent view is to stress existence itself as grace. The secrets of justice and mercy are recondite; a human being must be grateful just for life. The Jew echoes the statement of Rabbi Akiba and Nahum Ish

Gamzu: "Whatever God does is done for the best" (TB *Ta'anith* 21a). God is a righteous judge whose mercies are over all creation. These affirmations are made in the face of life's problems. The Jew does not ignore those problems—Job, Psalm 73, and even Rabbi Akiba raise Abraham's question "Shall the judge of the earth not do justly?" (Gen 18:25). The point, however, lies in raising the question rather than in answering it. The Jew is to affirm God's grace in creating the world but still demand to understand the incomprehensible ways of God's justice.

That paradoxical demand is essential because while God's ways are beyond human understanding they are also the basis for human life. Judaism sees one of the most powerful signs of divine favor in the human ability to imitate God. Each human being is an image of God; the human task is *imitatio Dei*, imitating divinity. The Jew affirms God's grace and questions God's justice because human beings must take divine action as a model for human behavior. The rabbinic tradition asks how it is possible to cleave to God who is a consuming fire (cf. TB *Sotah* 14b). Is it possible for human behavior to emulate the divine? In the sphere of justice such imitation is clearly impossible. Raising questions about divine justice serves this purpose. No answer can be given. Human beings, then, dare not "be righteous overmuch" (Ecclesiastes *Rabbah*). Because King Saul tried to be more just than God and spare Agag, king of the Amalekites, he became the slaughterer of the priests of Nob. When humans attempt to take justice into their own hands they become destructive and unrestrained.

Human beings, however, can and should imitate God's attribute of mercy. The Torah, strictly understood as the first five books of the Bible, begins and ends with divine acts of mercy. God clothes Adam and Eve; God buries Moses. A human being imitates God by clothing the naked and burying the dead. As God's day is spent caring for the creatures and feeding the hungry, so the human being should care for others and feed them. Just as God visited Abraham after his circumcision, so human beings are to visit the sick. Imitation of divinity means cultivating merciful sensitivity. The test of a person's "image of God" is neither intellectual nor strictly religious—it is attitudinal. When a person shows a lack of mercy, that discloses an underdeveloped divine image.

The Talmud tells of Judah the Prince, a scholar and member of the rabbinic elite, who once rejected a calf who had run to him for protection. Showing no compassion Rabbi Judah declared, "You were created to be slaughtered" (TB *Baba Meziah* 85a). Because he lacked mercy God punished him. Only when he intervened to save some mice who were being drowned was the punishment curtailed. Through mercy rather than through rabbinic leadership or even scholarly ability a Jew activates the divine image. The quality of mercy is the mark of being godlike just as recognition of God's unfathomable justice marks the limitation of human ability.

The two principles of God's incomprehensible justice and of divine mercy as the paradigm for human action need to be reaffirmed in the Jewish-Christian dialogue. Christians are often tempted to charge Jews with a primitive notion of a vengeful God. Such a view is mistaken as the emphasis on divine mercy demonstrates. Divine compassion is the primary attribute of God in Judaism. Justice, however, needs to be taken seriously. If human beings underestimate the distance between divine and human judgment, then arrogance, emotionalism, and self-satisfaction result. The Jew insists on God's prerogative as Judge because that insistence moderates and limits the extent of arbitrary human judgment. The Jew cautions the Christian against the excesses of identifying any human understanding of government and justice with the divine will.

The second principle—that of imitating God's merciful qualities—also needs to be stressed. Christians sometimes feel that Jews lack a coherent model for imitating God because Jews reject the idea of incarnation. In both the Hebrew Bible and in rabbinic writings Jews find concrete images of divine mercy. God's example of such mundane concerns as feeding the hungry, visiting the sick and comforting the bereaved is both accessible and powerful for Jews. The Jew, however, warns that imitation of God is productive only if it is limited. The danger involved is self-identification with God. A divine example too accessible would lead to deifying human beings. Jews are restless with incarnation as the basis for *imitatio Dei* because it may confuse imitation with identification. For the Jew the distance between the divine and the human must be preserved even while imitation of divine mercy is encouraged.

S. Daniel Breslauer

CHRISTIAN VIEW:

Justice or "righteousness" refers primarily to God. It is contrasted with faithlessness and wickedness (Rom 3:3, 5). The righteousness of God is shown forth in the death and resurrection of Christ. Human beings are justified in the event (Rom 3:22–26) and are reconciled to the Father (2 Cor 5:18–21). Thus a situation of estrangement is altered and people are brought into right relationship with God; they are justified.

Grace is God's free self-gift to us. It translates the Latin *gratia,* used by the Vulgate to render *charis.* Thus, we understand that *charis* is relational rather than abstract in meaning.

New Testament writers, especially Paul, use *charis* to render several words from the Hebrew Scriptures and the Jewish tradition: justice or righteousness (*tsedaka*), which signified the "uprightness" of God who judges, acquits and saves; mercy or covenant love (*hesed*), through which God initiates the covenant relationship; and steadfastness or fidelity (*emet, emuna*), through which God maintains that relationship. All three qualities refer to God as the one who acquits and saves his people. They refer secondarily to human persons insofar as they stand innocent before God and in covenantal relationship to him.

The relational quality of these words indicates that grace signifies our relationship with God and his primacy in that relationship. We are in relationship to God because he has first loved us. Christians have articulated the experience of grace in various ways in the development of their traditions. Paul uses *charis* for the gift of God's love to humankind in Christ, and three other words to describe various aspects of that gift: righteousness or justification (*dikaiosynē*), sanctification (*hagiasmos*), salvation (*sotēria*).

Justification is appropriated by faith, a surrender in confidence to God and union with the crucified and risen Jesus (Gal 2:11–21). Justification implies sanctification (1 Cor 1:30; 6:11), the operation of justification in a life of mutual concern and service. This is both the work of the Spirit in the hearts of the justified and their active response to God's gracious gift. Justification and sanctification are fulfilled in salvation, which is not yet fully accomplished.

Augustine articulated his experience of grace in different terms. The final development in his theology of grace may be described thus. God gives free will to humankind in creation. Nonetheless, people are powerless to do good or to orient themselves toward God because of radical sinfulness. God calls them to faith through the Word which is Christ. Those who receive this call turn to God in faith. The Father pours out his Spirit in their hearts, and this outpouring of the Spirit again results in the response of faith. The new relationship is reflected in good works and habits, and is fulfilled in union with God.

Interiority and gratuity characterize Augustine's consideration of grace. He understood that it is a radical orientation of the free will, not individual bad deeds, which distances human beings from God. He emphasized the primacy of God's action by describing free will, the call to faith, and the outpouring of the Spirit as gracious gifts of God.

Whereas Augustine spoke of grace in psychological terms (desire, delight, healing), Thomas Aquinas spoke of it in Aristotelian philosophical terms (nature, potency, habit). According to Thomas, human nature is open to grace as its fulfillment. However, because nature is human and not divine, and because it is sinful, persons are unable of themselves to come to intimacy with God. God heals and elevates the person's inmost being through "habitual" or "sanctifying" grace so that it can come to fulfillment in union with God.

God is also present in graced acts ("actual grace" in later theologians). He moves persons from within their new spontaneity and provides the external help through life's events so that they can perform acts which are in harmony with their transformed being.

Writings of later medieval theologians show us that some came to regard grace as a possession and cause of merit rather than as the result of God's loving self-gift. Luther developed his theology of grace partly in response to this distortion. He emphasized the fact that the person is saved by grace alone (*sola gratia*), not by any merit of his own. Human beings are in bondage to sin before justification, unable to move toward salvation. God, however, gives his Son Jesus so that people may abandon themselves to Jesus in faith. Human beings are justified, forgiven, and saved by God in his abandonment to Jesus. Justification is thus by faith in Christ Jesus, and not by merits or works. Good works, however, while not a cause for merit, do reflect the condition of justification.

Our brief reflections reveal that various Christian traditions articulate the experience of grace in different terms. All of these traditions begin with the experience of sin and alienation as a starting point. However, there is a divergence in the language used as well as in the description of various aspects of grace. Divergence in the understanding of grace has been a source of polemic since Luther. It can still cause misunderstanding between Christians of various traditions.

Despite a history of polemic and the danger of misunderstanding, it is possible to speak of a "Christian" concept of grace. People experience themselves as broken, inauthentic, fragmented. Individuals are unable to realize their fullest potential: relationship with God and community with others. God, however, is gracious and merciful. People are thus reconciled to God through the divine initiative in the death and resurrection of Jesus and the outpouring of the Spirit. This is the gift of grace, and the only response is a surrender in faith. In the dynamic of God's loving call and the response in faith, the situation of alienation and fragmentation is corrected. The new situation of reconciliation is reflected in people's lives in loving concern for others and in responsible action in the world in which they live.

The presence of grace does not depend on people's explicit religious awareness or belief because it is *God's* merciful and forgiving love. That love is both abundant and surprising. It is seen wherever people respond in unexpected ways, living in hope in situations which should produce despair, forgiving those who have hurt them, working constructively for justice despite overwhelming opposition. In other words, wherever people live in a truly human way, one can perceive God's merciful love healing human hearts and bringing them to new authenticity.

That authenticity is, however, still incomplete. While living in loving relationship to God and others, human beings still know within themselves and in society some areas of fragmentation. People live in a tension of "already" and "not yet." They know the "already" of the death and resurrection, of Jesus, of the outpouring of the Spirit, of their own love and responsibility for one another. But they also know the wavering of their faith and the cooling of their love. Thus, the fulfillment of grace, of God's love for us and our response in faith, awaits the future in the full manifestation of God's Kingdom.

Celia Deutsch

Law, Halakha

JEWISH VIEW:

When the word Torah was translated as *nomos*—law—a serious injustice was done. The Torah, of course, includes laws, but it is far broader than the term *nomos* implies. Torah includes history, religious concepts, ethical teachings and so much more. By defining it as law, the critics of Torah hoped to narrow the Torah's scope, to depict it merely as a system of ritualistic laws, numerous and cumbersome. By limiting the Torah to law, they could more easily contrast their own emphasis on faith and spirit. They conveniently ignored the elements of faith and spirit in the Torah itself. Therefore, the popular translation of Torah as law, *nomos, ley, loi,* etc. is erroneous. Unfortunately, after centuries of general usage, Jews also have tended to translate Torah as law. Since the translation is fundamentally wrong, it should be dropped.

Halakha (literally "way") is the term generally used to designate Jewish legal statutes relating to religious and community existence. But Halakha, too, is a term which carries different meanings. The following paragraphs will provide the basis for understanding the nature of Halakha in its various ramifications.

God provides the people of Israel with Torah—a teaching. The Torah gives an historical context for the people of Israel, describes their covenant with God, and elaborates rules and patterns of behavior (cf. Bible). The oral Torah accompanies the written Torah and provides explanations and elaborations which make the written Torah more intelligible. Since the Five Books of Moses do not contain a systematic code of laws, and since many of its phrases are vague or poetic, the oral Torah is vital to an understanding of the written Torah. The oral Torah was revealed to Moses along with the written Torah and has equal status with it.

Aside from providing definitions and explanations of the written Torah, the oral Torah also has a different function. It is not only a body of knowledge, but is also a process. The Great Court in Jerusalem in Temple times was empowered to interpret the written Torah and to create legislation based on its understanding of Scriptures. As time passed, new problems and questions arose. The Great Court of each generation had the authority and the responsibility to interpret the written Torah and to derive laws from it. The proceedings of the Court formed part of the oral Torah.

In the second century CE, Rabbi Judah the Prince organized the Mishnah, which includes the legal decisions and discussion of the rabbinic authorities up to his time. Due to the persecution and exile of the Jews, the Great Court no longer functioned, and the status of the oral law was jeopardized. By creating the Mishnah in a specific form, Rabbi Judah preserved the oral law (*Torah Shebe-al Peh*) which had developed until his day. From his time onward, rabbinic authorities no longer derived laws based on interpretations of Scripture itself, but rather relied upon the formulations in the Mishnah. Subsequent generations of rabbis (*amoraim*) thoroughly analyzed the Mishnah as well as other teachings and traditions of the rabbis who lived during the time and prior to the formulation of the Mishnah (*tannaim*). The analysis and discussion of the Mishnah is known as *Gemara,* and the Mishnah and *Gemara* together are known as the Talmud. The Talmud includes laws and teachings of rabbis spanning a period of about a thousand years.

The Talmud has become the basis of Halakha, Jewish law. Yet, because of its vast size and complexity, the Talmud is relatively inaccessible to the general public as a code of law. Rabbis throughout the generations have studied the Talmud and have given their rulings on various questions of Jewish law. From Talmudic times until our own day rabbinic responsa have formed an important feature of Halakha. Individuals asked questions of Jewish law to the great rabbinic authorities of their time. These rabbis wrote responses, drawing on the Talmud and other rabbinic literature. Often these responsa were published, and a vast literature of responsa exists.

A number of codes of Jewish law have been compiled in order to make the Halakha accessible to everyone. The most famous medieval codes are those compiled by Isaac Alfasi, Moses Maimonides, Jacob ben Asher, and Joseph Karo. Each of these codes has been the subject of numerous commentaries. There have been many other attempts to codify Halakha, and codes have been written or translated into many languages.

Halakha essentially tells the Jew how to behave, what God expects of him. It is vital that each Jew be able to know the law. Historically, the central role of the rabbis has been to guide people to live according to Halakha.

Halakha also includes several other dimensions. *Minhagim* are customs which have developed in various communities and which have taken on the character of legal dispositions. No one claims that these customs have divine origin; yet, since they have become so ingrained in people's religious behavior, they have gained the status of legal requirements. A well-known rabbinic statement is: *Minhag avoteinu beyadeinu,* the custom of our ancestors is in our hands. The weight of tradition gives *minhagim* their special meaning.

Takkanot, communal ordinances, form another aspect of Halakha. Each community passed laws applicable to its own specific needs. These ordinances were enacted to insure proper religious behavior, and each member of the community was required to observe communal laws. Like *minhagim, takkanot* are not claimed to have divine origin. Their impact is felt primarily within the communities which have accepted them.

Halakha provides an important insight into Jewish existence. In spite of being dispersed throughout the world for centuries, the Jewish people maintained its unity through its commitment to Torah and Halakha. Different communities have different customs, yet the essential laws have had universal acceptance.

In modern times, non-Orthodox Jews have moved away from the traditional understanding of Torah and Halakha. There has been a tendency to discount the divinity of the oral Torah and even the written Torah in some circles. Reform Judaism has by and large abandoned a commitment to Halakha, leaving individuals to decide for themselves what observances are meaningful for their own lives. Conservative Judaism maintains a commitment to Halakha, but offers legal decisions and interpretations which attempt to adapt Jewish law to contemporary life. Orthodoxy maintains a strict adherence to Halakha. Since Halakha is at base a divinely revealed system of life, Orthodoxy argues that it is not legitimate to compromise these laws.

The authority of Halakha, then, is an issue of controversy among the various groups of Jews. The way one understands the nature of Halakha will profoundly influence the way one lives his life.

Marc Angel

CHRISTIAN VIEW:

When the Jews of Alexandria, in the third century BCE, translated the Torah (the Way of life after God's will) by *nomos* (law), they endorsed an understanding of the Torah prevalent at their time. With the return from exile, as a matter of fact, the Torah had become the "law of the land," the by-laws by which the Jewish "church" regulated its life and defined what it is to be a perfect Jew. The accent was definitely put on performance, itself a *conditio sine qua non* of belonging to the community of the saints. Hence, although repentance remains indispensable for obtaining a "clean slate" at the beginning of the new year, the fulfillment of the *mitzvot* accumulates merits before God.

Besides, in such a conception of the Torah, it is of primordial importance to delineate with precision the contours of each *mitzvah*. What exactly constitutes the ritually pure diet? What exactly is it to observe the Sabbath rest? What exactly is the definition of the category "neighbor," and what are the minimal expressions of love expected from me, to satisfy the demands of the Commandment about him? That casuistry constitutes the "oral Torah" traditionally given to Moses on Mount Sinai along with the written one.

That understanding of the Torah—which Paul later calls a system of salvation through works (performance)—is the background for the New Testament protest of what it considers to be a distortion. In the development which follows, however, a distinction must be made between Jesus' and Paul's attitude, the latter being much more radical than the former.

Despite the dialectical complexity of Jesus' discourse on the Torah, as reconstructed with bits and pieces scattered over the Gospels, his stance appears rather straightforward. Himself a practicing Jew, he goes to the synagogue on the Sabbath (Mk 1:21; 4:16; 13:10), and to Jerusalem on the days of the festivals (Lk 2:41ff; Mk 11:1ff); he wears the ritual fringes on his garment (Mk 6:56; Lk 8:44). When he seems to break the Law (as understood by some Pharisees—q.v.), it is not by antinomianism, but in the name of a different interpretation of the nature of the Torah (cf. Mk 3:1ff, the healing of a man on the Sabbath, etc.). In brief, his criticism of the Law comes from within the framework of the Law (Mk 2:23–26; 3:1–6; 10:2f). He is indignant about the codification of the "oral Torah" which he is not ready to recognize as given to Moses on Mount Sinai (cf. Mk 7:5–13; cf. Col 2:8; against casuistry, Mt 23:14–33). On the contrary, that casuistry for him is a sheer "tradition of men" (Mk 7:5, 8). It therefore usurps a position of honor which belongs only to God's teaching. About the latter, moreover, it must be said that it does not readily coincide with the written Torah. Although in the main we only know

God's will through what has been transmitted in the text, there is to the Torah a provisional dimension of transience (cf. Mk 7:15; Mt 5:31, 38). Furthermore, the Torah cannot constitute a means for salvation. The Covenant is not based upon the Jews' dignity but upon God's free election which men are only to accept in their lives (Mt 11:7, 15; Lk 16:16; Mk 2:21). Within the Covenant, obedience to the Torah means the adoption of the proper behavior. As such, it is commendable albeit totally insufficient, for perfect obedience would mean self-oblation to God and to fellow men (Lk 10:25ff; Mk 10:20–22). The only recourse left is to implore forgiveness, or even to die on the Cross (*le shem shamayim*). Thus, Jesus radicalizes the Torah which, for him, demands total love. Such an extravagant requirement on the part of God means that no one can fully obey the Torah nor set up any claim for merit (cf. Lk 17:10).

For Paul, the Torah is excellent and divine (cf. Rom 3:2; 7:12, 14; Gal 2:21, cf. Mt 5:7). But its impact on the human beings is ambiguous, as it reveals their sinfulness without curing that state of affairs, even becoming an incentive to sin in providing its opportunity (Rom 4:15; 5:20; 7:13; Gal 3:19), while condemning them for it (Rom 2:18; 3:19; etc.). Hence, the Law creates powerless guilt in man, i.e., while being positive in itself, it has a negative effect, due to the weakness of the "flesh" (Rom 8:3).

Thus, from a benediction as a gift of God, the Torah becomes a curse, for we are as human beings prone to "eat the forbidden fruit," and reluctant to do the good we would like to do (cf. Rom 7:18f; 8:3, 7, etc.; cf. Mt 26:41). It remains, however, that the dispensation of the Law was necessary: it put squarely on man's shoulders his own responsibility before God. It was man's very nature to be a free partner of God but man's sinfulness succeeded in reversing the Torah's effect expected by God. Instead of making "Adam" a full partner in the dialogue with the Lord, Adam used the commandment to further alienate himself from God. Therefore, it is clear that the dispensation of the Law could not be final. It had to lead to something else, to another dispensation, whose type we find in what preceded the order of the Law, viz., the gracious promise to Abraham (cf. Gal 3:1ff; Rom 4:20). The Torah, thus, is a teacher unto the new era inaugurated by Christ (Gal 3:23f; 4:1–7, Col 2:17; cf. Heb 10:1). Here, the whole initiative is God's again. Any expectation that Adam could in any way satisfy the demands of God's will is forfeited. In conformity with the apocalyptic world view, *Heilsgeschichte* (history of salvation) had had its chance; with Christ, it is over. Now, the Torah belongs to the *stoicheia tou kosmou,* i.e., the elements of the world (Gal 4:3–4). It is even of the essence of creation, which, in the dominant strand of Jewish tradition, God uses as the means for redemption. But those *stoicheia* were incapable of delivering any fulfillment of the promise they contained. This is why a new era had to be initiated. God intervenes himself. He puts a stop to the endlessly unsuccessful attempt by Adam to fulfill the divine expectations. For Paul, God has done so in Christ, who is the Second Adam, or the first one of a new humanity entirely under the divine grace (Rom 5). What happened, as the initial and final act in that new and decisive economy, is that Christ transcended all limitations in human obedience to the Law: he died on the Cross. This indeed is the ultimate act because one cannot give more than one's life (Rom 8:34ff). Thus is revealed the ultimate purpose of the Torah (Rom 3:21) and, by the same token, the Law has become without object. For, on the one hand, any partial obedience to the Law falls short of what the Torah actually demands, and, on the other hand, any total obedience implying martyrdom can only duplicate what Christ has already done. (The Law has had its dead: cf. Gal 2:19; 3:13).

The new dispensation, according to Paul, consists for us all in existentially communicating with Christ's death and resurrection (Gal 2:19; Rom 7:4, 6; Col 2:20). Living before God means not rightly performing before him, but essentially loving—loving fully, loving endlessly, loving limitlessly. Thus, the Christian is not without Law-Torah, but the Torah has become an historical person, Christ. To be his disciple is a far cry from obeying a code; it is to become "Christic" (Col 3:1f; Phil 3:9). Is this overthrowing the Law? "By no means! On the contrary, we uphold the Law" (Rom 3:31).

André Lacocque

Love

JEWISH VIEW:

Jewish tradition understands the word *ahavah* (love) to encompass several meanings and terms. In its first sense, *ahavah* refers to human love: Jacob loved Joseph, Isaac loved certain foods, Jonathan loved David, and the author of the Song of Songs loved his beloved.

In its second sense, *ahavah* refers to God's love for man, particularly for Israel. Here *ahavah* encompasses three terms: *hesed, rahamim,* and *tsedek. Hesed* is the undeserved love which God has for his creation. It is ontological, part of the structure of reality. Thus, "Give thanks to the Lord...for his *hesed* endures forever" (Ps 118:1). *Hesed* is parallel to the "and it was good" of creation (q.v.).

Rahamim is also an undeserved love, deriving from the word for "womb." If refers to God's mercy toward man and is a moral, not an ontological, term. When we have exhausted all our merits and efforts, we still are as nothing before God, and he must have *rahamim* upon us. He must, in the metaphor of the rabbis, move from the throne of judgment to the throne of mercy.

Both *hesed* and *rahamim* are undeserved. They flow from God because he is who he is. *Tsedek* is interactional. God has given humankind standards by which to live, a Torah, and we must do the best we can to live up to these standards, moral, ritual, and intellectual. When we do so, we have a right to God's love. We have earned it by our hard work. In this perspective, we ask God only to deal with us in *tsedek* although we know that ultimately we cannot be fully righteous before him. *Tsedek* is a moral term, and because of it, we receive deserved love from God. This love is a function of the covenant (q.v.).

The terms *ahavah rabbah* (great love) and *ahavah olam* (eternal love)

123

express the peculiar love that God has for his Chosen People, the Jews. This love is both superabundant and abiding. It is his gift to his people, hidden at times, yet always-present, never-ending. It is his promise of a time of renewed intimacy at the end of days.

Two verses—one commanding love of God and the other love of one's neighbor—deserve special attention. The first is: "You shall love your neighbor as yourself" (Lev 19:18). Jewish tradition is not of one mind on the meaning of this verse for several reasons. The Talmud points out that one's own life takes precedence over that of one's neighbor. Sometimes one's neighbors are evil. If love is a feeling, it cannot be commanded. If love is empathy with the other, a human being would break under the burden of a universal empathy. How, then, can one love one's neighbor as oneself?

Several answers have been offered. Some reply that one should love one's neighbor but only if he or she is good. If the neighbor is bad, one is bidden to follow the verse "You who love God, hate evil" (Ps 97:10). Some reply that loving one's neighbor is not so much a matter of acts as of attitude. Thus, we might wish for all good things for ourselves but begrudge such largesse to our neighbor. The verse, then, urges us to wish our neighbor all the good we would wish for ourselves. The classic answer is that, since the other is "as yourself," i.e., created in the image of God, you should at least not do unto him/her anything that you would not have done unto yourself. This is the well-known dictum of Hillel, "What is hateful to you, do not do to your neighbor" (TB *Shabbat* 31a). This negative formulation has the advantage of being practicable and concrete. It has an inner logic of its own.

The other verse is "And you shall love the Lord your God with all your heart, and with all your soul, and with all your might" (Deut 6:5). Here, too, there are some knotty problems: How can love be commanded? How would one love God? Are there special activities that are defined as loving God?

Again, there are diverse answers. Some say that to love God is to perform the commandments with an intense sense of God's presence, with *kavanah* (devotion). Some say it is a dedication of all the forces of the body and—if necessary—with one's material wealth to God. Some say that love of God is surrender of the soul and will to God. Some say it is a rapture. And some say that it is a contemplation of God's ways in creation, in providence, and in Torah.

Part of the concept of *ahavah* seems to have a parallel in Christianity. *Hesed*, as the ontological love of the Creator for his work, seems parallel to grace (q.v.). *Rahamim,* as the moral love of the Father for his children, also seems parallel to grace. *Tsedek* as the motif of moral righteousness that evokes a justified love from God seems to have a parallel only in the early

Christian sources, before the primacy of faith over deeds became central to Christian self-understanding. The presence, however, of these early Christian sources, together with the books of the prophets, in the Christian canon leaves open the possibility of renewed sensitivity to these formulations.

David Blumenthal

CHRISTIAN VIEW:

Agape, whose infinitive is *agapan,* is the Greek translation of the Hebrew *āhab,* which in English is "love." Although it was not the most frequent Greek word for love, in the New Testament it is used so often that it becomes almost a technical word for love.

In discussion, Christians often distinguish *agape* from the other frequent Greek words for love, *eros* and *philia. Eros* refers to the kind of love which looks for some sort of return, some response from the other. *Eros* is not exclusively sensual love, although sensual love is one of its components. *Philia* is more properly that love which obtains among family members, as a child has *philia* for its parents, or brothers and sisters have *philia* for one another. Against these *agape* is often pitted as selfless love which does not look for a return on its giving; it is a total gift of self to the other without any strings attached. This meaning of *agape,* combined with its frequent use in the New Testament, gives the impression to many Christians that love as *agape,* selfless giving, is a peculiar insight of Jesus and of the Christian tradition in general.

One of the most prominent examples of *agape* in the New Testament is 1 Corinthians 13, wherein St. Paul describes love as the bedrock of all virtues, the one absolutely essential Christian trademark, without which all other gifts are meaningless. Addressing a congregation torn apart by division, Paul writes, "If I speak in the tongues of men and angels, but have not love, I am a noisy gong or a clanging cymbal...Love is patient and kind; love is not jealous or boastful...Love never ends" (13:1–8). This is perhaps one of the most memorable passages in the New Testament, often used at Christian wedding services to challenge the newly married to steadfastness and perseverance.

For the Christian, not only is *agape* a virtue—it is the very definition of God (if one can speak of a "definition" of God). In a letter replete with "agape language," St. John counsels "Beloved, let us love one another; for love is of God, and he who loves is born of God and knows God. He who does not love does not know God; for God is love" (1 Jn 4:7f). Indeed, in another place, the same writer speaks about the knowledge which one has of God as equivalent to loving God, for the one who loves already knows God, for God is love.

Agape is also the kind of love which God has for humankind. God's first expression of love for humankind was creation itself, when God created man and woman "in his image" and set them over all the rest of creation. For the Christian, the ultimate expression of God's love was the sending of Jesus into the world: "God so loved the world that he gave his only Son, that whoever believes in him should not perish but have eternal life" (Jn 3:16). Jesus Christ is the embodiment, the very incarnation of God's love in the world. In his teaching, Jesus called his followers to love one another. This love was to have no bounds: it was to include even one's enemies (Mt 5:43f) and it was to go beyond the usual definition of loving one's neighbor (cf. Lk 10:29–37).

In his teaching, Jesus made the intimate connection between loving God and loving one's neighbor (cf. Mt 22:36–40; Jn 4:20). Some Christians think that the connection between these commands was Jesus' peculiar contribution to rabbinical teaching. Recent historical study has called this uniqueness into question.

Like the Jewish tradition, the Christian tradition sees the love command as essentially an invitation to imitate God in his love for all nations, in his "sending rain on the just and the unjust." Furthermore, in imitation of God, the Christian sees that while love begins as *intention*, it is never complete without action, without moving from intention into reality. Christians try to imitate the way Jesus lived the love command, particularly in his willingness to lay down his life for his friends and in his willingness to serve others (cf. Jn 13). The total gift of self stands as the irreducible model of what the Christian life entails (cf. Mk 10:45; Jn 15:13).

The Second Vatican Council understands the love which Jesus has for his Church as the model of Christian marriage. For the Christian, marriage is not simply the public expression of lifelong fidelity between a man and a woman; it stands always as the enfleshed sacrament or sign of Christ's love for the Church. Thus, *agape* is the total gift of self, as Christ has given himself for his Church.

Recent Christian scholars have suggested that the distinction between *agape, eros,* and *philia* has been overdrawn. While each word radiates different connotations, they are not to be so sharply contrasted. Furthermore, recent translations of the New Testament have refrained from rendering *agape* as "charity" because "charity" too quickly connotes "philanthropy."

The importance which *agape*/love may have in the Jewish-Christian dialogue may be manifold. First, Scripture scholars need to further explore the many parallels and overlappings between the love commands in the Hebrew Scriptures and the New Testament. Christians in particular are often victims of the impression that the God of the Old Testament was a God of wrath and anger while the God of Jesus was one of love and mercy. Further explorations of the relation between *agape, hesed* and other Hebrew notions might relieve Christians of this impression.

Second, Christians need to hear from their Jewish counterparts how the link between loving one's neighbor, and one's God is adumbrated already in the Hebrew Scriptures. Indeed, in Luke 10:26, it is a Jewish lawyer, not Jesus, who combines the two commands (besides the fact that Jesus himself was Jewish).

Third, a deeper understanding of the Law (*halakha* in Hebrew—q.v.) will help Christians understand that following the Law, far from the opposite of love, can be an expression of love for God. The myth of the "legalistic Jew" might more easily dissolve for some Christians if they understood better the reason for the Law.

Michael McGarry

Martyrdom

JEWISH VIEW:

The Hebrew term for martyrdom is *Kiddush ha-Shem* ("the sanctification of the Name of God"). The opposite term is *Hillul ha-Shem* ("the desecration of the Name of God"). Both terms include all acts—ritual and ethical, intrapsychic and overt—which have the capacity to bring honor and glory or, conversely, disgrace and shame to God's Name. Thus, for instance, an act of extraordinary piety honors God's Name while an act which is immoral—even if legal—disgraces it. The highest form of sanctifying God's Name is to give up one's life for God.

The issue, however, is not simple because the Jew is commanded to preserve life at all costs. Thus, for instance, the Sabbath *must* be violated if a life is at stake. Conversely, suicide is forbidden and considered a very grave sin. The rabbis, therefore, had to articulate rules under which martyrdom was obligatory and rules under which it was forbidden to martyr oneself. They are the following: (1) Martyrdom is obligatory if the option is to commit an act of idolatry or apostasy, an act of incest or adultery, or murder. One must prefer death to committing such acts. Any other demands made as a condition of continued life must be met, e.g., violation of the ritual laws. (2) If the non-Jewish authorities make a public issue of matters of Jewish observance not included within the three mentioned above, martyrdom is obligatory. Relatively minor acts can become a disgrace to God's Name when they take on the political character of a public performance, and under such conditions one must prefer death. If the threat, however, is made in private, one must bend and conform in order to preserve life. (3) If a whole community is being actively persecuted, threats made in private, even on matters other than the three listed above in (1), must be resisted. In such circumstances, sanctifying

God's Name is very broadly construed. The best advice of the rabbis is to avoid situations of persecution, to flee.

Historically, the possibility of martyrdom appeared for the first time in the Book of Daniel where Shadrach, Meshach, and Abed-Nego resisted idolatry and endangered their lives (Dn 3:8ff) and also in the case of Daniel in the lion's den (Dn 6). The first cases of martyrdom appeared during the revolt against the Syrian-Greeks under the leadership of the Maccabees. For the first time, Jews actually gave up their lives rather than commit acts of pagan worship or give up the study of Torah. Since then, the history of Jewish martyrdom has included grievous episodes under the Roman emperors, terrible moments under Christian rulers particularly during the Crusades, and shocking incidents under modern nation states. Throughout, Jews have taken the broadest definition of martyrdom, preferring death to desecration of God's Name, of his Torah, or of his people.

Two paradigms developed out of this history. First, there is the model of Masada. In the course of the great war against Rome (66–73 CE), the Jews chose the desert fort of Masada as a focal point for their resistance. Its importance increased after the fall of Jerusalem (69–70 CE) because it was one of the few fortresses left. The defenders fought bravely and, when all appeared lost, committed mass suicide. The story of Masada has become a central symbol in modern Jewish culture, especially in Israel. Jews travel from all over the world to visit the site. The Israeli army inducts its soldiers there. Masada, representing martyrdom linked with armed resistance, is one type of *Kiddush ha-Shem*.

The other paradigm is the story of the Jewish settlements along the Rhine River during the Crusades. The Jews were few in number and defenseless; the Crusaders were a wild and murderous band. Acts of murder and terror became common and word spread from community to community. The Jews of many of these towns resolved not to fall into the hands of the enemy who demanded apostasy or death. They prepared themselves carefully for death by ritual bathing, prayer, and fasting, and then killed their friends, their families, and themselves. The story of these communities became, and continues to be, a central symbol in Jewish religious culture. Their histories are preserved in the Ashkenazi liturgy and are recited every year. The memory of the holy ones molds the religious consciousness of the Jew. The communities of the Crusades represent martyrdom linked with piety—a second type of *Kiddush ha-Shem*.

The Holocaust, however, called both paradigms into question and created a new one. True, there were martyrs of both of the older types. There were those who died in armed resistance to the Nazi onslaught in the ghettos, in the forests, even in the camps. And there were those who died affirming their piety in the very face of Satan. The stories of both groups are deeply moving and need to be told and heard. But there were many Jews who died denying, or ignorant of, their Jewishness. And there were millions who never really had the choice of martyrdom; they were just summarily murdered. For them, there was no glory, no sanctification. Contemporary Jewish theology and liturgy, however, has reached out to these people and has called them martyrs, martyrs for the Jewish people and its God. They are involuntary martyrs, unwitting sacrifices, but they sanctified the Name of God nonetheless.

In Hebrew, the word holocaust, *shoah*, means a "destructive windstorm" (Is 74:11; Zeph 1:15; Ps 35:8). The English term "holocaust" is used to designate the sacrificial offerings that were wholly burnt on the altar. Since, however, Jews do not see anything sacrificial in the events of 1933-1945, the English word is not quite appropriate. But *shoah,* "destructive windstorm," does not really capture the impact of the event either. The Jewish people lost one-third of its world population. It lost much of the very best of its civilization. And it sustained these losses under conditions that defy the imagination for cruelty and debased behavior, including the passive acceptance of the facts of extermination by those who knew what was happening. Even the expanded paradigm of *Kiddush ha-Shem,* of unwitting martyrdom does not quite encompass the event or comfort those who remain and those who live in the shadow of that event.

The State of Israel has fixed the twenty-seventh day of the month of Nisan as *Yom ha-Shoah,* Holocaust Remembrance Day. It thus always falls just after Passover. This day is almost universally observed by Jews. Prayers are recited, liturgies have been composed and services are held at local cemeteries. The United States President's Council on the Holocaust established a Holocaust Memorial Museum in Washington, D.C., that is open to the general public. Many Jewish communities have established memorials for the victims of the Holocaust. The central memorial is Yad Vashem in Jerusalem. The purpose of the memorials and events, together with the annual lectures and other programs on the Holocaust, is twofold: to remember and to educate. The dead must be memorialized, the survivors comforted, and the living public warned. "Never Again" has become the motto, *Kiddush ha-Hayyim* ("the sanctification of life") the by-word.

The martyrdom of the Holocaust is the deepest motif in the contemporary Jewish psyche. No dialogue can even begin without opening this wound gently and with healing intent.

David Blumenthal

CHRISTIAN VIEW:

The word "martyr" comes from the Greek word *martus,* which means "a witness." In the early Church, and even within the New Testament, a martyr was one who witnessed to his faith by suffering persecution and death for the sake of faith in Christ. The word "martyr" is not used in the Hebrew Scriptures in the sense of "one who dies for the faith," although certainly that reality was adumbrated in such passages as 2 Maccabees 6–7.

In the New Testament, giving witness and being slain for the faith were associated in Acts 22:20 and Revelation 2:13, 11:3. The early Church saw the combination of witness and death in imitation of Christ, as in Revelation 1:5 where Christ is referred to as *martus,* witness. Christ was the first "martyr" in this root sense. Thus, one can see the importance in the early Christian imagination for Jesus' saying: "Love one another as I have loved you. Greater love has no man than this, that a man lay down his life for his friends" (Jn 15:12f). Thus, while from the outside martyrdom is a witness to faith, from the inside it is a witness to love. At the moment of his condemnation, Jesus referred to his mission as one of witness (Jn 18:37). But the combination of witness and death would not belong to the Messiah alone; the followers would have the same fate: "Remember the word that I said to you, 'A servant is not greater than his master.' If they persecuted me, they will persecute you" (Jn 15:20).

Although death by persecution for the faith is a specific understanding of witness, martyrdom became synonymous with death by persecution for the faith during the first few Christian centuries. Such a death was a sign that nothing is more important to the Christian than to be faithful to his/her belief in Christ, even if it means death. Such a death was a guarantee of instant communion with God in imitation of the death of Jesus.

A cult of martyrs soon emerged in the Christian Church which recounted the faith and death of the early martyrs. These stories were sources of encouragement and were prods to perseverance for Christians in their faith; those who died for their faith were held as models of the ultimate cost of discipleship. The cult of martyrs, like the cult of the saints, is a characteristic among Roman Catholic Christians before and since the Reformation. Protestants have observed certain excesses of devotion to saints, including the martyrs, among Roman Catholic Christians, and thus they have questioned their veneration of them. This does not mean that Protestants admire the early Christian martyrs any less; it means only that Protestants seldom have allowed their admiration to become veneration. It is more frequent among Roman Catholic Christians that one hears the stores of the martyrs, although this dimension of

Catholic life is less prominent in the United States today than it was thirty years ago.

Martyrdom, among the early Christians, was sometimes compared with baptism, and even called "baptism by blood" because such a fate sometimes befell those who were preparing for water-baptism. Such a martyrdom was seen not as a cause of salvation, but as a sign that God's grace/strength already enveloped the individual to the degree that he/she could give his/her life. With the rise of the cult of martyrs in the early Church, there also arose informal criteria by which a true martyr could be designated. According to T. Gilby, three conditions obtain for a Christian to be a martyr in the strict sense: "(1) that physical life has been laid down and real death undergone; (2) that death has been inflicted in hatred of Christian life and truth; (3) that death has been voluntarily accepted in defense of these."

While the definition of Christian martyrdom is rather strict, the word has come into ordinary language to mean anyone who dies for the sake of a principle of belief. Close to this ordinary usage of the term is the understanding that the person put to death is aware of his beliefs and holds them firmly; hence, one would not speak of a black person shot to death as a martyr simply because he was black. But one could speak of Martin Luther King as a martyr since his life was marked by fighting for the rights of black people for which he gave his life. Thus the intention of the person is essential to even the ordinary understanding of the term.

The notion of martyrdom has sometimes been metaphorically applied to those Christians who, although not suffering death physically, nevertheless endured many "small deaths" during their daily lives. Gospel phrases such as "carrying one's cross daily" and "dying to self" were correlates to this notion of metaphorical martyrdom. It was related to what the Desert Fathers called "white martyrdom" which is not as frequent in contemporary usage.

It may be the expanded notion of martyrdom—one who dies for what he believes—that could be a fruitful topic in the Jewish-Christian dialogue. While it is true that some of the early Christian martyrs died at the hands of their Jewish brothers and sisters, Christians have amply returned in kind in later history through forced baptism, killing of Jews during the Crusades and other periods, and various forms of persecution. The history of martyrdom is a very sensitive one in the Jewish-Christian dialogue because we stand under the sign of the Holocaust. But discussion of martyrdom between the two parties can raise the issue how the God we mutually believe in accepts that love which both parties have given throughout their respective histories.

Michael McGarry

Messiah

JEWISH VIEW:

The word Messiah derives from the Hebrew *mashiah,* anointed. Kings were anointed with oil as a sign of being chosen to rule. The Messiah of the future, the one who will bring peace and glory to Israel, will be the anointed one, the chosen descendant from the House of King David.

Jewish Messianic thought is hardly monolithic. A study of biblical, rabbinic, medieval and modern texts will reveal a wide variety of opinions and attitudes concerning Messiah. Israeli scholar Gershom Scholem has indicated two general tendencies within Jewish Messianic thought: restorative and utopian. The first envisions the Messianic Era as a return to the ancient greatness of Israel. The House of King David will be restored. The ancient Temple will be rebuilt. The restorative aspect finds expression in the popular words of Hebrew prayer: "Renew our days as of old." In short, there is a deep yearning to return to a golden age in the distant past, and the Messiah will make this restoration possible.

The utopian aspect, though, is very different. It supposes a cataclysmic break with normal historical process. The Messianic Era will be introduced and maintained by miracles and wonders. Human life as we know it—even the laws of nature—will be radically transformed according to this apocalyptic vision. The Messianic Age will not be reached as a natural process of progress in human civilization but rather will come spontaneously, as a total break with the past. And it will be introduced by catastrophe. Jewish tradition speaks of the wars of Gog and Magog as the preliminaries to the arrival of the Messiah.

The attitude concerning the Messiah has not been constant in Jewish history. At times it was utopian and apocalyptic, at other times it was restorative and rationalistic. Often the vision contained elements of both tendencies.

The idea of Messiah, however, provided all the Jewish people—regardless of their specific opinions and attitudes relating to Messiah—with the hope for better times, a dream of an ideal world which would someday surely come into being. Especially in times of oppression, the suffering and aching Jewish people could lift their eyes and see the ultimate redemption which would definitely be coming. Whether his coming would be natural or miraculous, whether he would be endowed with supernatural powers or merely be a charismatic human being, the Messiah would bring peace to Israel.

The historian Bension Netanyahu has written that "from a religious standpoint, the Middle Ages were in a permanent state of war, and as far as Jews and Christians were concerned, Messianism, the most exasperating and explosive issue, was the chronic cause." Indeed, this conflict dates back to the rise of Christianity and has been a perennial area of conflict between Jews and Christians. For Christians, the Messiah has already come. For Jews, the Messiah is still awaited. For Christians, the Messiah represents a spiritual salvation; the Messianic idea is universalistic and, in a sense, other-worldly. For Jews, the Messiah will restore the people of Israel to its Kingdom. He will bring peace in this world. Since the people of Israel has not lived in peace, since the Kingdom of Israel has not been restored, since Jews have been persecuted and oppressed, it is clear to Jews that the Messiah has not yet come.

The medieval philosopher Moses Maimonides included the belief in the coming of the Messiah as one of the thirteen basic principles of the Jewish faith. Indeed, the Jewish prayer book contains many prayers for the restoration of Jerusalem, the rebuilding of the Temple and the coming of the Messiah. The Messianic idea had a major impact on Jewish history and has played a vital role in the religious and national life of the Jewish people over the centuries.

The longing for the Messiah tended to intensify during periods of persecution. Following the expulsion of Jews from Catholic Spain in 1492, Jewish Messianic speculation increased. Rabbi Isaac Abravanel, the leading Jewish personality among the exiles from Spain, wrote a series of three books in which he predicted the coming of the Messiah in the year 1503. Although there is a strong tradition forbidding speculation as to the date of the coming of the Messiah, Abravanel felt compelled to make his prediction due to the crisis of the time. The Jews were in despair and felt abandoned and lost. By informing them of the imminent coming of the Messiah, Abravanel hoped that Jews could restore their faith in the future. Other writers of the time likewise predicted the imminent coming of the Messiah.

The more Jews needed and wanted the Messiah to come, the more likely it was for pseudo-Messiahs to arise. There have been numerous pseudo-Messiahs throughout Jewish history, and their falsehood was always ultimately revealed by their failure to bring peace to Israel, to restore the Kingdom of Israel, and to end foreign oppression of the Jews.

In modern times, the Messianic idea has received additional nuances. Classical Reform Judaism eliminated the idea of a personal Messiah, preferring to teach of a Messianic Era with universal peace. This Era would naturally flow from the progress of human civilization. Classical Reform also removed the nationalistic elements from the Messianic idea. However, with the ascendancy of Zionism, Reform Judaism has generally become more responsive to a Messianic idea which would involve the Jewish homeland, Israel. Among many Orthodox Jews, the rise of the State of Israel is viewed as the first sign of the imminent coming of the Messiah. This is the first period in nearly two thousand years when the Jewish people has regained sovereignty over its own land. Since one of the goals of the Messiah is to restore the Kingdom of Israel, the rise of the State of Israel can be seen in a pre-Messianic context.

In conclusion, we still live in an unredeemed world. War, violence, persecution, oppression: all are the unfortunate features of our world. The land and people of Israel are not free of enemies. Anyone recognizing the realities of Jewish life today will recognize that the Messianic Era has not yet arrived, that no one has brought the peace and tranquility expected of the Messiah. And, therefore, the Jews continue to wait for the coming of the Messiah.

Marc Angel

CHRISTIAN VIEW:

According to the Hebrew Scriptures God will establish, through a descendant of David, called the Anointed or "Messiah," his everlasting reign on earth. This will be characterized by perfection in the material and moral realms, i.e., by peace, bliss, happiness, abundance, and, above all, by a face-to-face encounter with God (cf. especially Is 9–11). The notion of Messiah is complex in its origins and its development. Suffice it here to recall that the pressure of events brought Israel to accentuate successively different aspects of its messianic expectation. At the time of the Hasmoneans, the priestly dimension came to supersede the royal, without eliminating it, and, at Qumran, there is even the question of a double Messiah, a son of Aaron and a son of Judah.

Early Christianity is heir to the so-called "intertestamental" set of ideas as found in the Apocrypha and the Pseudepigrapha, especially those writings reacting against the Roman occupation of Palestine. Previously, the Enochian literature had exalted a messianic figure called, after Daniel, "Son of Man" (or the Elect One). With it, we are almost at the other extreme of the spectrum from the anointed king, son of David, restorer of Israel's glory, and exterminator of godless nations, as he was still expected, e.g., by Psalms of Solomon (cf. especially chapters 17–18). Both conceptions are represented in the New Testament. Let us also mention the Philonic "Logos" which the Alexandrian Jew hypostatized as ambassador of God, Prime (*arche*) of the world, and even "second God." For the Logos in Philo corresponds to the *tabnit* (archetype, antitype) in apocalyptic literature, i.e., the primordial and ultimate reality of all things, for all things have been modeled after it.

So, as far as the Church's understanding of Jesus is concerned, the title "Messiah" was competing with other titles. In fact, these enrich the meaning given by the Christians to the term "Messiah" which is now definitely eschatological. The activity of the Messiah concerns the Kingdom of God (cf. Eschatology) which he inaugurates in all kinds of ways. He *is* that Kingdom in his person; he spreads it around through healing and through restoring life; he teaches with a sovereign authority (cf. Mk 13); he forgives the sins of all (cf. Mk 2:10); he has power over nature (cf. Mt 8:18ff; Jn 6:1ff, 16ff); he "preaches good news to the poor" (cf. Is 61:1 quoted in Mt 11:5); in sum, he is filled with the Holy Spirit (cf. Mk 1:10; Lk 3:22), so that those who attach themselves to him are adopted in his likeness as sons of God (cf. Rom 8:15ff).

But, at the time of the Nazarene, the word Messiah had a definitely political connotation. Palestine had lost its independence for centuries, with some remission during the Maccabean era, and was then occupied by the most hated of foes, Rome. The expectation of the Messiah was naturally connected, in the popular mind at least, with liberation from the enemy. For that very reason, Jesus clearly loathes the title that some would like to give him.

It is all the more remarkable how irresistible the title was, for soon it became in the eyes of the early Christians like a second name for Jesus. The reason for this is no doubt found in Judaism, from where they came and to which they addressed their apologetics in the first place.

John presents the most developed Christology of the New Testament.

For him, Christ is the Logos incarnate (chapter 1). He is life, light, salvation, truth. He is the agent of creation (an identification with Wisdom and with Torah), the Way, the Door. Furthermore, he is equal with God and can even be called God (3:35; 5:18; 10:34–36; 20:28). We are well on our way to the Christological speculations of the Apostolic Fathers on the Trinity, the Virgin Birth, and the Double Nature in Christ (cf. 1 Clement 58:2; Didache 7:1, 3; Ignatius of Antioch to the Ephesians 7:1; 19:1; 20:1). It is in general this maximized conception of the Messiah which prevailed in Christianity.

It might be surprising to find a body of Jewish literature—whether or not written by Jews, all the New Testament documents present a distinctive Jewish character, if only for the topics treated there—stepping over the forbidden boundary of monotheism. But it is clear that for John or the Church Fathers, this was not a way to go back to polytheism. Christ was seen as the hypostasis of the one God, being more so than Ben Sira's Wisdom or Philo's Logos, or again the rabbis' Memra/Torah.

The scriptural context for this is manifold, but one text in particular must have played a central role, viz., Zechariah 12:10. It is alluded to in Matthew 24:30; but more directly pertinent are John 19:37 and Revelation 1:7. Clearly, the mysterious personage of Zechariah was identified by the early Church with Jesus because of his tragic destiny. Furthermore, the very ambiguity of the text underlines the awesome identity claimed by God with his envoy: "They will look at me (about) the one whom they pierced." Whatever the Zecharian text may originally have meant, it is of course secondary for Midrashic reading as practiced by both the New Testament and rabbinic Judaism. Most of the Johannine Christology is encapsulated in the text of Zechariah. No other Gospel or Epistle writer in the New Testament insists more than John on the humanity of Jesus and the "divinity" of Christ simultaneously.

The text of Isaiah 52:13—53:12 is here presenting the same perspective. Incidentally, Zechariah 12:10 depends upon the Isaian text. In both places, it should be noted, the original meaning of the figure is (probably in the case of Isaiah, certainly in the case of Zechariah) *collective.* The Messiah, to the extent that he takes over the symbolism attached to the Servant figure, is never separable from his Messianic people. Jesus gathers around himself twelve Apostles, according to the number of Israel's tribes, and they share in the Holy Spirit like their Master (cf. Jn 14:15ff, etc.) and receive powers similar to his (cf. Lk 9:1 and parallels, etc.). The main dimension of the Church is to be collectively what the individual Christ was and is (cf. Church/Synagogue). The Church, says Paul, is the "Body of Christ," i.e., his protracted embodiment in history (cf. 1 Cor 12:27; Eph 1:23; 5:30; etc.).

By John and since John, Christ has been seen as the meeting point of God and man, i.e., Christ is the one being in whom God is humanized and man is divinized. Philo had done almost the same thing with the figure of Moses, which he nearly identified with Logos (in *Life of Moses*). Later, around the close of the first century CE, the Hebrew Book of Enoch (III Enoch) introduces the figure of Metatron whom the text goes so far as to call "the lesser Yhwh" (12:5). It is also probably legitimate to bring forth in connection with this the rabbinic conception of the Torah, a human book with a divine origin; however, to the Church, anything pre-existent or not, to which the supreme quality of divinity could be attributed, was still a far cry from its Messiah. The Christians proceeded by way of *kal va-homer* (a fortiori reasoning) to consider Christ as superseding anyone or anything but God himself (cf. Col 2:9; Phil 2). Paul traces, however, the limit of such a "divinity" of Christ in stating that the messianic rule comes to an end when the Kingdom is handed to God himself who then is all in all (1 Cor 15:24–27).

André Lacocque

Mission

JEWISH VIEW:

Israel's mission and vocation is the testimony of its covenantal relationship with God. The Jew fulfills the divine task by remaining a Jew, thus bearing witness to the creation and God's commandments. The Mosaic covenant creates Israel as "a kingdom of priests and a consecrated community" (Ex 19:6). Deutero-Isaiah sees the reborn Judaism of post-exilic times as "a light unto the nations" (42:6).

The biblical suggestion that God makes Israel's very existence the divine witness finds support in rabbinic Judaism. Exile according to some rabbis is for the good of Israel, mitigating punishment in the next world through punishment in this. Other sages, however, suggest that exile is for the good of the nations. Rabbi Joshua ben Levi commented that if the nations knew how much they depended upon Jewish existence they would defend it with two armies (Tanhuma Buber, *Teruma* 47a). Their destiny depends upon their action toward Jews.

While Jewish existence is the primary aspect of Jewish mission, it is not merely a passive vocation. Israel's identity depends upon its fidelity to divine law. God made Jews a divine witness only on condition that they carry out divine will. God's name is exalted only when Jews fulfill God's teachings.

By fulfilling those precepts the Jew remains distinguishable among the nations. Amos compares the Jews to the Ethiopians, and the rabbis explain that just as the Ethiopian is distinguished by skin color, so the Jew is distinguished by obeying Halakha. As long as Israel remains unique in the world, then jews give witness to the uniqueness of God. If Jews assimilate and become indistinguishable from others, then God's uniqueness is obscured in the world.

The Jewish task is spiritual rather than political—addressing the Master of the universe and thereby bearing witness to divine involvement in human life. Israel's suffering, prayer, and continued survival testify to the ongoing presence of God in the midst of world history. When Jews pray, all humanity benefits; when Jews suffer, it is for the sake of all nations. Judah Halevi (1075–1141) compared the Jews to the heart within the body. Just as the heart is both the most essential and the most vulnerable organ, so too the Jews are both indispensable and vulnerable.

Jews who recognize this aspect of Jewish existence embrace both suffering and martyrdom (q.v.) as part of their divinely assigned task. Jewish tradition cites a long list of such martyrs. Abraham, the first Jew, is said to have been willing to submit to Nimrod's fiery furnace rather than deny God or perform idolatry. The biblical hero Daniel and the Maccabean martyrs were considered witnesses in the same Abrahamic tradition. Rabbi Akiba, whose martyrdom to the Romans serves as a basic example of heroic witness, saw in such self-sacrifice a means of fulfilling the command to love God with all one's soul. Medieval martyrs followed in this tradition, gladly dying as testimony to God's reality. Such deaths were called *Kiddush ha-Shem,* sanctification of God. By steadfast refusal to sacrifice distinctive Jewish life in the name of divine commandments, Jews publicize the unique reality of the divine governance over all creation.

This willingness to accept suffering, persecution, and even death in the name of witnessing to God's commanding reality has been the mark of Jewish life. Expectation of such self-sacrifice cannot be recommended to all humanity. Jewish mission concerns Jewish existence; the world requires the presence of Jews, not the conversion of non-Jews. Traditional Judaism, therefore, has approached the making of proselytes with caution. A potential proselyte is warned about the realities of Jewish life—exile, suffering, and vulnerability are stressed (cf. TB *Yebamoth* 47a-b). Only if the would-be proselyte responds to these warnings by saying, "I know and I am not worthy," are basic laws and precepts then explained and taught. Upon entering the Jewish community a new Jew accepts all Jewish responsibilities, becoming a full heir of Abraham. Because modern Jewish groups differ on their interpretation of Abraham's heritage, expectations of new Jews often differ. Traditional Jews still require circumcision for a male, immersion in a ritual bath for both males and females, and a determination to fulfill all the laws of Jewish life. Non-traditional Jews often establish different criteria for conversion, but many require circumcision and ritual bath. What remains constant in both traditional and non-traditional approaches to the new Jew is the contention that the proselyte has done more than undergo a change of "faith."

Entering Judaism means accepting the consequences of belonging to the people of Israel and accepting the suffering, responsibilities, and promises associated with that people.

Jewish mission understood as survival has become a crucial concern for Jews in an era of Auschwitz. Christians may wonder why Jews take their physical survival so seriously despite a tradition of martyrdom. Modernity has shown that genocide is a real possibility. While martyrdom sanctifies God's name, the destruction of the entire Jewish people would be a failure of mission. The Jewish vocation includes survival as a distinctive group within humanity. Christians may see the Jewish support of the State of Israel as parochial nationalism. For Jews to whom political survival is a religious requirement the spiritual necessity of the Israeli state seems undeniable. No dialogue between Jew and Christian can proceed unless Christians can understand why Jews find a threat to their continued existence as a threat to the *religious* vocation. Christian missionizing is often incomprehensible to the Jew who sees no necessity for converting others and is repelled by the idea of such conversion as a religious task. Christians need not accept this Jewish view of conversion—indeed Jews must respect their right to a different view of mission. They should, however, understand why Jews find the Christian combination of religious task and proselytism a strange one. At the heart of the Christian-Jewish dialogue must be the willingness to understand the very different presuppositions about religious vocation and witness to God in each tradition.

S. Daniel Breslauer

CHRISTIAN VIEW:

"Mission" is derived from the Latin word *mittere* (to send), while "vocation" is taken from the Latin *vocare* (to call). Vocation refers to the call of God to human persons to various walks of life; we speak of a vocation to married life, to the ministry, to service of the poor. Christians also speak of the Christian vocation, that is, the call to follow Jesus in a life of discipleship. This call is formalized and ratified in the Sacraments of Baptism and Confirmation.

Christian vocation implies mission because it is a call to follow Jesus, the one sent by the Father. The New Testament describes Jesus' mission as the proclamation of the good news that the Kingdom of God has drawn near (Mk 1:15). Jesus proclaims the Kingdom, not only in his teaching, but also in his table-fellowship with outcasts and sinners, and in his ministry of healing, forgiveness, and exorcism.

John's Gospel tells us that the Father has sent Jesus in order that those who believe in Jesus might have eternal life (Jn 6:38–40). Jesus is sent to save the world (Jn 3:16–17). In the Synoptic Gospels, as well as in John, Jesus' mission is related to a saving death. Jesus has come to serve and to give his life as "a ransom for many" (Mk 10:45). He is the Good Shepherd who lays down his life for his sheep (Jn 10:1–18).

All four Gospels describe discipleship as a sharing in Jesus' mission. Jesus chooses Apostles. The very word "Apostle" means "one who is sent." The Synoptic Gospels describe Jesus as sending the Apostles to preach, to exorcise and to heal (Mk 3:14–15; Mt 10:1; Lk 9:1). In other words, their activity is patterned on that of Jesus. John's Gospel describes Jesus as bidding his disciples to love one another as he has loved them, that is, in humble service (13:14), to the point of laying down their lives for one another (15:12). The Synoptics as well as John describe the disciples' ultimate fate as sharing in the saving death and resurrection of Jesus (Mk 8:31–38; Mt. 10:38; Jn 12:24–26).

The Synoptic tradition reflects the insight that the disciples are sent forth by Jesus to "all nations" (Mt 28:16–20). This insight is grounded in the primitive Church's belief in Jesus as Lord of all, as the one to whom the Father has given all authority in heaven and on earth. Because discipleship is a share in Jesus' life and mission, the disciples thus go to the "nations," empowered by the gift of the Spirit.

Paul's life exemplifies the perception that the Christian community is sent out to all nations to proclaim the Gospel of the Kingdom of God. Paul understands his call to be an Apostle as inextricably linked to his initial experience of the Risen Christ (Gal 1:16). Indeed, he understands that he has experienced the Risen Christ precisely in order that he might preach the Lord among the Gentiles. He describes himself, not as called to follow Christ, but as called to be an Apostle of Christ, that is, one sent forth on his behalf (1 Cor 1:1; Rom 1:1).

The earliest Church, then, understood discipleship as mission. It understood that to follow Jesus meant to be sent forth by him to those who had not heard the good news of the Kingdom of God. Thus, mission was understood to be integral to the Christian vocation to discipleship. The Christian vocation, then, has a centrifugal dimension; it requires that those who are part of the Christian community go beyond the confines of that community to those who have not heard that the Kingdom of God has come in Christ.

Despite historical misunderstanding of the meaning of mission, the New Testament understanding does not imply proselytism. That is, it does not imply the use of coercion in any form, be it under the guise of a promise of spiritual, psychological or material gain, or the exploitation of people's guilt or anxiety in order to acquire new members for the Christian community. Quite the contrary, because Jesus' mission was one of service, it was not characterized by motives of gain or domination, but by the proclamation of the Kingdom of God.

Proselytism has no part of authentic Christian mission, then. Christian mission is, rather, identified by witness. As Jesus bears witness, or testifies, to the Father who has sent him, so do Christians bear witness to Jesus who has sent them (Jn 17:18; 20:21). The Christian's call is to proclaim the "wonderful deeds" of God in Christ Jesus (1 Pet 2:9–10). Such a call implies that Christians have indeed experienced the Gospel as "good news" in their own lives and that they know that the Father's work in Christ Jesus manifests a fidelity which is stronger than death. Christian witness implies a knowledge of Jesus, not simply as an historical figure, but as a risen, living person.

Christians bear witness to Jesus through a life in service of others, that is, in a life which bears the pattern of Jesus' own, and thus manifest the presence of the Kingdom of God. Christian witness is characterized by the centrifugal dynamic of Christian mission. That is, it is not meant to be concerned primarily with the maintenance of the structures of the Christian community, but with the service of the broader human community.

Human beings not only act out of their experience; they speak about themselves and their experience. Thus, Christians bear witness in words as well as deeds. In addressing the ultimate questions of human existence, Christians must be true to their experience of God in Christ. That is, they proclaim the Gospel. This is not to say that Christians engage in proselytism. It is, rather, to say that they are true to themselves in sharing that which they know from their experience to be "good news." (Cf. "Study Outline on the Mission and Witness of the Church" by Tommaso Federici, prepared for the Vatican Commission for Religious Relations with the Jews, *Face to Face,* Fall/Winter, 1977, pp. 23ff.)

An adequate understanding of Christian mission and witness has profound implications for Jewish-Christian dialogue, indeed for any inter-religious dialogue. Dialogue requires mutual openness, trust and respect. Thus, dialogue becomes impossible when one of the parties is acting out of a desire to proselytize.

Authentic dialogue requires that the parties share their experience of their own religious traditions. Thus, dialogue becomes proclamation or witness, to use Christian vocabulary; it moves to the level of sharing one's own experience of the ultimate.

Christians involved in inter-religious dialogue, however, recognize that authentic witness is also dialogical. It is receptive to the witness of people from other traditions; it is characterized by concern for the other as other, and by a willingness to be challenged and called to growth by other religious traditions.

The Christian vocation thus implies mission because the call to discipleship is a call to share in Jesus' own life and mission. It implies witness as fidelity to the Christian experience of God's work in Christ Jesus. Christian mission and witness, however, are not to be identified with proselytism, but are instead dialogical.

Celia Deutsch

Personhood

JEWISH VIEW:

The personhood of God and humankind are very closely intertwined in both Judaism and Christianity. Each defines and explicates the other. It is appropriate, therefore, to consider first God's personhood and then that of humankind.

The *locus classicus* for the discussion of God's personhood in Jewish tradition is Genesis 1:26–27: "And God said, 'Let us make man in our image, after our likeness. They shall rule the fish of the sea, the birds of the sky, the animals, the whole earth, and all creeping things that creep on the earth.' And God created man in his image; in the image of God he created him; male and female he created them." The discussion of the meaning of this verse is the history of God's revelation to us and of our perception of him.

Not only in Genesis but in almost every verse of the Bible, God is referred to in anthropomorphic and anthropopathic terms. In these texts God presents himself, and is understood by the reader, in personalist terms. In the Bible, personhood is core and central to the understanding of the divine. In scriptural tradition, theology is anthropology.

Personhood in the Bible, however, has a different connotation from "personality" in modern parlance. The term personality is commonly used to refer to characteristics and patterns of behavior manifested by individual people. The term personhood, however, reaches out to include the spiritual, the moral, and the intellectual dimensions of existence. In the biblical world-view, it is these dimensions which shape the personhood of God (and humankind), not a set of given characteristics which are then more-or-less molded by environment. The Bible understands personhood as a response and a responsibility; modernity often understands it as an empirical evolving structure within a natural being.

God, then, in the Bible, is understood as a person. By this we mean that he is a being who is holy, capable of feeling, possessed of mind, and moved to moral judgment.

In the Middle Ages, under the influence of Greek thought as transmitted through Islam, Jewish thinkers took up systematically a motif that is already present in the Bible, to wit, how can one really describe God. Biblical writers recognized that personhood was a limiting category for a being who transcends all categorization. Medieval philosophers took up this motif very seriously and reached the conclusion that it is improper to understand God with the category of personhood. Maimonides, the most systematic of those thinkers, even went so far as to point out that oneness is a human category and that existence too is a human construct, not to speak of the more avowedly anthropomorphic and anthropopathic modes of understanding God. It was, therefore, on the basis of logic that medieval philosophers excluded personhood from God in their theologies, though, interestingly, they admitted the use of such terms in their liturgies.

The modern period brought several major factors into the consideration of the modes in which we understand God. The enlightenment stream of modern culture tended to deny the use of personhood as a category on two grounds: First, the use of personalist language implies a certain supernaturalism that empirical thought does not allow, and, second, the study of comparative literature leads one to conclude that such terms are merely metaphors and do not indicate any truly existent being beyond them. The romantic stream of modern culture tended, on the other hand, to reassert the personhood of God on the ground that humanness is the category *par excellence* for understanding anything, including God.

Two specific developments in modern culture have considerably sharpened our focus on God's personhood as a category. First Sigmund Freud, in his view of the human personality which has proved so genuine in its insights and so helpful to so many, proposed that organized religion and especially the God-concept were projections of human needs. They function as a support for our weakness in facing harsh reality. Freud also maintained that a human person's relationship with his/her parent forms the controlling mode of his/her understanding of God. Second, the development of the feminist movement sensitized all of us to the distinctly male-dominant language of even the biblical texts. We use the pronoun "he," for example, taking it for granted that that is the correct designation. Similarly, the images and metaphors we use are male-dominant. Both sets of claims have brought into question the use of personhood as a legitimate mode of understanding God.

It is my opinion that serious language about God simply cannot abandon personhood as a category. Personhood, as understood in the Bible, includes spirituality, feeling, mind, and moral judgment. It is the basic category of God's self-revelation. It is also the basic category of humankind's own self-understanding. Contemporary theology must take seriously the claims of science, Freud, and feminism. It must beware of turning one's personal perception of one's parent into a definition of God's personhood; that would be theological idolatry. It must beware of using exclusivist language; that too would be theological idolatry. But the holy in Jewish tradition—biblical, rabbinic, and liturgical—is inextricably bound up with the personal. In this matter, Christians, who understand God in incarnational terms, cannot be far from Jews, and there is room for meaningful exchange.

Humanity too, in Jewish tradition, is defined by the *locus classicus* of Genesis 1:26–27. It is not defined by the empirical realities of behaviorist psychology, social psychology, or psychoanalysis. The image of God in which humanity is created is personhood, that is, spirituality, feeling, mind, and moral judgment. The presence of the image of God in humanity implies the imitation of that image. Humankind was created to be spiritual, feeling, intelligent, and moral. Personhood is core and central to the biblical conception of humanity.

The burden of being human, in the sense of molding oneself to the personhood of God, is enormous. We may fantasize about omnipotence, but never about omni-responsibility. We may fantasize about omniscience, but never about omni-morality. Yet, that is the burden of the image of God in humanity. As Abraham Joshua Heschel put it, "A Jew must strive to be Torah incarnate," to embody the very presence of the divine.

Even if the burden is rejected, however, Jewish tradition teaches that the image of the personhood of God is still present in humanity. The human being is, therefore, ultimately sacred. For this reason, the rabbis teach that "whoever saves one life, it is as if s/he had saved the entire universe." It is in this perspective, too, that traditional Jewish ethics views such problems as the dying patient, the fetus, and even the corpse. The image of personhood is given and cannot be tampered with. Here, too, serious Christians cannot be far from serious Jews, and there is room for fruitful dialogue.

David Blumenthal

CHRISTIAN VIEW:

Christian thought concerning the person has a long and convoluted history. While the Christian may begin with a biblical idea of person, much of later Christian thought was formed by the discussions and controversies over the Trinity in the first few centuries of the Church and carried on through the Scholastic period in Europe.

According to Christian theology, the person is created by God for God. While theological exploration is most properly an exploration about the ways of God, to explore the meaning of the creature made by and for God is to discover something about God. Thus to understand the person is a properly theological task.

The human person's orientation is toward God. Humankind has never lost that, even with the committing of the first sin. Many Christian thinkers call this divine orientation the "transcendental dimension of man." In fact, one may define the person, according to these Christian thinkers, as precisely this transcendental vocation. The meaning of the person is beyond the sum of its theological parts. That the person is oriented to God is not enough, however; the person must be enabled to follow this orientation. Since this is literally "beyond him," God's grace is necessary for the human person to be who he/she truly is. This grace enables the human person to exercise his/her freedom. Here Christians of different traditions are in some disagreement. In the Calvinist and Lutheran traditions, Christians are keenly sensitive to how paralyzed and fractured the human person has become because of sin. Others, starting from the abundance and sweep of Christ's saving activity, have spoken of the person, although wounded, as still free to some extent. The human person, then, made in the image and likeness of God, shares in the vocation to think, create, choose and act in this world.

The foundation for these thoughts about the nature of the person are to be found in the Bible. Genesis 2:7 assures us that the person is created by God. But this fundamental assertion was filtered through a Platonically-influenced Christianity: the person is a being consisting of body and soul. For the Jews in ancient times there was no way to exist other than bodily. The biblical view of the person as an animated body was lost sight of. Some of the dimensions of the person found in the Hebrew Scriptures include sexuality, freedom to respond to God's call to relationship, freedom to sin, and an historical perspective.

St. Paul, accepting the insights of the Hebrew Scriptures to be sure, further contemplated the person in the light of the Christian resurrection experience. For example, in 2 Corinthians 5:17, Paul writes, "If anyone is in

Christ, he is a new creation; the old has passed away; behold, the new has come." That is, the dimension of the person affected by sin has somehow been addressed by the transforming work of Christ, which has been variously argued in the Christian tradition with great nuance. This biblical view was ratified in the early Christian creeds which spoke of the "resurrection of the body" or the "resurrection of the dead (person)." These credal formulations hearken back to the hopes expressed in Isaiah 26:19 and Daniel 12:2–3.

In the Roman Catholic tradition, there is a tendency to speak of the human person as wounded by sin and afflicted by the propensity to sin, but healed by Christ. The Protestant tradition has tended to emphasize the corruption of the human person, first manifested and caused by Adam's sin, and ratified individually by each person's sin. God in his graciousness and because of the sin of Adam treats the human person as if he/she has been transformed and welcomes him/her into everlasting life if he/she believes in Jesus. Oversimplified, but in the main, these two strains represent Christian anthropology of the person.

For a biblically-based understanding of the human person, both Protestants and Catholics look to Paul, particularly in his four major Letters. Much discussion between the two main Christian perspectives has revolved around the relationship between sin—personified in many places by Paul—and the gracious love bestowed by God in Christ Jesus.

The early Fathers of the Church continued the biblical tradition, but they adopted the Greek categories and formed the questions as they would be addressed for centuries to come. Many of the later deliberations about a Christian notion of person emerge as the Christians try to figure out what it means for God to be three "Persons" in one nature.

Many are the modern Christian theologians who warn against adopting a modern notion of person (e.g., a person as a psychological center of consciousness) with the Christological and Trinitarian controversies of the first few centuries. Therein, "nature" and "person" had technical meanings which can be retrieved only through careful historical and theological study. In the Middle Ages, the arguments became even more nuanced about the precise definitions of "nature" and "person." These arguments may strike us moderns as overly technical, but they reflect those Christian theologians' effort to maintain the Jewish insistence on the oneness of God combined with the Christian revelation that there is something three about God as well. That is, God is one, but God has been revealed as Father, Son, and Spirit. The nature of God is one, but the Person is three.

When the early Christian Fathers discussed the *human* person, many of their treatises show a marked influence of neo-Platonism with its disdain for the human body. The person in such tracts came to be known as a combination of body and soul. Things fleshly were denigrated. Some penitential practices, intended to reflect the Christian yearning for heaven, appear in retrospect to cast doubt on the goodness of the human body. The better parts of Christianity disputed with these strains, but never completely overcame them. The continued influence of the body-soul dichotomy can be seen in such Christian expressions as "saving souls," the "poor souls in purgatory," and "gain the whole world but suffer the loss of one's soul."

Modern Christian thinking on the human person has been influenced by the movement in psychology called "personalism." The Church has placed more emphasis on the dignity of the human person, especially in view of industrialization, nihilism, and other anti-human philosophies. In the Roman Catholic tradition, one sees a decidedly person-oriented movement. Recent papal encyclicals call attention to the subjective side of the human person in all its complexity and dignity. This emphasis on the dignity of the human person has renewed Catholic interest in the freedom of conscience and social and political dimensions of personhood.

In the Jewish-Christian dialogue, mutual exploration of the dignity of the human person can only be a positive sign for the world shocked by torture, repression, and indignity. Furthermore, in the more narrowly theological discussion, Jews and Christians may wish to ask each other: In what sense can we call God "Person"? Finally, it may very well turn out that an unsought for, but welcome, by-product of the dialogue would be the time when Jews and Christians would approach each other as persons loved by the same God.

Michael McGarry

Pharisees

JEWISH VIEW:

The Pharisees were a religious grouping of the Jewish people in Israel during the period of the Second Temple. The group seems to have emerged as a particular entity shortly after the Hasmonean revolt (165–160 BCE).

The word Pharisee is believed to derive from the Hebrew root word *parash,* meaning separate. The Pharisees, then, were a group which was set apart, which was separated from heathens, from heathen tendencies, from impurity.

In Talmudic literature, the Pharisees are known primarily as the antagonists of the Sadducees. The Sadducees formed an aristocratic priestly group that controlled the Temple and much of the religious life of the nation which revolved around Temple ritual. The Pharisees attempted to wrest religious authority from the Sadducees and away from the Temple. They taught the Torah throughout the country and were particularly interested in stimulating the religious devotion of the non-priestly Jews. The growth of synagogues in Israel may have been due to the influence of the Pharisees. They felt that religious life should not be controlled exclusively by those in charge of the Temple in Jerusalem.

There were continuous struggles between the Pharisees and Sadducees. Under John Hyrcanus, the Pharisees were expelled from the Sanhedrin, the governing religious body. Yet, in time, the Pharisees gained in influence and eventually completely eclipsed the Sadducees. There is a touching description in a *mishnah* in the Talmudic tractate *Yoma* (1:5) dealing with the ritual of Yom Kippur. It indicates that the scholars (Pharisees) had to make the High Priest take an oath that he would follow the procedures of the Pharisees. The oath was necessary in order to preclude the possibility of the priest following the rules of the Sadducees. Since at that time the high priest was a political appointee of Rome, it was possible that he lacked the knowledge of the Yom Kippur ritual, and it was also possible that he had Sadducee tendencies. The *mishnah* concludes with the statement that after the oath was taken, the High Priest would cry and the scholars who accompanied him would cry. It was tragic that the High Priest had to be under suspicion and could not be depended upon to perform the ritual correctly in accordance with the teaching of the Pharisees.

By the first century of the Common Era, the Pharisees had become the dominant group of Jews. They stressed holiness, devotion to the study of Torah, and righteousness. The great Pharisee teachers such as Shammai, Hillel, Akiba and Ishmael have left an enormous impact on Judaism. Orthodox Jews certainly consider themselves to be in the tradition of the Pharisees.

Among the distinctive teachings of the Pharisees was the belief in the divine origin of the Oral Torah. The Pharisees also stressed belief in resurrection of the dead, reward and punishment in the afterlife (q.v.), and Messianic redemption. The Pharisees argued that God was omniscient, yet he granted human beings free choice. The Pharisees stressed piety and education, giving the highest respect to scholars. The spiritual leadership of the nation belonged to those who learned the Torah and taught it. Anyone, rich or poor, could attain leadership through study. Religious leadership was not restricted to a hereditary priestly class.

The Pharisees added a considerable dimension of spirituality to their people. Although there may have been Pharisees who were not sincere or who were not entirely righteous—as in any other religious group—the overall impact of the Pharisees was positive.

The reputation of the Pharisees has been tarnished by pejorative comments in the New Testament. Describing Pharisees as "hypocrites" does a disservice to the entire group, most of whom were devoted and pious people, trying to live their lives in righteousness. There is a growing awareness that Christianity was influenced by the teachings of the Pharisees. Paul himself had been a Pharisee, was the son of a Pharisee and was taught by one of the great Pharisee teachers of the time, Gamaliel. Pharisaic concepts such as messianism, afterlife, and resurrection of the dead influenced Christian religious thought significantly. The Pharisees, therefore, have left an impressive legacy to Western civilization.

Marc Angel

CHRISTIAN VIEW:

Christian antisemitism found one of its fiercest expressions in the polemics against the Pharisees. This misunderstanding is so deep and so widespread that it has invaded even the definitions of the word in the dictionaries of all European languages. There, with rare exceptions, the term Pharisee is given the synonym of "hypocrisy."

This is not only totally unjust with regard to the nature of the movement or sect of the Pharisees, but mistaken with regard to the nature of New Testament polemics against them. It is important to realize that Pharisaism is a revolt against the priestly class, comparable to the sixteenth century Lutheran Reform. The parallel between the two goes even further in their respective stands about the unmediated relationship with God, and about the internalization of the legal (halakhic) system, understanding *mitzvah* (good deed) as giving expression to the privilege of being God's own. The ultimate source of human action is God's grace, as it is for Luther.

Paul must be exonerated for one thing and reprimanded for another. First, those he calls "Judaizers" are not former Pharisees who attempted to minimize the utter novelty of the economy initiated by Jesus Christ. The Judaizers were non-Jews. Though Paul acknowledged the necessity for himself qua Jew of performing the *mitzvot,* he maintained that Gentiles were saved in Christ without the burden of all the commandments, as it had been made clear from the time of the Noahide covenant (Gen 9).

But the same Paul allegorized the story of Hagar and Sarah (Gal 4). He thus introduced the reductionist interpretation of the Jew as a mere figure, an image, a typology. This misinterpretation on the hermeneutic level has since been immeasurably compounded by the Christian tendency to regard Judaism as dead from the time of Jesus, and hence the synagogue as without any religious meaning today.

Moreover, Paul had been a Pharisee himself, disciple of Gamaliel. All the more surprising, therefore, is the way he speaks of the role of the Torah in Jewish life. It is not easy to recognize there the conception shared by law-abiding Jews. Some of Paul's modern opponents insinuate that he did not understand the teaching of his master(s) and became a Christian on the basis of a previous misunderstanding of Torah. In fact, the explanation lies in the stark contrast drawn by Paul between the time *before* he met Christ and *after*. The hinge is at the point when he accepted to be graced and justified in Christ. Giving up all striving to perfection through the accumulation of merits and the display of righteousness, he looks to the past and regards the Pharisaic system of *mitzvot* as preposterous at best, if not outright blasphemous (cf. Phil 3:7f and context). From that perspective, as a matter of fact, the Pharisees are to be pitied for their unintelligent or unenlightened zeal (Rom 10:2), or vilified for their arrogance and hypocrisy (cf. Lk 12:1; Mt 23:27–29, etc).

So-called "Christian" antisemitism is only too happy to use New Testament texts to nurture its heinous slandering of the Jews. When love and compassion are absent, however, the condemnation of the Pharisees is itself foolish, uninformed, or outright cruel. It comes from spurious Christians, prompted by prejudice at the antipode of Christ discipleship. To avoid this, it is necessary to replace the New Testament polemics within their actual context of internecine strife between Jewish "sects."

First, the Christian hostility to the Pharisees is no prejudice. It is born of the experience of their rejection of Jesus as Messiah. The early Church—Jewish for the most part—was flabbergasted by what it saw as a taut paradox. Those who were the better trained in the tenets of Judaism, "la fleur de la fleur" of the Jewish people, were blinded by their own science and status. They even used these as defenses against the grace of God manifested in Jesus Christ. They were so busily working at their self-righteousness that they bypassed the justice granted graciously to them and to all by God in Christ (cf. Rom 9:30—10:4).

What could be forgiven coming from publicans or notorious sinners (not to speak of prostitutes, rogues, and Gentiles) was unforgivable in the case of Pharisees. Hence, "the tax collectors and the harlots go into the Kingdom of God before you," Jesus tells them (Mt 21:31).

Once more, it is made clear that the crux of the matter is the Pharisaic system of accumulation of merits, either by themselves, or by the fathers, which implies the rejection of the pessimistic anthropology shared by Paul (cf. Rom 1:18; cf. Mt 3:7; Lk 19:9f). This leads them to level off, so to speak, all the commandments, the minutest and the greatest, so that the obedience to any is on a par with the obedience to another. But in the New Testament's hermeneutics, this is myopia or micrology, if not sheer escapism. The principle —commendable in itself as it may appear—allows, in the practice of some, to balance off the most sacred humanitarian duties with a sheer legalistic *mitzvah* such as: "You say, if any one tells his father or his mother, 'What you would have gained from me is given to God,' he need not honor his father" (Mt 15:5), or, "The man went away and told the Jews that it was Jesus who had healed him. And this was why the Jews persecuted Jesus, because he did this on the sabbath" (Jn 5:15f). Jesus denounces time and again putting the Sabbath rest and keeping of the purity laws above human compassion. And, more fundamentally, he establishes a hierarchy in the commandments. The summit and the core of them all is love, i.e., the love of God manifested in the love of the fellow human being. This is the container and content of the Law.

André Lacocque

Prayer

JEWISH VIEW:

Human beings direct words toward God in praise, petition, and thanksgiving. These words are known as prayer. A human being who prays assumes that his words are heard by eternal God, that God has the power to answer his prayers.

The Psalmist is sensitive to the paradox involved in prayer: "God, what is man that you should know him, the son of man that you should think of him?" (8:4) It is not at all obvious that a human being should have the right to pray, should expect God to hear human prayers, let alone to respond to them. Yet, in spite of this paradox, human beings have engaged in prayer from time immemorial.

Judaism takes it for granted that God and human beings are involved in a continuous dialogue. In the Bible, God speaks to humans and directs their affairs. Likewise, human beings pray to God, ask for his intercession, offer him praises and thanksgiving. Throughout the Bible, biblical characters engage in prayer. The Book of Psalms is essentially a book of prayers.

In biblical times, people offered prayers relating to their own life crises. Isaac prayed that his wife would bear a child. Jacob prayed that God would provide him with his material needs. Moses prayed that God would forgive the sins of the children of Israel. Prayers were essentially spontaneous emotional outbursts.

In time, prayer became more formalized. The sacrificial system should be seen in relationship to prayer. Through sacrifices, people hoped to come closer to God, to gain his atonement, to offer thanksgiving, etc. Moreover, as prayer became more formalized there grew a need for sacred places in which to pray: the Temple in Jerusalem, synagogues.

Jewish tradition ascribes the formulation of prayers and blessings to

Ezra and the great scholars of his generation. They provided a formal structure to prayers and set the pattern for all future generations of Jews. While each individual might use his own words, he was still expected to follow the organizational structure established by Ezra and his successors. It was not until the ninth century CE when an authentic Jewish prayer book was issued by Amram Gaon in Babylonia. Others followed Amram in compiling books of prayers so that individuals could read the required texts without have to improvise with their own words. In the course of time, a variety of prayer books emerged among the Jewish people. Though all of the essentially follow the same structure, there are variations. There are specific prayer books for the rites of Sephardic, Ashkenazic, Italian, Yemenite and other groups of Jews. There are prayer books which include daily prayers, Sabbath prayers, prayers for all of the holidays. Thus, the process of formalization of liturgy and synagogue prayer services occurred over a period of many generations.

Jewish tradition prescribed three daily prayers: one in the morning (*shaharith*), one in the afternoon (*minhah*), and one at night (*arvith*). The prayers in the morning and night include the recitation of the *Shema* ("Hear, O Israel, the Lord our God, the Lord is One..."). All three daily prayers include a silent devotion known as *Amidah*. The Amidah includes introductory blessings in praise of God, petitions to God, and closing blessings of thanksgiving. Jewish law stresses the need for *kavanah*, proper intention while praying. The prayers are not seen as magic formulae or incantations. Rather, they are seen as expressions of deep human feelings toward God. In general, Jewish prayers are recited in the plural. An individual does not ask God merely for his own welfare, but for the well-being of all Israel.

Public worship among Jews served as a great uniting element among the diverse Jewish communities scattered throughout the world. The prayer book emphasizes the unity of the Jewish people, the responsibility of Jews to help each other. Prayers are recited facing toward east—toward Jerusalem— hence maintaining the Jewish aspiration for the restoration of the people of Israel in their own homeland. The prayer book includes texts which are not, strictly speaking, prayers. The *Shema,* for example, is composed of biblical passages which teach the unity of God and the importance of observing his commandments. The prayer book includes other scriptural passages, as well as selections from rabbinic literature. The Jewish form of worship, therefore, involves the Jew not only in prayer but also in study.

Obviously, one is free to pray at any time, not only within the context of formal communal worship. Each individual may address God in his or her own way. Private prayer has always been highly regarded among Jews. In the Talmud tractate *Berekoth* (16b–17a), there are recorded a number of the private prayers composed by great rabbis. Some of these prayers were eventually incorporated in the prayer book.

In Jewish tradition, each individual may pray directly to God, without needing an intermediary. The *hazzan*, the leader of services in the synagogue, has the responsibility of conducting the services while congregants read along with him. Those who are unable to read Hebrew may listen to the prayers of the *hazzan* and answer amen. By saying amen, it is considered as though the individual himself had said the prayers. Even if one cannot recite the Hebrew prayers, he is still expected to offer his own prayers sincerely and humbly. In the words of the Psalmist, "God is near to all who call upon him, to all who call upon him in truth."

Marc Angel

CHRISTIAN VIEW:

In Christianity, as in Judaism, prayer is a direct address to God, and its nature is entirely dependent upon the nature of the addressee. God is spiritual and transcendent, which means that prayer cannot be manipulative; also, he is personal and not an idea, so that prayer is a dialogue, not a monologue. The combination of the two makes the prayer influential. God lets himself be influenced by the human being. Moreover, such an influence is not only upon the design of God, but also reflexively upon the disposition and the being of the pray-er. In Hebrew, the verb "to pray" is in the reflexive mode (*hitpael*), for the nature of the addressee reverberates on the addressor: the human being is responsible before God; that is why, as said above, prayer is a dialogue and not a monologue.

The more the Bible insists upon the transcendence of God, the more paradoxical the prayer appears. John 4:24 says: "God is spirit, and those who worship him must worship him in spirit and truth." But the Bible does not shy away from that difficulty. For God has made the human being in his image, so that although the Creator is infinite and the creature finite, there is the possibility of communication between them. As a matter of fact, the whole of Revelation, and consequently the whole of Israel's existence since the beginning, find here their *raison d'être*. What is beyond logic and expression is made true in the very existence of Israel who not only entertains a dialogue with God, but actually *is* that dialogue. In that sense, the people are prayer inserted in human history.

Not any kind of prayer. For in Israel's prayer, God is speaking to God, for "we do not know how to pray as we ought, but the Spirit himself intercedes for us with sighs too deep for words" (Rom 8:26). To express this metaphorically, the New Testament says that true prayer is the cry of the Son to the Father, "Abba!" (Gal 4:6). In this way, of course, the New Testament emphasizes also the intimacy and the trust which preside over the act of prayer.

The paradox of prayer made possible to the transcendent God is further deepened by the statement that he cares for the smallest of his creatures: "Look at the birds of the air...your heavenly Father feeds them" (Mt 6:26; cf. 10:29). Here lies one of the fundamentals of Christian prayer: God is gracious, providential, prepossessing. He forestalls man's prayer: "Ask and it will be given you...for everyone who asks receives...If you, then, who are evil, know how to give good gifts to your children, how much more your Father... (Mt 7:7–11). The accent is on "how much more" which constitutes one of the main characteristics of the New Testament as a whole (cf. Jesus' parables, Paul's argumentation). The goodness of God is not proportionate to the virtues of man, not even with his best intentions, but goes "how much more" beyond anything "deserved," for, indeed nothing is deserved.

Hence, the main aspect of Christian prayer is thanksgiving. Paul exhorts people to pray ceaselessly to God with thanksgiving (1 Thess 5:17f; 2 Cor 1:11; Rom 12:12; Col 4:2; Phil 4:6, Eph 5:4, 20). Petition is not excluded, but it is secondary (cf. Mt 6:34), and made with utmost soberness, without multiplying words and formulas as do the heathens (Mt 6:7f). The Christian knows that he/she has received everything in advance in Christ: all the rest—even the food and the clothing—"are added unto" him/her (Mt 6:33). That is why the model of prayer is here the Lord's prayer (Mt 6:33ff), which starts and ends by glorifying God and turns to our needs and petitions within that framework of the will of the Lord. What it says, thus, is that God is Alpha and Omega, the beginning and the end, the only one Being who fills the horizon, in whom we all are. Prayer among the pagans is a manipulative formula. In the best of cases, it still borders on magic. The divine powers are mobilized to man's service. In brief, prayer is anthropocentric. In Judaism and Christianity prayer is freed from such monologous discourse with alternate voices. In itself, prayer in Judaism and Christianity is already a miracle.

There is, of course, nothing adverse to individual prayer, but due to its glorification of God, prayer is essentially collective, deeply rooted in tradition. Thus, even when the individual is isolated, the prayer's address is to

"*Our* Father." Now God is acknowledged by Christians as "Father" and "ours," because he is Christ's "Father" and "his." The Christian prayer is thus said "in the name of Jesus Christ." It is Christ's prayer, i.e., prayer because of Christ, through Christ, and ultimately of Christ (cf Gal 2:20).

Such a communion with God's Son, as experienced in prayer, is also manifested in the Sacraments (q.v.) of Baptism and Eucharist. The Christian lives with the consciousness of having been plunged into the person of the Messiah, so that I live, but "it is no longer I who live, but Christ who lives in me" (Gal 2:20) and of feeding on him who is the everlasting manna (cf. Rev 2:17). Although not yet enjoying the limitless vision of God, the Christian is already a heavenly being, resurrected and sitting at the right hand of God (cf. Col 1:12f; 2:12f, 20; 3:1–4). As such, the Christian prayer is an everlasting hymn of praise.

André Lacocque

Repentance

JEWISH VIEW:

The Hebrew word designating repentance is *teshuva*. It derives from the root word *shuv*, meaning return. The Hebrew prophets often called on the people of Israel to return, to turn away from evil and to act righteously. The message of the prophets was aimed at their contemporary Israelites (and, in the case of Jonah, at the people of Nineveh), but their teachings have had a lasting influence on world civilization.

The very word *teshuva* has significant implications. It assumes that people naturally tend to righteousness, that they want to live according to God's laws. A sin, then, is a deviation from the normal pattern of life. To repent, one must *return* to his previous state of righteousness.

Teshuva also implies that it is possible for a human being to restore himself to righteousness (q.v.). A sin (q.v.) is not a permanent stain, but a straying from the proper path. People have the power to redirect their own behavior, to repent for errors and to return to a correct way of life.

Judaism does not believe that human beings are born with the taint of original sin. On the contrary, one of the first prayers in the Jewish prayer book, to be recited each morning, states: "My God, the soul which you have endowed me with is pure." In the Jewish view, each human being starts life with a clean slate. He has the power to do good or evil, but knows that he should do good. When he does commit evil—and it is inevitable that everyone will sin—then he has the responsibility and opportunity to repent, to return to the proper path. Repentance is performed by the individual himself. There is no need for any intermediary between a person and God, but each individual does *teshuva* in his own direct relationship to God.

Rabbinic literature, following biblical precedent, describes God as wanting human beings to return. A well-known rabbinic parable provides good insight into the traditional Jewish attitude: "They asked of Wisdom: what is the punishment of the sinner? Wisdom replied: evil pursues sinners. Then they asked Prophecy: what is the punishment of the sinner? Prophecy replied: the soul that sins shall die. Then they asked the Holy One, blessed be He: what is the punishment of the sinner? He replied: let him repent and he will find atonement."

Within Jewish tradition, there are at least three distinct stages in the process of *teshuva*. First, there must be regret for one's sinfulness (*haratah*). One must recognize clearly the nature of his errors and truly feel the significance of his wrongdoings. Then, he must confess his sins (*vidui*). There is some debate among rabbis whether the confession may be general or whether it must describe the sin in detail, whether it should be done privately or publicly. Yet all opinions agree that one must confess his sins, actually stating what he has done wrong. By verbalizing his errors, he will necessarily come to a clearer understanding of exactly what he has done. Finally, there must be a commitment not to repeat the sin in the future (*kabbalah lehaba*). True repentance can be tested if a person finds himself in the same situation as when he originally sinned and is able to resist the temptation to repeat his sin.

The obligation to repent is always applicable. Whenever someone sins he is immediately required to do *teshuva*. Sins committed against human beings will not be forgiven by God until the sinner first receives forgiveness from the person he has wronged. Sins against God may only be forgiven by God.

Rabbi Eliezer, in the tractate of the Mishnah *Ethics of the Fathers* (2:15), is quoted as saying: "Repent one day before your death." Since a person never knows when he is going to die, he should engage in repentance each day. Thus, when the time does come for him to die, he will be able to face God in purity, having atoned for sins which he has committed during the course of his lifetime.

While repentance is applicable every day, the season of the High Holy Days gives particular emphasis to repentance. During the month prior to Rosh Hashana, many Jews have the custom of reciting *selihot,* penitential prayers. Popular symbolism has it that on Rosh Hashana—the Jewish New Year—God sits in judgment, evaluating each of our lives. Through repentance, we ask God to judge us mercifully, to forgive our sins, to bless us with good health and happiness. The ten days between Rosh Hashana and Yom Kippur (Day of Atonement) are known as the Ten Days of Penitence. Jews are expected to devote these days to thoughtful introspection, to ask forgiveness from those they may have sinned against during the year, and to resolve to be more righteous during the coming year.

The Day of Atonement is a day of fasting and prayer. It is the classic day on the Jewish calendar devoted exclusively to repentance. Interestingly, rabbinic tradition teaches that the Day of Atonement is ineffective if one says: I will sin and then repent on Yom Kippur. The fasting and prayer have value insofar as the individual is sincere in his repentance.

Jewish law forbids one to remind a penitent of former sins. There is discussion in the Talmud whether a repentant person is greater than a righteous person who had not sinned. All agree, however, that one who has repented sincerely will have his sins forgiven.

During the periods of the First and Second Temples in Jerusalem, animal sacrifices were brought as sin offerings. However, the sacrifices themselves did not create automatic atonement; rather, atonement was dependent on the sincerity of the repentant individual.

Throughout the generations, Jews have created a significant literature dealing with repentance. During the nineteenth century, Rabbi Israel Salanter inspired the Musar movement, a movement dedicated to self-analysis, piety, and the pursuit of righteousness. Almost every Jewish author of significance has dealt with the subject of repentance, from antiquity until the present time. The quantity and quality of this literature is incontrovertible evidence of the Jews' eternal commitment to righteousness, to returning to the ways of God.

Marc Angel

CHRISTIAN VIEW:

It is in terms of the Kingdom of God, rather than in terms of the fulfillment of the Law, that Jesus calls to repentance (cf. Mk 1:15; Mt 4:17; Lk 15:19). The Hebrew word *teshuva* means also *response;* for Jesus, it is the response to the Kingdom which has come near; it is thus "the response to gratuitous love, not its condition" (S. Terrien). That is why it is also an endless process (cf. Jer 18:11; 25:5; etc.). The redeeming good news for the Christian is that God does not love the ideal me but the sinful me. I repent to have so little to offer in return. I would like to be like the Hasidic Rabbi Sussya who, when reading in the Scriptures the name Elohim (i.e., the third word of the text), was unable to go further in his reading because of his overwhelming enthusiasm. I would like to be like St. John of the Cross and let

God fill heaven and earth and the whole of me, or like St. Francis of Assisi and tell the Glory of the Lord to the birds. I would like to be like the Nazarene and offer my soul as a living sacrifice—and I repent of my mediocrity.

But the Christian knows with Paul that he "does not live any longer but Christ lives in him" (Gal 2:20). Christians' repentance is to let Christ fill the place. If they are not good, Christ is. If they are not holy, Christ is. If they are not intelligent, Christ is. If they are not acceptable, Christ is. "Christ is in me more myself than I" (Paul Claudel). The atonement is not an individual or collective achievement, but God's forgiveness is granted as an undeserved gift (cf. Mt 18:23ff; Mk 10:26f and par.) This gift is manifested in Christ (his life, teaching, healing, death, and resurrection). That is why God's grace is "conveyed" in the prepossessing sacraments of Baptism and Eucharist (Acts 2:38; Mk 1:4; Mt 26:28).

The Christian emphasis on God's grace and human undeservedness has proven to be very ambivalent throughout history. That was meant to signify, for the repentant sinner, the impassionate and profound sense of comfort and of compassion that God himself feels vis-à-vis his creatures. That is the meaning of the verb *naham* which accompanies semantically *teshuva* (cf. Jer 31:13; Is 40:1; Ps 90:13). It soon, however, became understood as a sign of God's giving free hand to human actions of all kinds, and nominal Christians took advantage of their "liberty" for indulging in the perpetration of monstrous crimes.

After the terrible Holocaust of European Jewry, perpetrated by the Nazis in the midst of universal indifference, the relevance for the Church of *repentance* is not to be demonstrated. Were it not for such contrition, one could say that the extermination camps have not only cremated six million Jews but also Christianity itself. It was then fully revealed that antisemitism is a stronger feeling in human hearts than the love of Christ and, consequently, that the Christian faith among the nations is only a thin coat of varnish over deeply ingrained pagan mythologies. For millions of human beings, Christianity is indeed a disposable luxury-good filling the empty space left by distinguished former idols, but advantageously itself replaced by old-new religions of blood, race, and self-divinization.

In fact, the analysis must reach deeper levels yet. The Holocaust has ushered in a new era. Its initial act which is also its "setting in life" and its *raison d'être* has been the most daring attempt ever to kill God in the persons of his representatives. The German rage against the Jews had ultimately no other ground but to eradicate what they have historically been signifying. Whether the victims themselves were religious or not, whether even they had or had not been baptized in a Christian church, had become totally irrelevant, for through them it was what or whom they represented that was under attack. In brief, with the innocent ones, was killed the Innocence (or should we say the Innocent?).

By the same token, Christianity has since been compelled to proceed to a painful soul searching, indeed to an excruciating search for identity. "Christianity" does not rhyme with popularity or State religion. Christianity is only authentic when repenting, when becoming a living act of contrition for the crimes of humanity against humanity, ultimately against God. Christianity can never be at ease, because it has contemplated the Kingdom of God and witnesses to peace, love, and hope, in the midst of war, hatred, and desperation. When Christianity itself becomes an instrument of the latter instead of facilitating the former, there's simply no Christianity left, but a hoax. Then only the repentance of some can *perhaps* (an important word in the Bible and for the rabbis) save Sodom and Gomorrah.

André Lacocque

Revelation

JEWISH VIEW:

Revelation occurs when God shows himself to a human being. The concept of revelation supposes the possibility of an eternal, spiritual God communicating with mortal, limited human beings. It also supposes that human beings have the capacity to receive communications from Almighty God.

The Hebrew Bible takes for granted that God communicates with humans, just as human beings pray to God. When God speaks to biblical characters, he does so quite naturally. The Bible generally does not express surprise or awe at God's speaking to people.

Biblical words expressing revelation suggest God's being seen (*nirah*) or making himself known (*noda*). At times, the Bible describes God speaking directly to individuals. On other occasions, God reveals himself through objects, e.g., the burning bush, a pillar of fire. Moses is described as the individual who received the highest level of revelation possible to a human being. While others received God's communications in dreams or visions, Moses saw God "face to face," and he is therefore considered by Jews to be the greatest of all prophets.

The classic example of revelation in Jewish tradition is known as *maamad har Sinai,* the standing of the people of Israel before Mount Sinai. On that occasion, God revealed himself to an entire people, not merely to unique, gifted individuals. All the Israelites—men, women and children—experienced the presence of God and received Commandments from him. Judaism is based on the authenticity of that divine revelation at Sinai. The Torah and its Commandments were revealed by God to Israel and therefore represent God's own guidance on how Israel should live. The medieval Sephardic poet and thinker, Yehudah Halevi, pointed out that the revelation at Sinai was experienced by thousands of Israelites, and that these individuals passed down the content of this revelation to their children and grandchildren throughout the generations. Judaism is based, therefore, not on abstract philosophical speculations, not on the testimony of a revelation received by an individual or a few individuals, but by the experience of an entire people who received the word of God at Sinai. This evidence, Halevi asserts, is irrefutable and serves as the true basis of the Jewish religion.

Aside from direct communications with human beings by means of words, God reveals himself in other ways. The Ten Commandments open with the statement: "I am the Lord your God who took you out of the land of Egypt" (Ex 20:2). God can be seen through his role in history, through his redemptive acts. He can also be seen through his miracles, through his direct participating in the affairs of human beings.

Talmudic literature does not offer a systematic discussion which explains the process of revelation. Yet several concepts are discussed which are relevant to the topic. *Bat kol* is a heavenly voice which sometimes makes itself heard to humans. *Ruah Hakodesh,* holy spirit, is a quality which some individuals have whereby they receive specific divine guidance. *Nevuah,* prophecy, is a gift which God bestows on certain individuals whereby they receive specific messages from God. It ceased with Haggai, Zechariah and Malachi (TB *Sotah* 48b) and its return will be eschatological (Jl 3:1–2).

God no longer communicates to human beings through the means of prophecy. Yet there are many examples in Jewish history of individuals who believed they were receiving direct communications from God. Rabbi Joseph Karo, author of the standard code of Jewish law, *Shulhan Arukh,* authored a book known as *Maggid Mesharim.* In this volume, Rabbi Karo records messages he received from a Maggid, a divine voice which gave him guidance. Other mystics claimed similar experiences. Although formal prophecy in the biblical sense has come to an end, God's revelation to human beings has certainly not ceased.

During the Middle Ages, Jews and Christians were concerned with the relative importance of revelation versus reason. Some writers stressed that all true knowledge was available through revelation, and that reason was an uncertain guide. Others argued that reason was preeminent and that the truths of revelation could not conflict with reason. Maimonides attempted to give reason supremacy over revelation, although he fully accepted the truths taught through revelation. For Maimonides, a prophet gained his position through the perfection of his intellectual faculties. The prophets attained the highest level of development of human reason and therefore were able to attain prophecy. Other writers, of course, disagreed with Maimonides, and did not view the prophets necessarily as being men of reason and intellect, but rather of poetry and imagination.

During modern times, there has been a tendency to define revelation in personal terms. An individual may have an intense experience—poetic and subjective—in which he feels he has received a message from God. While this experience cannot be objectively proven, yet the individual may be convinced that he has experienced a revelation from God.

While Judaism is based on revelation, there has been a tendency to play down the role of personal revelations. There is a fear that individuals may espouse absurd opinions or engage in improper behavior—claiming that they do so at God's command. Since revelation to an individual can never be proven objectively, much confusion and evil can occur by giving credence to everyone who claims to have had a special revelation. The world could hardly be orderly if everyone claimed that his opinions and actions were dictated to him by God himself.

Marc Angel

CHRISTIAN VIEW:

God is the subject and the object of revelation. He is a hidden God (Is 45:15) who uncovers himself to his beloved people (Dt 29:28; Gen 35:7).

As God is one, revelation also is one, but the means of revelation are diverse. First, a distinction is to be made between divine revelation in nature and in history. For nature, cf. Psalm 19:1–6, Isaiah 40:26, and especially Romans 1:19f. But nature is not *par excellence* the shrine of theophany, a feature which runs counter to the naturalistic orientation of religions in the ancient Near East as elsewhere. Nature's laws are sometimes violated by the divine fiat (cf. Jos 10:12f; Is 38:8). History is the scene of revelation, as eventually the meaning of life here and now is that the Kingdom of God will be ushered in on earth (cf. Is 7:7ff; 8:10ff; 14:24–27; 19:22; 23:8f; etc.). But history becomes revelation only through the Word which creates and interprets the world (cf. Gen 1; Am 3:7). Through the Word, an episodic, accidental, or fortuitous occurrence becomes a unique, momentous, and meaningful event. True, events accumulate, events pile upon events, so that we run the risk of being deafened by the multiplicity of meanings which surround us. But, revelation insists that history is one, and that the Word, which creates history, permeates it, and makes it significant, is one. Hence, all events tend toward *the* Event, i.e., toward the fullness of meaning.

The Church has recognized as the bedrock of its foundation the Christ historical event. This *kairos* (momentous happening) is the apex of history and the pivot of time. The whole of history is seen as situated before or after the Christ event. Before Christ comes the promise (Lk 10:24; Heb 11:1; 1 Pet 1:10–12); it is a time of darkness for the nations. With Christ comes God's full revelation (1 Pet 1:20) and the "ultimate" time (cf. Jn 3:36). Here, there is no distinction made (by God) between Gentile and Jew (Rom 10:12; Gal 3:18, Col 3:11). For the full revelation of God to all human beings does not come as a reward for human righteousness (*dor kulo zakkai* of the rabbis), but as pure grace, moved as God was, so to speak, by the innocence (*tsedakah*) of his Son (Mk 1:11).

This is not another revelation, but a fuller revelation. There is superiority of this mode of revelation in Christ over all other modes, because Christ is *one* with his Father (Lk 10:22–24; Jn17:6–8). So, those who share in his Spirit have a full knowledge of God (Mt 11:27; 1 Cor 2:10ff; 12:3). For such a Spirit is none else but God's Holy Spirit, so that God subjectively reveals through his Spirit the One he is, objectively, in Christ.

For Christianity, there is equivalence in knowing God's Son or God himself (Jn 14:9; Gal 1:16), a far-reaching statement which has nothing to do with an ontological identity of God and Christ, albeit this has been historically taught in the mainstream Christian churches. It is more fitting to think in biblical terms of Christ as the true and perfect image of God (cf. Phil 2), which means that his way of being belongs to God, is permeated by God, and reveals God.

This revelation is made to all (Lk 2:31; Jn 1:9), i.e., first to all Israel, and, through Israel, the revelation reaches the confines of the earth. The only "condition" for benefiting from it is no condition, but the very structure of its reception by man, i.e., *faith* (cf. Rom 3:21f; Cor 2:9). That is why the revelation is for the humble and for the "babes" (Mt 11:25). There is a sophistication in handling God's business which blinds the mind instead of illuminating it (cf. also 2 Cor 3:14).

As the revelation in Christ itself is a "stumbling stone" (Rom 9:33), it is clear that the day will come when revelation will achieve its full glory and unveil everything which is "covered" (cf. Mk 4:22; Lk 12:2, 1 Cor 3:13; 4:5). Meanwhile, we are living in the tension between 'already" and "not yet," by which is meant that we know what the full revelation shall be, without however yet fully comprehending it. Then, "the Son himself will also be subjected to him who put all things under him, that God may be everything to everyone" (1 Cor 15:28).

André Lacocque

Righteousness

JEWISH VIEW:

The English term "righteousness" does not have an exact parallel in Hebrew and, hence, in Jewish tradition where there are four terms which explicate the constellation of value-concepts involved.

The first term is *tsedek.* It is best translated by "precise justice." Thus, for instance, "precise (just) balances, precise (just) weights, and precise (just) measures shall you have" (Lev 19:36), and "justice, justice shall you pursue" (Dt 16:20) (cf. Justice).

The second term is *rahamim.* It denotes "undeserved love of a moral nature" (cf. Love). The closest English equivalent would be "merciful love." Thus, for instance, "let us fall into the hand of the Lord, for his mercies are great; and let me not fall into the hands of men" (2 Sam 24:14), "her mercy was aroused on behalf of her son" (1 Kgs 3:26), and "he will grant you mercy and be merciful unto you" (Dt 13:17).

The third term is *mishpat,* which means judgment, that is, the flowing together of "precise justice" and "merciful love." Moral judgment, if it is to be fair and true, must always be a fusion of justice and love. Thus, for instance, "shall not the judge of all earth render judgment?" (Gen 18:25), "for all his ways are judgment" (Dt 32:4), and "he shall judge between the nations" (Is 2:4). This idea is embodied in the daily liturgy in which the Jews ask God, *tsadekenu ba-mishpat,* which may be rendered, "treat us justly in your judgment," or "give us our due in your judgment." The prayer implies a deep faith in God's willingness to fuse precise and merciful love into a fair decision.

In some biblical texts and in later Jewish mystical texts the terms change but the idea remains the same. One alternate set of terms is *din* (precise justice), *hesed* (merciful love), and *rahamim* (judgment).

The fourth term is *tsedekah,* referring to "supererogatory effort" and, hence, "righteousness." Thus, for instance, "he (Abraham) put his trust in the Lord, and He (God) reckoned it to him as righteousness" (Gen 15:6), "it will be righteousness before the Lord our God to observe faithfully this whole instruction, as he has command us" (Dt. 6:25), and "you must return the pledge to him (the poor man)…and it will be an act of righteousness before the Lord your God" (Dt. 24:13). In later usage, the word *tsedekah* (also spelled *zedakah*) came to be used to refer to charity, and that is its usual usage today.

The biblical-rabbinic concepts of *tsedek, rahamim, mishpat,* and *tsedekah* are grounded in Torah, that is, in the revelation of God interpreted through the prophets, the priests, and later the rabbis. These concepts are not grounded in nature, logic, society, or history, as are the concepts prevalent in Western culture. Hence, such terms as "distributive justice," "natural law," and "situational ethics" are very hard to apply to Jewish tradition.

Sometimes the teachings of Christianity are understood to imply that there must be love even without justice. There are, however, Christian thinkers who say that there can be no true love if it is not also a just love. There is room for fruitful discussion of the relationship between love and justice in Judaism and Christianity.

The Hebrew term for good is *tov*—but there are two kinds of goodness. First there is the goodness of Genesis 1—"and God saw that it was good." This goodness precedes the Fall. In fact, it precedes the creation of human beings. This goodness, then, is an ontological goodness. It is the goodness of the very act of creation, of the very act of being. This type of goodness appears again clearly when Moses, having asked to see the Glory of God, is told: "I will make all my goodness pass before you" (Ex 33:19).

The other kind of goodness is moral goodness. Thus, for instance, "see, I set before you this day life and goodness, death and adversity" (Dt 30:15), "refuse the evil and choose the good" (Is 7:15–16), and "do good, O Lord, unto the good" (Ps 125:4). (The word *tov* has other meanings too as in "good houses," "good vineyards," etc.).

Again, the ontological goodness of creation and the moral goodness of God and humanity are not functions of nature, logic, society, or history. They are functions of the will of God, expressed in creation and articulated in revelation. Judaism and Christianity share these concepts and, insofar as contemporary Jews and Christians doubt them, their doubt is a function of a common secularization of these concepts. There is much room for discussion of these topics.

David Blumenthal

CHRISTIAN VIEW:

When one investigates the Christian approach to the notion of righteousness, one finds a veritable constellation of words meaning the same as, or implied by, that notion. The word-field around "righteousness" includes "justification," "justice" (q.v.) "salvation" (q.v.), and "reconciliation." In fact, these words are often used to translate the Greek *dikaiosune* which, in turn, often has been passed over from the Hebrew *tsedekah.*

In more recent Christian history, the meaning of righteousness has been fed and formed by the Catholic-Protestant debate over "justification (righteousness) by faith." Since the Reformation, especially in English-speaking countries, "justification" has been more of a "Protestant" word than a "Catholic" one. Catholics speak more often of "salvation" or "going to heaven," Protestants more of "justification by faith."

When one sees the expression "justification by faith," it is usually an interpretation of one of the main insights of Paul's Epistles: Christians are not saved by the works that they do, but by the faith that they have been given in Christ Jesus. Even in that expression, however, it is rather vague as to just what righteousness/justification means. In recent years, the battle over the precise meaning of justification has quieted down, but for centuries Protestants—in the main—argued that the word *dikaiosune* meant "to acquit" or "to treat as if one were righteous." Catholics—in the main—taught that not only did God declare the believers righteous, but he actually *made them* righteous. However, in a Pauline understanding of righteousness, a Catholic-Protestant consensus is emerging that "the righteousness of God" is to be understood as "power," in which the gifted recipient lives and from which he draws from the very power of God.

Part of the argument between Catholics and Protestants has been whether righteousness and sanctification coincide—that is, if one is justified, is there anything else to be added? And in what sense can one still grow if one is justified? In Protestantism, there has been the tendency to say that the grace of justification *is* the grace of sanctification: God does not turn back on his choices and require further testing. Catholics have tended to say that, while God's initial choice is found in justification, human freedom is not thereby negated, and the person, in freedom, is called to cooperate with that grace, growing into deeper love, growing in sanctification. One can see that, in this simplified description of positions, perseverance is a superfluous, even blasphemous virtue in the first position, and a sorely sought virtue in the second.

A classical argument between Catholics and Protestants has been whether righteousness as applied to the sinner really changes the person ontologically (Catholic) or merely changes the way God treats him, sometimes referred to as "forensic justification" (Protestant). What Catholics have emphasized is that when God declares something, it is really so. Catholics have been particularly sensitive to the performative function of human language. Protestants, on the other hand, have been very sensitive to the ineradicable indebtedness which man has for his salvation and that there is no way that the saved person can call righteousness his own. Rather, God in his gracious mercy accounts, or regards, or treats him as righteous. All that man can claim as his own is his sin.

In common language, among less biblically-oriented Christians, the righteousness/justice of God is wrongly allied with his wrath or anger. One reason for this misalignment can be traced to the Vulgate translation of *dikaiosune* as *justitia,* too quickly then understood within the framework of the Anglo-Saxon notion of justice and criminal procedure. As we know, the judge in ancient Israel was not so much an impartial arbiter as he was an advocate and executor of what was right. If the accuser was found to be unjust, the judge would execute judgment on him for falsely accusing the defendant. The good judge, then, would be one who had an innate bias in favor of the poor, the widow, and the orphan. It was not a positive value that the judge be totally impartial in a dispute between a rich and poor person. Rather, the Israelites revered the judge who took the side of the poor and powerless. One can more easily see, then, how far from being allied with wrath and anger justice is; rather, righteousness is intimately related to God's mercy (cf. Justice) and compassion. St. Paul himself carried this theme forward in his Epistle to the Romans; this Epistle has been the major battleground for Christians deciphering the meaning of "righteousness" (cf. Rom 1:17, 21).

In recent years, Christians who connect themselves with the movement of "liberation theology" have hearkened back to the Hebrew Scriptures' notion of righteousness, particularly as it is seen as God's "preferential option for the poor." That is, to know God, one must act justly. To be committed to the God of Abraham, Moses, Jeremiah, and Jesus is to be committed to feeding the hungry, taking care of the widow, sheltering the homeless, and assisting the poor. Frequently however, Christians have fallen victim to the misunderstanding that justice and righteousness are biblically synonymous with vengeance and wrath. Thus, among liberation theologians, more attention needs to be paid to the close affinity of God's righteousness to his compassion.

Righteousness is an important word in the Jewish-Christian dialogue for the following reasons. First, the Hebrew understanding of the dynamic quality of the word might help arbitrate the classic Catholic and Protestant polemics about so-called "forensic" and "real" justification. This is not to say that the Jews are to be referees in an intra-Christian theological debate, but that the religious insight of the Jews may help to break up a four hundred year logjam. Second, the retrieval of a more focused and conscious notion of *social* justice among Christians can only be advanced by dialogue with Jews about the sense of peoplehood which comes from the social understanding of justice in the Hebrew Scriptures. Third, some Christians need to move away from the incorrect notion that righteousness is a negative term. Fourth, as Christians reflect on the centrality of righteousness revealed in St. Paul's Letter to the Romans, they must investigate ever more deeply how God's righteousness applies to Jews. Fifth, in some explanation of righteousness, particularly from Paul's Letters, Christians tend to compare adversely Jewish and Christian forms of righteousness; for instance, some Christians might say, "Righteousness under the 'Old Law' was impossible because it was legalistic and narrow, a matter of attainment rather than gift." Or, "The Pharisees thought one could attain salvation by good works rather than by faith." Christians need to talk with Jews about righteousness in order to rid themselves of such misleading caricatures.

Michael McGarry

Sacrament

JEWISH VIEW:

Although Judaism does not use the term "sacrament," it is a religion of the sacred deed, the *mitzvah*. The transforming power of religious action finds expression in the Bible through the sacrificial cult, prophetic ethics, and prayer. The offering of sacrifices as described in Leviticus 16 has a purifying effect upon the entire community of Israel as well as upon individuals. The sacred calendar links the Jew with sacred time and transforms mundane existence into part of divine eternity. Prophetic protest, however, was often raised against the sacramental view of sacrifice. Prophets like Hosea, Amos, Isaiah, and Jeremiah saw history as the context of God's activity. When Jews act in history they perform sacramental deeds, transforming profane time and space into hallowed life through ethics. Toward the end of the biblical period private prayers, as evidenced in the Book of Daniel, took on sacramental significance. Through such prayers an individual is lifted beyond earthly experience to the spheres of God.

Later Judaism took over the same scheme of sacramental thought. In the place of sacrifice a remembrance of sacrificial worship was established. In liturgical memorials to the earlier tradition a Jew could re-establish the cosmic link that sacrifice had forged. The ethics of the prophets was converted into a system of detailed commandments. The idea that Jewish *mitzvot* are mere empty form is far from the truth. These commands organizing every aspect of life make ethics a means of transforming daily existence into a shared experience with God. *Mitzvah* achieves *tikkun olam*, the improvement of the world. Personal prayer is not only formal recitation but intimacy with God. The Jew is warned against making prayer mere rote—it must be a sacramental experience of meeting with divinity, of sharing eternal time with God.

The key concept transforming Jewish liturgy, law, and piety from external action to sacramental deed is *kavanah,* literally translated as intention. The mere doing of a *mitzvah* is only a beginning, only the opportunity for sacramental experience. The deed must be filled with awareness of the divine; it must be directed toward God. The actual deed performed is less crucial than the *kavanah* which fills it. Judaism is a "moral mysticism" in which every human act is the key to self-transcendence. Every deed is potentially sacramental—all it needs is to be done with *kavanah.* Daily life provides many doors to cosmic experience, and human deeds filled with religious intention open those doors. "One person may perform more, another less," the tradition claims; "they are equal if their hearts are directed to heaven" (TB *Berakoth* 63a).

Jewish sacramentalism, then, is oriented toward the quality of a deed. More prosaic attention to detail, however, is also present. While intention is primary, specific commandments do have specific cosmic worth. The very enumeration of the commandments reflects their sacramental power. There are 613 commandments corresponding to the days of a year (365) and the traditional number of limbs in the human body (248). When Jews neglect the commandments or perform them inadequately the world and humanity are impaired. Jewish mystics went to great lengths to describe the intricate relationship between the details of Jewish observance and cosmic effects; war and peace, prosperity and adversity, redemption and exile, all depend on how Jews follow the divinely bestowed commandments, how they transform the world through sacramental deeds.

Later mystics saw the value of sacramental deed differently. According to them creation precipitated a crisis. Holy sparks were scattered throughout the world. When Israel performs the commandments it is also performing a type of exorcism. The holy sparks trapped in the alien matter of creation are liberated. Every deed—whether sacrificial, ethical, or liturgical—lifts sparks back to their source. Some actions—particularly those of the Zaddik or holy leader—even transform corrupt matter into holy spirit; the dross is burned away and becomes spiritual. For the mystic this type of sacramental deed is the true *tikkun olam.*

Christians who sometimes brand Judaism as a dry legalism need to take note of the sacramental intention in Jewish deeds. Not only is the system of commanded sacrifices, ethics, and piety not legalism, it is also seen Judaically as a necessity for the redemption of the world. *Mitzvah* transforms the world by giving human beings an opportunity to move from this mundane sphere to cosmic life. Through holy deeds the Jew purifies the world and redeems the trapped sparks of divinity. Although specific commandments are given detailed attention the vitalizing element is not mere action but *kavanah,* inner attention. When Jews enter into dialogue with Christians this depth-dimension of Jewish action must be respected. Christians can hardly talk sympathetically with Jews without respecting their religious commitment to Jewish law (q.v.) as a transforming sacrament.

S. Daniel Breslauer

CHRISTIAN VIEW:

Sacraments are signs, ritual actions through which God's self-communication (grace) to the Church and the Church's response to God are focused at critical moments of Christian life. These ritual actions are moments of explicit encounter with God at work in the Christian community to offer salvation.

Human existence is bodily; thus, people can communicate thoughts, images, and feelings only in an embodied fashion. They need words and gestures to express realities which would otherwise remain hidden. These words and gestures are signs that point to something beyond themselves. Religion requires embodied forms, or signs, under which people can perceive God's presence and respond to it. Thus, Christians believe that God's self-communication occurs in the sacraments, which are signs containing what they signify. The waters of baptism e.g. embody the action of God who justifies persons and introduces them to new life.

Sacraments signify God's action and the presence of Christ in the Church. God's saving grace is always present in sacraments, independently of the personal merit or disposition of the recipient; however, sacraments do not work magically. They are truly encounters, and thus free acts of God and recipient. While grace is always available, the recipient is free to respond more or less generously.

Sacraments also signify the belief of the Church, and the unity of believers with one another and with Christ, in worship. Sacraments are, thus, the action of God; but they are also the action of the Church so that we can say that, in the sacraments, God's presence is actually mediated, or transmitted, through the Church. This corresponds to the ecclesial nature of Christian faith. Key moments of Christian life are celebrated in communal acts because Christian faith is essentially ecclesial and communal; that is to say, it is lived by individuals as members of a believing community which mediates God's active presence in Christ.

Christian denominations differ on the number of sacraments. All, however, agree on the sacramental nature of Baptism and Eucharist, for these two rites are clearly represented in the New Testament as being instituted by Jesus (Mt 28:16–20, Mk 14:22–25 and parallels). Baptism is the Church's initiation rite. It has historical roots in the first-century Jewish practice of ritual immersion and proselyte baptism. Christians understand baptism as that sacrament through which persons are justified and sanctified; they enter explicitly into life with Christ as a sharing in his death and resurrection. Christians do this by being received by the Church as the community which confesses Jesus as Lord.

The Eucharist is the remembrance of the Lord's Last Supper, his death and resurrection. It has origins in Jewish synagogue worship as well as in the Seder. The Eucharist is not merely the recalling of past historical events, but it is a remembrance through which Christians themselves both enter into the reality of those events and anticipate the full coming of the Kingdom of God. At Eucharist the Christian community recalls its union with Jesus present in its midst, and the members of the community enter more deeply into union with one another.

Confirmation, which was originally part of the rite of baptism, is the sacrament which completes, or confirms, baptism as rite of initiation. In confirmation, the person is empowered through the outpouring of the Spirit, to assume full responsibility as a member of the Christian community. The nature of confirmation as part of the rites of initiation is evident in the fact that, among Orthodox Christians it is always received with baptism, and among Roman Catholics it is received with baptism in the case of adult initiation.

The Sacrament of Reconciliation, or Penance, is the sacrament of forgiveness (cf. Sin). Serious sin estranges the person, not only from God, but also from the Christian community. The Sacrament of Reconciliation, is the rite through which the person is reconciled, not only to God, but to the community. With regard to less serious matters, the Sacrament of Reconciliation is a moment in which the person formalizes his desire to live his Christian commitment more deeply and receives, through the ordained minister, the assurance of God's forgiveness and that of the community.

The Sacrament of the Sick (also called the Anointing of the Sick), is the rite through which the Christian community prays for the healing of the person who is seriously ill or dying. It is an expression of the person's union with the suffering of Christ, of the Church's support of the sick person, and of God's healing grace which helps the person to endure suffering, and sometimes heals him physically.

The Sacrament of Marriage celebrates the union of the partners, and the particular way in which their love for one another is a sign of the Lord's love for the Church. The couple receives strength and grace to live their commitment to one another as integral to their commitment to Jesus Christ. The presence of the Christian community is sign that the marriage is significant, not only to the partners, but to the entire faith community.

The Sacrament of Orders is the sacrament through which a person is made an ordained minister. All Christians are called to ministry by virtue of their baptism; that is, they are called to serve others in the Christian community and beyond. However, some members are called to serve the community through the ministry of word and sacraments. This calling is ratified in the Sacrament of Orders.

The sacraments are thus signs of encounter with God at important moments of Christian life: initiation (baptism, confirmation), ratification of vocation (marriage, Orders), reconciliation (Sacrament of Reconciliation), serious illness (Anointing of the Sick). The difference in the sacraments is to be understood in the context of their unity, which corresponds to the whole range of Christian life. That fundamental unity is focused in the Eucharist which celebrates the death, resurrection, and final coming of Christ as the focus of Christian existence, both individual and communal.

There is considerable debate as to which sacraments were instituted explicitly by Jesus. However, we can say that Jesus instituted sacraments, whether two or seven, insofar as he instituted the Church; that is, insofar as he gathered a community of people who believed that, in him, the Kingdom of God had arrived. That Church is itself sacramental; in it God's action is visible, to be encountered in concrete and tangible ways. Because the Church is sacramental, its nature is manifest in sacraments.

Sacraments embody God's action and the Church's response according to the specific nature of the individual sacrament. Thus, in baptism God shows His saving love offering new life, and the believing community is seen as the community constituted by that new life which welcomes others. In the Sacrament of Reconciliation, God shows mercy to the sinner, and the Church acts as the community of forgiveness and healing.

Sacraments are thus signs of God's active presence, and the expression of the Church's nature. Through sacraments the Church as believing community mediates the presence of God at important moments of Christian life. At such moments there converges the initiative of God's saving love, the individual's response, and that of the community.

Celia Deutsch

Salvation

JEWISH VIEW:

The Hebrew Bible uses different terms to express nuances in the idea of deliverance, *yeshuah and geulah*. Two overlapping types, however, can be discerned—one concerned with the individual and one focused on the nation. The former looks to the well-being, security, prosperity and vindication of the individual. Many of the Psalms, a greater part of the Book of Proverbs, and scattered indications in the historical and prophetic books emphasize God's power to provide individual success. A theme in the Pentateuch is that obedience to divine teachings and commandments (*halakha*) will lead to personal vindication and prosperity. This set of concepts can be said to refer to salvation.

A second cluster of ideas focuses on national life. Covenantal promises in the Torah sometimes focus on communal prosperity rather than individual success; the royal Psalms look to national victory rather than personal vindication; prophetic promise and threat is often addressed to the nation as a whole. Messianic expectations of a renewed national life, of a restored judicial and royal system, and of a revitalized religious cult are part of this second type of deliverance. Understood as national achievement success can be called redemption.

This double approach to deliverance found in the Bible was reaffirmed in rabbinic Judaism. The *Shema*—a central liturgical unit made up of selections from Deuteronomy and Numbers—includes, first, divine promises directed to the individual and then immediately afterward the communal expectation of redemption and the divine requirements for it. An even more pointed prayer focuses on eschatological hope. This prayer, *Uva LeZiyon Goel* (And a Redeemer Shall Come to Zion), is central to Jewish liturgy. The prayer begins by stressing national redemption through the use of selections

180

from Isaiah, Micah, Psalms, and 1 Chronicles. The prayer ends, however, by praising Torah—meaning all Jewish teachings—as the means to personal salvation which enables an individual to "inherit the life of the world to come." The final section of the prayer uses Isaiah 42:21 which brings to mind the words of Rabbi Hananya ben Akashya, "God wanted Israel to acquire merit and therefore gave a multitude of teachings and commandments" (TB *Makkoth*). Torah is God's gracious gift to the Jewish people and each individual whereby salvation is made possible.

Torah represents God's grace to the individual; messianic redemption is God's grace for the people of Israel as a national whole. Jewish tradition emphasizes the hidden, recondite, nature of that redemption. The statement of Zechariah 4:6, "Not by might, nor by power, but by my Spirit, says the Lord," was pivotal for traditional Judaism. With Zechariah and his contemporary Haggai, Jewish leaders stressed the subservient nature of God's chosen leaders. There were, as Zechariah and Haggai suggest, to be two messianic leaders—an anointed Davidic king and an anointed priestly Aaronide teacher. The Hasmonean kings who had claimed to restore peace to the land and usher in the time when "each man sat under his own vine and fig tree with none to make them afraid" (1 Macc 14:11–12) were rejected on the grounds of this understanding of redemption. The Hasmonean leaders had gained authority through their own force and power; they also sought to unite both priestly and royal messianic prerogatives. During the Second Jewish Commonwealth numerous elements rejected the Hasmonean claim to have led the people to redemption, the Pharisaic teachers and the Dead Sea Sectarians being only two more widely known representatives of this rejection. Redemption is God's secret gift which will be given in God's own time. Despite certain medieval meddling in messianic expectation and some dubious calculating of the time of messianic fulfillment the normally accepted principle was that of respecting the mystery of the Messiah. Only God knows when and why the messianic redemption will be granted.

While redemption is a future, undisclosed hope, salvation is a gift made immediately accessible in the present. Through Jewish teachings and instructions—through Torah—a Jew becomes a *ben Olam Haba* (son of the world to come, i.e., member of those worthy of salvation). While Torah is the means to salvation, the measure of a person's worth is not the quantity but the quality of Torah living. Some people attain in one moment of self-sacrifice what it takes others a lifetime to achieve. Faith rather than works is primary as the story of Elazar ben Durdia makes clear. Elazar ben Durdia was a well-known reprobate who frequented every house of ill repute. Once after traveling far to a famous courtesan he was moved to repent and cried aloud until his heart broke and he died. A heavenly voice at once declared, "Rabbi Elazar ben Durdia is a ben Olam Haba." In amazement Rabbi Judah the Prince remarked: "Not merely is a penitent accepted into the world to come but he is also called rabbi" (TB *Ta'anit* 16a). The highest merit a person can acquire depends on the movements of faith, not on quantitative accumulation of deeds.

Judaism posits a subtle connection between personal salvation and national redemption. Transformed human beings do become the basis for God's gracious redeeming act. Joshua ben Levi living in a time of Roman domination and suffering under Roman siege once demanded when the Messiah would come. The answer was given through Psalm 95:7 "Today, if only you would hearken to God's voice" (TB *Sanhedrin* 98a). A world obedient to God is a world in which messianic fulfillment is more possible. A Hasidic rabbi once commented on 1 Samuel 20:27, "Why has not the son of Jesse come…either yesterday or today?" (Martin Buber, *Tales of the Hasidim*). The messianic redemption has not occurred because we today are no different from what we were yesterday. Personal acceptance of religious responsibility becomes the prerequisite for God's redemption of the entire national body.

The Jew does not *earn* either salvation or redemption, but Jewish deeds are understood as the *preparation* for each. Torah prepares an individual to turn in faith to God; the turning of individuals to God prepares the way for God's gracious act of redemption. The stress in Judaism is on discovering *opportunities* in personal life for the response of faith and *opportunities* in political life for God's reaching out of redemptive power. This emphasis on the need to create opportunities, to prepare the way for both human response and divine activity, helps explain why Jews find the existence of the modern State of Israel so important in the context of both salvation and redemption. The Jewish State is first and foremost a spiritual opportunity. Within its borders a Jew can experience an all-embracing Jewish life. Sabbaths and holidays, laws regarding the land of Israel itself, communal obligations and social injunctions from Torah can be fulfilled in a Jewish political setting. Zionism is not a human attempt to usurp divine prerogative. It rather offers a unique opportunity for faithful turning to God and the unique challenge of constructing a political system ready to respond to the divine redemptive act. Modern statehood is thus neither the fulfillment of messianic hopes nor a substitute for individual salvation. It is rather a reflection of modern political realities which dictate that neither salvation nor redemption can be possible without a concrete framework of Jewish existence, a framework which must be assured in these post-Holocaust days by a secure national body and communal structure.

Christians in dialogue with Jews often confuse this emphasis on the need for concrete opportunities in which personal salvation and national redemption can take place with a humanistic arrogance. True ecumenical sharing can begin only when the spiritual element of the Jewish hope for salvation and redemption is clearly understood. Christians need to realize that Judaism stresses deeds as means to faith, not as substitutes for it. Salvation is made possible because God graciously gave a Torah in which opportunities for a faithful turning to God are numerous. The Jew does not earn salvation by multiplying large quantities of sterile actions. Only one action, faithfully performed, is sufficient. God's grace, however, has made the faithful turning possible through the instrument of Torah.

A second important issue in the Christian-Jewish discussion concerns life in an unredeemed world. The Jew refuses to acknowledge that this world of war and tension is God's promised redemption. The biblical messianic expectations are still unfulfilled from the Jewish point of view. Life in an unredeemed world, however, does not preclude *individual salvation.* The Jew finds personal self-fulfillment possible even in a world which is not yet touched by God's final act of political redemption.

A final point needs to be made. Torah presents the Jew with opportunities for turning in salvific faith. All human beings, however, are graced with opportunities of their own. At the very least the seven divine instructions given to Noah provide non-Jews with such opportunities. A basic Jewish presupposition is that the righteous from all nations inherit the world to come (cf. TB *Sanhedrin* 105a). While redemption may be national and particular, salvation because it is individual and personal is universal. The Jew denies salvation to no human being. Religious traditions may vary, but salvation is possible for the non-Jew no less than for the Jew.

S. Daniel Breslauer

CHRISTIAN VIEW:

Salvation and redemption are two words which express the liberation of human persons by God. These words imply the poles of sin and grace, alienation and reconciliation.

Human beings are open to the transcendent, to God who is wholly

Other. This is evident in the person's desire to know and understand. This desire is never fully satisfied, a situation which presses the person to question further. Openness to the transcendent is particularly evident in extreme situations, moments of crisis such as birth, serious decision, and death, when the question of life's meaning can be answered only by silence.

Openness to the transcendent is also evident in the desire to love and to be loved, another desire which is never fully satisfied. Both desires, understanding and love, show that persons are truly human only in self-transcendence. It is the impulse to reach beyond themselves toward others and, ultimately, toward God who is Other.

Experience shows, however, that people also flee questions of life's meaning. And, while desiring love, both given and received, they retreat into a self-enclosed world. In the wish to use creation's goods, they spoil the wealth they grasp. Thus, human beings know a radical alienation from God, from others, from creation, and ultimately from self. We call this situation of alienation "sin." People are born into the situation of alienation, and they ratify that state of being in personal decisions when they make selfish choices. Human beings are thrown, or throw themselves, back on their own resources. If they try to overcome their alienation, they know only their own helplessness; they cannot achieve their own fulfillment as self-transcendent beings.

God offers redemption to humans precisely in their state of alienation; he liberates them from sin. Christians believe that God has redeemed people through the death and resurrection of Jesus. In order to understand the way in which the Cross is redemptive, however, we must understand it in the context of Jesus' life.

Jesus' life is marked by self-transcending love. He is truly the "man for others" and he lives in solidarity with them. He shows this by his attention to the needy and through his fellowship with the dispossessed. He teaches that the Kingdom of God has been inaugurated, and he manifests this not only in his words but in spending himself on those who need healing and forgiveness. Jesus' life, then, is a reversal of human experience of alienation from others.

Jesus' life is also marked by obedience. He is the beloved Son sent by the Father. Tempted by power and wealth, he remains faithful to the Father as his ultimate concern. In the dread of approaching death, he yields to the Father's will, and in his obedience he reverses human alienation from God.

Jesus meets his death as the end of an entire life of self-transcending love and obedience. Even in death he is in solidarity with others; thus, he experiences that death as they experience it, as ultimate alienation and separation, helplessness and disintegration. He cries out to the Father in his abandonment (Mk 15:34).

Jesus' death, then, is redemptive because it is an act of obedience to the Father in accepting the consequences of his ministry, and an act of solidarity with people in experiencing with them ultimate alienation. Jesus has truly died "for us" (1 Cor 15:3). Redemption is not complete in the Cross, however. The Resurrection is integral to redemption, for it is the "other side" of the Cross. In the Resurrection, the Father gives Jesus new life. That life is the consummation of Jesus' earthly life and death. Obedient unto death, he is now exalted (Phil 2:6–11). Jesus, whose earthly life was spent in solidarity with others, is now so much one with them that Paul can say we are baptized "into Christ Jesus" (Rom 6:3).

Redemption through Jesus' Cross and Resurrection is a once-for-all historical event. Yet it is also an eschatological event. Thus, it is present as well as future. Although God has already redeemed people in the Cross and Resurrection, Christians believe that they must also appropriate that redemption in the present. They do this in baptism and in following Jesus. Redemption thus has a twofold dynamic. It is free gift, grace. People who cannot save themselves, who know only alienation, are saved by God. Yet, redemption also calls for response; it demands that graced and redeemed persons surrender themselves to God in faith and follow Jesus as his disciples. This means that Christians take on Jesus' own way of life, that they too live in obedience to the Father and in solidarity with others. The reversal of the situation of sin and alienation thus becomes concrete in Christians' lives.

Redemption is liberation of the whole person from sin and alienation. Human beings are embodied. Thus, redemption is not liberation from the body or from the world, but liberation of the person *in* the body and *in* the world. The act of redemption and its appropriation sets free the whole person to live at one with God, with others, and with the material universe. The redeemed person appropriates fully his redemption, not only in a life lived for others, but in responsibility for the material order. Through the redeemed person, redemption is extended to the realm of non-personal being.

Redemption is a past event because Jesus' death and Resurrection have already occurred. It is present in people's appropriation of it. Redemption is also future, for redemption of the entire created order awaits consummation in the unspecified future (Rom 8:18–25). This dynamic, which shifts between the "already" (that which has been accomplished in Jesus' death and Resurrection) and the "not yet" (future fulfillment), is reflected in the experience of Christians. Although they respond to God in faith, and try to follow Jesus, they yet know the ambiguity of sin. Even their most loving acts are influenced by selfish motives. Although Christians know that they are redeemed, they wait for the fullness of redemption.

Christian life is essentially communal. Though Christians appropriate redemption personally and individually, redemption is mediated through the Church as the community of those who believe in redemption through Jesus. Furthermore, because redemption reverses the situation of alienation, it implies that Christians live in solidarity, not only with those of their own faith tradition, but with all others.

Christian belief in redemption through Jesus, when understood inadequately, has often caused harsh judgments of other religious traditions. A new climate of understanding, however, calls for a rethinking of such attitudes. Theologians are exploring new ways of understanding redemption which maintain the integrity of Christian belief while reflecting the changed climate of interfaith dialogue. While such explorations are still in a preliminary stage, we may say that any Christian understanding of redemption must reflect the solidarity with others and obedience to the Father, which are the hallmarks of redemption itself.

Celia Deutsch

Sin

JEWISH VIEW:

A culture can be measured by the phenomena for which it has a rich vocabulary. Jewish tradition has a very intense vocabulary for the complex of ideas: sin—transgression—repentance—forgiveness. No really thorough typology exists for this motif, yet its centrality demands some presentation.

There are two typologies of sin which deserve special mention. The first is the differentiation between "sins between persons" and "sins between persons and God." "Sins between persons" include all offenses that people commit against their fellow human beings: depriving them of a living, insult, injury, gossip, and so on. Jewish tradition is very clear that God cannot forgive such a sin; only the offended party can do so. Thus, if I sin against a fellow human being, I am responsible to seek his/her forgiveness. Seeking forgiveness from another is not easy because we are resistant to admitting that we are wrong, even more resistant to apologizing, and still more resistant to asking for outright forgiveness. Yet it must be done, and in some circles it is customary to do this during the period before the Day of Atonement.

"Sins between persons and God" include all those offenses which bring dishonor and shame to his Name: ritual sins, offenses against other human beings insofar as they are also rebellion against God's aspirations for us, sins which no one sees, even sins of the mind and heart. These sins can be atoned for through repentance (q.v.) which includes confession. This confession is normally not a private confession but a liturgical formula recited in the course of communal worship. The formula is in the plural, thus avoiding any emphasis on one's own sinfulness. There is no confession to a rabbi or other figure, and there is no absolution granted by a rabbi or other figure to the individual in the name of God or Judaism. Rather, thoroughgoing contrition for past wrongs and complete resolve not to sin again will arouse God's merciful love and bring atonement for sins against him.

The second typology of sin is the distinction between *pesha,* a transgression of the Law, and *hatat,* a defilement of one's true inner self. *Pesha* implies a theology of revelation (q.v.). The sins it includes are all the transgressions of an ethical, as well as a ritual nature. These sins are defined by the tradition and not by social consensus. They are a function of the Law. *Hatat,* by contrast, implies the theology of goodness, that is, the theological recognition that creation (q.v.) is good, that "nature," including human individual and social existence, is "naturally" holy (cf. Righteousness). In this understanding, sin defiles, or pollutes, creation. Here, sin is more than traditional-revelational; it is ontological-creational.

In this typology, God acts in two ways. He foregoes the accumulated debt which humans build up by transgressing the Law, just as a human creditor may forego a human debt. He does this by an exercise of judgment which is itself composed of the fusion of precise justice with merciful love. This is called *mehilah,* "the forgiveness of debts." God also acts to rectify our sense of inner defilement. He accomplishes this by purifying our inner spiritual selves through an act of gracious love. This is called *taharah* (cf. Repentance).

The Jewish concept of sin-repentance-forgiveness is, then, based on three theological truths: (1) that God has revealed his way to humankind but that he has also granted us the "right" to choose to follow that way in varying degrees or to reject it: (2) that when humankind rejects the way of God, there is always a remedy; (3) that the remedy is based upon a tension between human responsibility for redressing wrongs (repentance) and God's grace (forgiveness). Humankind and God share in rectifying wrong. Humankind is worthless in comparison with God, yet it is also co-responsible for the governance of creation. God is Judge, yet he also acts out of mercy.

There is, therefore, no concept of "original sin" in Judaism. It is precluded by the theology of goodness of creation and the co-responsibility of humankind. It is also the case that sex and sexuality are not a sin in Judaism. On the contrary, sexuality was socialized into Jewish religion as the proper form of human relatedness. God commanded us to marry and to be fruitful and multiply. Hence, sex is within the concept of the goodness of creation. There are forms of sexuality which are forbidden, but there is adequate room for legitimate sexuality so that none need think of it as sinful.

It is further the case that ego and personal ambition are not a sin in Judaism. On the contrary, personal ambition was socialized in Jewish religion. Thus, a person who has strong ego drives should use them to build Torah institutions, to increase moral authority, to work for the greater security of God's people, etc. God commanded us to rule creation (which includes society and history) as long as we do it within the confines of his guidance. Hence, ego is within the concept of human co-responsibility for creation. One may not be vulgar about it, but there is adequate room for legitimate expression of personal ambition so that none need think of it as sinful.

"Evil," as used in biblical and rabbinic tradition, is closely related to sinfulness. It is not inherent in the universe, in humankind, or in society or history. On the contrary, these phenomena fall under the rubric of creation which is *tov*, good. Evil, in this theological framework, is the result of bad judgment exercised by human beings. It is not a radical force, independent of man and certainly not of God. Evilness can exert a terrible force within the human personality. But that force can, and must, be resisted. It is an intra-human force and, hence, can be controlled by strong moral consciousness and discipline. It is generated by humankind and can, therefore, be managed by it.

In later Jewish mystical tradition, the problem arose of radical evil— that is, the question of whether some evil exists which precedes, and influences, humankind. In its simplest form, the mystical answer proposes that finitude itself constitutes the root of evil, that the self-imposed limitation of the divine allows for the principle of evil. Never, however, is evil a force co-equal in power with God. It is always subject to his judgment which, in turn, is affected by humankind's exercise of its co-responsibility for creation.

David Blumenthal

CHRISTIAN VIEW:

In the Hebrew Scriptures, the word for sin (*het*) meant literally, "to miss the mark." This "missing the mark" meant to do evil, especially evil which carried social consequences. It was to sin against God or against one's neighbor. It was breaking the law, especially laws which had social consequences.

Christians, in speaking of sin, frequently refer to "original sin," Adam's sin which has had dire consequences. It let loose the whole history of human sins and set the atmosphere for an inclination to commit sin. From this, the Christian concern about "forgiveness of sins" emerged as one central way of understanding the work of Christ: Christ came to "save us from our sins." Indeed, in Pauline thought, particularly in his Letter to the Romans, we see two notions of sin side by side: sin as an act, more or less freely done, which breaks the law or relationship, and sin as a power which envelops the Christian and from whose power he/she is saved.

It is Paul's notion of sin as power that most closely resembles a Christian understanding of evil. As a power which seems to influence us and comes from outside of us, evil is a force which few could deny; as an undeniable fact, however, evil is quite difficult to define, still more to understand. There are evils that are natural, such as storms and earthquakes, and there are moral evils such as selfishness and lust. Evil seems to be a personified combatant for persons who seek to live lives marked by goodness, justice and love. Sometimes such persons experience evil almost as an overpowering force which is not simply the sum total of the sins or imperfections of humankind. Events such as the Holocaust and the bombings of Hiroshima and Nagasaki spontaneously raise the question: How can there be such evil in the world?

For the Christian, the explanation of evil may be no easier than for other humans, but its solution somehow is tied in with what Jesus has done for us. His death crushed the final power of evil, the final power of sin, even though all the effects of evil have not been annihilated. For Christians, the death and Resurrection of Jesus Christ means that, in the end, God, goodness, and life will triumph, and evil, sin, and death will be defeated. It is the virtue of hope, then, which Christians have, not as the answer to evil, but as a constant companion for strength in the struggle.

Christians differ as to how they assess the damage caused by Adam's sin and from which, they believe, they are saved by Christ. Protestant Christians have tended to emphasize the total corrupting power of sin which God in his righteousness and compassion through the life, death, and Resurrection of Jesus Christ, has chosen to save us from and disregard. Even though we are still in the vise of sin, God the Father, through Christ, treats us as though we were not corrupt. Roman Catholics, on the other hand, fully acknowledging the power of sin since and through Adam, more often have expressed the belief that sin has wounded us and Christ's redeeming acts have healed us, although scars still remain. Thus, Roman Catholics have more often spoken of sanctification as a process and lifelong project. Perseverance is the virtue which God grants to those who are being sanctified. Protestants seldom speak of perseverance and more often speak of justification (cf. Righteousness) as the moment when one in faith accepts Christ who grants salvation and which faith can never be lost. Obviously, in this oversimplified description of Catholic-Protestant divergence, the operative definition of sin is Paul's second emphasis, sin as power which has humans in its grip.

Since the time of John's Letter to his community, the meaning and remission of particular sins committed after one's baptism have been problematic for Christians. The Christian may be forgiven of all sins through Baptism, but what about those lapses in love, honesty, chastity and integrity afterward? In the Roman Catholic tradition, such sins have been in the province of the Sacrament (q.v.) of Penance (a blessed ritualized moment of forgiveness of sin by the priest which includes confession of particular sins) and moral theology (that branch of Christian theology which deals with right and wrong, virtue and morality). Moral theology, like other sciences, engages in definition and classification. Thus, moral theology has seen sin as "an offense against God and/or neighbor," a "breaking of the moral law." Some of the classifications which moral theology has used include sins of omission (the good we neglected to do) and sins of commission (the evil we perpetrated). Another fundamental classification we have already alluded to is original sin (the sin of Adam and Eve whose effects have given us an inclination to sin and over which Christ has triumphed) and actual sin (those acts more or less freely done which break the law of God, of the Church, and which harm our neighbor). Another, more recently emphasized classification of sin is personal (those sins I commit which are of an individual nature whose social effects are minimal) and social sin (those sins which are "bigger" than the individual and which seem to have a hold on persons and social structures—e.g., racism, sexism, etc.). The final classification which has much meaning for contemporary Catholics is that of mortal, venial and (most lately) serious sin. These categories are ways for Catholics to understand the seriousness of their sinful actions, particularly with regard to confessing them in the Sacrament of Penance and examining their conscience. Mortal sin is that kind of sin which breaks one off from friendship with God; it is lethal, deadly. Examples of mortal sin include murder, adultery, ruining another's reputation, etc. The traditional criteria for mortal sin are: (1) it is a serious issue, (2) you have to know it is serious, (3) you have to really intend to do it. Venial sin is often a matter of where these three criteria—one, two or all of them—are not met. For example, if the issue is not serious (e.g., a "white lie"), then the sin is not mortal. In recent years, some Catholic moralist have spoken of "serious sin" as somewhere between the two; serious sin would be that sin which involves a serious matter but which, of itself, is not sufficient to cut us off from God's good friendship. This would be the case especially where, against the backdrop of one's whole life situation, a particular act does not have the effect of changing our "fundamental option" for

God, but which is a serious breaking of God's law.

Protestants have not been as eager about distinctions among sins as have Catholics, partly because their theology of righteousness does not require an elaborate detailing of sin: justification comes by faith, not by works. Since no works—great or small—can "merit" salvation, all sin—great or small—is evidence of one's need for the saving and forgiving gift of God. Second, the elaborate classifications of sins in Catholic moral teaching speak to the general custom of confession of sins in the Sacrament of Penance. Protestants have not continued that practice for a number of reasons. Third, Protestants have not emphasized law—natural or moral—because of its perceived affinity to Jewish law from which they have been "rescued." A concern for classifications of sins smacks of casuistry in the worst sense.

In the Jewish-Christian dialogue, Christians need to listen to the Jewish understanding of virtue and *mitzvot*. Second, dialogue about sin, particularly about social sin and its causes, can open doors for joint efforts for social justice. Third, renewed and joint study of Pharisaism (q.v.) will open up for Christians an understanding of law whose fulfillment flows from the heart and not just from concern for appearances.

Michael McGarry

Spirituality

JEWISH VIEW:

Jewish spirituality finds expression in two dimensions. One is the covenantal relationship God-Israel, the other its implementation in a daily actualization of the experience of God, his Call and Presence, in individual and community existence. Spirituality is an exercise of inwardness.

There is no precise theological expression for the term "spirituality" in Hebrew. Two words should be considered: *Halakha* and *Emuna*. *Halakha* often incorrectly translated as law or "nomos" by Biblical and Latin translators, means a way of being and doing, implementing the covenantal relationship. *Emuna*, "faith," is the experience of reliving the covenantal relationship in a spirit of hope and realization. *Emuna* and *Halakha* convey the whole range of Jewish spirituality.

Jewish spirituality is guided and inspired by Psalm 16:8: "I have set God before me continuously." The presence of God is a real experience in the daily existence of individuals and the community, and expressed in prayer and rituals that are sources to sanctify the world created by God, but damaged by human evil. The experience of "Presence" was affirmed and repeated in the Temple liturgy focusing on the redemptive value of the sacrifice. Prayer and the study of God's Word were two distinctive trends that developed after the destruction of the Jerusalem Temple by the Romans in the year 70 CE, and the disappearance of the sacrificial system.

Prayer becomes central in Jewish spirituality. Three times a day Jews gather in the synagogue to pray. The schedule coincides with the sacrificial offering in the Temple, proclaiming God in the morning, afternoon and evening services. The life of prayer is conveyed in a symbology present in specific objects and places. The most sanctified and prominent section of the synagogue is the *Aron Ha-Kodesh*, the Ark, in which are deposited the *Sifrei-*

Torah, the scrolls of the five books of the Bible. It is always built against a wall facing Jerusalem, and indicates the direction in which the service of the heart is offered.

The perpetual light in front of the Ark, the *Ner Tamid,* recalls the light which was ever kept alight in the Tabernacle and in the Holy Temple of Jerusalem. The eternal light represents the biblical text of Proverbs 6:23, "For the Commandment is a lamp and the Torah is a light." Next in importance is the wooden platform, *Bemah,* a place in the center of the synagogue around which the worshipers have their seats, and reminiscent of the altar. From the desk that is placed thereon, the *Torah* is read and the community is led in prayer; just as the sacrifices were offered on the altar "so will we render as bullocks the words of our lips" (Hos 14:3).

Prayer as an actualization of God's Presence and covenantal relationship centers on the *Shema,* Israel's declaration of faith with its three biblical portions, Deuteronomy 6:4–9; 11:13–21, and Numbers 15:37–41. It is followed by the *Shemoneh Ezre,* eighteen and later nineteen benedictions, and the final declamation of the *Kaddish,* a sanctification of God's name, considered since medieval times a prayer for the departed and martyrs. This basic structure has been augmented by additional prayers, psalms, petitions and hymns of thanksgiving.

The *Shema* proclaims in a daily act of committed spirituality God's Unity, Israel's allegiance to the Kingdom of God, and a joyful submission to God's Commandments.

Three main ideas relate to the *Shema:* creation, revelation and redemption. The morning service starts with the prayer *Yotzer Or,* the creator of light, a thanksgiving for the creation of the light of day, and the daily renewal of creation. This concept entails the obligation for a personal commitment to the goodness of creation and the Kingdom of God.

The second prayer is the *Ahavah Rabbah,* "With abundant love have you loved us, O Lord our God, and great and overflowing tenderness have you shown to us." It is an outpouring of fervor and thanksgiving for the moral illumination bestowed upon Israel, and an affirmation of the need to live revelation in a daily life of prayer and all of life's activities.

The final concept remembered in the recitation of the *Shema* is redemption. This finds expression in three prayers of the morning service. *Emeth veyatzib,* "true and firm, established and enduring, right and faithful, beloved and precious, desirable, revered and mighty, well ordered and acceptable, good and beautiful is this your word forever and forever." It is followed by *Al Harishonim,* "alike for former and later ages Your Word is good and endures forever and ever; it is true and trustworthy, an ordination which shall not pass away. True it is that you are indeed the Lord, our God, and God of our fathers, our King, our fathers' King, our Redeemer, the Redeemer of our fathers, our maker, the rock of our salvation; our Deliverer and Rescuer from everlasting such is your name; there is no God besides You." The final hymn of thanksgiving for redemption is *Ezrath Abotenu*, praising God as the shield and savior of the community, declaring once again that God is indeed the first and the last and that "besides you we have no king, redeemer and savior."

The central elements renewing the spirituality of prayer are *kavanah* and *minhag*. *Kavanah* is considered a unique attitude that must accompany religious devotion. The Hebrew term has no exact equivalent in the English language. The original Hebrew conveys the idea of concentration, devotion, intention or inwardness, encompassing a state of oneness in devotion and inner direction toward God.

This state of mind, a preparation for prayer and commandment, is not explicitly mentioned in the Pentateuch, but is clearly referred to by the prophets. Isaiah, for instance, criticizes those who "with their mouth and with their lips do honor me, but have removed their heart far from me" (29:13). Rabbinic literature, and specifically the Talmud, attaches considerable importance to *kavanah*. In TB, *Berakot* 5, 1, it is pointed out that the early *Hasidim*, the pious ones, used to wait an hour before and after prayer to achieve a state of *kavanah* and again, to emerge from it.

Minhag is one of the most important bases of *Halakha*. The word is found in the Bible (2 Kgs 9:2), meaning "the driving" of a chariot, but it was taken by the rabbis to refer to "usage." It denotes primarily the customs which, having been accepted in practice, became binding and assumed the impact of *Halakha*. The word *minhag* is also employed to designate the various liturgical rites which have developed.

Custom and usage are the natural, normal manners of expressing the contemporary experience of God, ways of conveying spirituality to ever new generations, without losing the links with tradition. *Minhag* relates the aspiration of one generation to the thoughts of the preceding ones, renewing the basic meaning of religiosity. Custom can also become an impediment, an end in itself, a ruling rather than an expression of religious experience. New forms of *minhag* express the mood and heart of a community. For instance, the inclusion of special prayers or a time of silence at the reading of the Passover *Haggadah* to remember the Holocaust has become a way to recall missing members of the family, a missing community of six million people, a reminder of the covenantal commitment to endure evil and the realities of history. The rich spiritual experience of Sephardic Jews from Northern

Africa, Greece, Italy and Southern France, and *Ashkenazim,* Jews from Eastern Europe and Germany, testifies to the richness of the *minhag* in the spirituality of the Jewish people.

Liturgy is a combination of word, song, and prayer; an exercise in religious commitment; it also translates a need. This is the human need for confirmation, the actualization of the Presence of God and the covenantal relationship, the encounter between person and Maker. Liturgy reenacts the primordial divine encounter, embedded in the Jewish historical experience with the world and with God.

The spirituality of liturgy is vividly expressed in four particular moments of prayer: the daily service, the celebration of the Sabbath, the redemptive power of Passover, and the renewed reckoning of the soul at Yom Kippur. Special attention will be given here to the Sabbath spirituality.

Observance and ritual are central elements in the religious life of individuals and communities. They are born out of experience of a unique moment in the human development, the meeting of God and human being. Words and symbols become the daily remembrance of that unique experience.

The Sabbath celebration is no exception to this religious phenomenon. The reference in Genesis 2:3, "God blessed the seventh day and made it holy, because on that day he ceased from all the work he had set himself to do," is the call for inwardness and the celebration of a particular time.

The Sabbath and its spirituality go beyond the commandment of halting work, to a commemoration of creation and freedom. On Friday night, the beginning of the Sabbath in the Hebrew calendar, each ritual and liturgical expression in the community and family is charged with eschatological dimensions, reminding Jews of the covenant with God, the ethical and religious fulfillment of their witnessing, their obligations toward God, and the establishment of his Kingdom in the universe.

The Hebrew Bible specifically refers to the Sabbath in two of its books, Exodus 20:8-11 and Deuteronomy 5:12–15. The latter introduces the concept of freedom from slavery that will take on a special meaning in the benediction of wine on Friday night, the *Kiddush.* Neither biblical source gives detailed rules concerning the observance of the day. The commandment is "to remember" and "to keep" the Sabbath, and to bring to a halt all work of the family and the community. The text does not indicate how to make effective in the daily experience the commandments established for the Sabbath observance. The rabbis and sages from Ezra's day to the compilation of the fifth century of the Talmud in Babylon developed a detailed account of precepts and dispositions regulating every aspect of Sabbath celebration. Their consideration covered every aspect of the life of the individual and the community, and gave to the celebration its eschatological overtones that permeate every part of the Sabbath celebration.

Two central themes are remembered in the spirituality of the Sabbath, *menuhah* (rest) and freedom. The German Jewish theologian Leo Baeck implies them in the following:

> The Sabbath does not mean a mere not working, nor empty idleness. It connotes something positive. It has guided the soul into its mystery so that it is not a day that just interrupts, but a day that renews, speaks through it, of something eternal. It is the expression of the direction for life, and not just an instituted day of rest. If it were only that, or if it became that, its essence would be taken from it. It would then be only a hollow shell.

The Sabbath rest brings to a halt the creative stream of the week, but it is more than a moment of relaxation: it is a time of inner activity. The authentic expression of *menuhah,* rest, requires the individual and the community to direct their creative strength, not to the work of the world but to the spirit. The creative energies are not suspended but subjected to a transformation whose object is the inner world of the spirit. The Sabbath is a day of interiority, of self-discovery, a time to restore individual integrity, after a week of work and alienation. It allows for a recovery of self out of the routine of weekday involvement.

The liturgy speaks of a phenomenon peculiar to the Sabbath: each one receives on that day a *neshamah veterah*, an additional soul, that requires cultivation and creative self-search. It implies *nomesh,* self-change, an inner silence that transforms the self in depth and meaning. The weekday is devoted to work which for the religious person is also a creative activity; but the Sabbath is a time for inner creativity.

The *Kiddush,* the benediction over wine in the Friday night ceremony at home, recalls freedom as the second basic element of the Sabbath. The blessing says that the Sabbath is "first among our sacred days," and "a remembrance of the exodus from Egypt." The Exodus narration, the liberation movement of the Jewish people as an example for all generations of humankind, relates the historical events that allowed them to continue their spiritual and religious commitment in freedom. Slavery implied subjection to a form of life that despised spirituality and the development of a religious attitude. The slavery in Egypt became symbolic of all forms of slavery, and the *Kiddush* reminds the Jew of subjection suffered throughout the centuries, from Pharaoh to contemporary antisemitism, and the devastating experience of Auschwitz.

Freedom is celebrated at home, and Jews are reminded of the creative possibilities of freedom for a religious commitment. Jews are well aware of the fact that the lack of freedom is an experience leading to spiritual suffocation and, eventually, spiritual death. It is only in an atmosphere of liberty and respect for others that a covenantal religiosity can reach high levels of inner activity and meaning.

Creative rest and freedom as elements of the Sabbath celebration have been expounded in liturgy and theological commentary for the last two thousand years. The Sabbath observance has been enriched by the liturgical experience of the Jewish people, and history has influenced its symbology and modes of commemorating. The present time, too, requires us to rethink the meaning of rituals and customs in relation to contemporary experience, mainly the Holocaust and the founding of the State of Israel and the unique experience of political freedom and pluralism.

Leon Klenicki

CHRISTIAN VIEW:

When we discuss spirituality, we are ultimately dealing with that aspect of reality which is the realm of the spirit (that is, the non-corporeal); for Christians, it also means being concerned with one's life in the Holy Spirit, the Third Person of the Blessed Trinity, to whom theology traditionally assigns the task of sanctification. St. Paul wrote in these terms: "Now we have received not the spirit of the world, but the Spirit which is from God, that we might understand the gifts bestowed on us by God. And we impart this in words not taught by human wisdom but taught by the Spirit, interpreting spiritual truths to those who possess the Spirit" (1 Cor 2:12–13).

Now, there is a danger inherent in the use of the word "spirituality" because, at certain moments in Christian history (especially under the influence of Platonic philosophy), spirituality came to be seen in a dualistic manner, so that it appeared that Christians had to "war" against their bodies to save their souls; that, to use Plato's own language, "the soul is the prisoner of the body"; that death was a most welcome, looked for relief from the struggle of our spiritual side against the forces of evil which resided principally in material things. To be fair, it is important to say that such approaches were not truly grounded in a sound Christian theology, but the temptation does exist in every age to create dichotomies where they need not and should not be. Indeed, Christianity at its best has always reflected the biblical/Hebraic notion of man as a body/soul unity and not a duality. That necessarily leads to the conclusion that one is saved as a whole person (body, soul, spirit); flowing from that is the conviction that to be human implies life "in a body"—a point of major convergence between Jesus and Pharisaic Judaism. In Catholicism, this conviction about human life and how it is lived even in the afterlife is so strong that Catholic dogma asserts that Christ reigns in his risen life now and for all eternity, precisely as embodied; the same is also true of the Blessed Virgin Mary who anticipates the full life of glory which is held out in promise to every believer—a life which she enjoys presently, both body and soul, like all others who will be so united after the General Judgment.

At any rate, in spite of all the caution built into the use of the term "spirituality" and concerned about the possible pitfalls, some prefer to substitute expressions like "ascetical theology" (but that also has a history which at times has become almost exclusively identified with mortification) or "life in Christ." While there is nothing objectionable to expressions like the latter, the usage of centuries has seemed to hallow "spirituality" and also provides bridges for discussions about this important topic within an interfaith context. With all the caveats in place, this article will proceed by relying on the use of "spirituality."

The desire for a "spiritual" existence for man is, first and foremost, God's wish for his children. In the Book of Leviticus, Almighty God invites, indeed commands, the Chosen People to "be holy; for I the Lord your God am holy" (19:2); following that same line of thought, Jesus urges his disciples: "You, therefore, must be perfect, as your heavenly Father is perfect" (Mt 5:48). Holiness and perfection are but two words for the same goal. In truth, all believers in the God of Abraham, Isaac and Jacob are called to imitate and reflect the holiness and perfection of God. In Christianity, that is considered to be a requisite for entering into eternal life, for one's holiness here on earth determines one's suitability for final union with God at the end of this earthly sojourn. And union with God is the very aim of spirituality—union now in veiled and fragmentary ways and total union in eternity, which is generally referred to as the beatific vision.

This communion with God for all eternity is the purpose of all human life and was begun in a unique manner in and through the Incarnation of the

Son of God. St. Augustine of Hippo declares, without fear of contradiction, that "God became man that men might become gods." Those same bold sentiments are reflected in the Church's liturgy as the priest mingles the water and wine, praying that "through the mystery of this water and wine, may we come to share in the divinity of Christ who humbled himself to share in our humanity." Eastern Christian spirituality speaks of this process as "divinization," not to be understood in any kind of crude or crass sense resulting in a pantheon in the afterlife, but seen as that slow but sure process whereby God and a human being share a relationship of intimacy. This process takes place in such wise that, as St. Thomas Aquinas put it, "grace builds on nature." In other words, God's grace or life is communicated to man so that the human person's identity is not overpowered or destroyed but brought to the perfection God intended from the creation of the first humans with whom he shared his life and love completely (cf. Gen 3); the repair of the sad breach was preeminently the work of Christ, "the last Adam" (1 Cor 15:45), who seeks to lead all back into full communion with his heavenly Father.

Although all Christian spirituality must be rooted in a relationship with Jesus Christ, the modalities vary according to individual circumstances of time, place and personality; hence, it is not incorrect to talk about "spiritualities." Furthermore, distinctions come up between Catholic and Protestant spiritualities at certain junctions; this essay is concerned predominantly with the Catholic dimension for two reasons: (1) the author is a Catholic and obviously can write with more authority on that method of spiritual growth; (2) Catholic spirituality has been rightly dubbed "a big umbrella" under which a host of spiritual techniques can be practiced and perfected—from which the several branches of Protestantism have taken and used according to their special dispositions.

Catholic spirituality (in both the East and West) is essentially liturgical and ecclesial, which is to say that the believer is led to a deeper life of faith in and through the Church and her liturgy, what the Fathers of the Second Vatican Council described as "the source and summit of the Christian life" (*Sacrosanctum Concilium*, n. 10). Thus one is introduced to a spiritual life through Baptism as one is brought into a saving relationship with Christ and his Church; that is sealed in the Sacrament of Confirmation; it is continuously nourished in the Eucharist. Corresponding to the exigencies of human existence, the sacraments of healing and mission fill out the means available to members of the Church as they travel the road to perfection.

Spirituality, however, is not limited to the Church's sacramental system or exhausted by it. It also involves what might be properly designated as interdisciplinary, first within theology itself—utilizing all the resources of the many branches of theological investigation (dogma, morality, scriptural studies, patristics); also helpful, however, are the insights which can be gleaned from the social sciences, especially psychology, anthropology and sociology. These latter disciplines are not to be used uncritically but submitted to a procedure of discernment which can take the good of these secular sciences and integrate them into a holistic vision of Christian faith. Because of the delicacy of the task, people serious about true and mature spiritual development are urged to seek out a prudent spiritual director, who may or may not be ordained.

Growth in one's life in Christ is aided, in an indispensable way, by one's life in the Church. Heeding the teachings of the Church and benefiting from her two millennia of leading men to God, the individual believer is led inexorably into more profound communion with Christ and his Church, for the two are inseparable. The witness of the greatest mystics, in fact, testifies to the indissoluble unity between a personal relationship with Christ and a strengthening of the bonds of ecclesial communion. As St. Cyprian expressed it centuries ago, "anyone who would have God for a Father must have the Church for a Mother." It is perhaps on this point that Catholic and Protestant spiritualities diverge the most; ironically, though, that is a point of convergence between Catholic and Jewish spiritualities, for Judaism views it as virtually impossible to relate to the God of the patriarchs in isolation from the People he has called to be his own.

Prayer is the most obvious element in the spiritual life, and this takes many forms (in addition to the sacramental types already treated). It may be spontaneous or formulaic, personal or communal; it may flow from sacred texts (like Scripture or the Fathers of the Church) or may result from meditation on the mysteries of the life of Christ or of the Christian Faith. Catholic prayer is likewise characterized by a reliance on devotions (of a more emotional nature) to supplement the more formal and even cerebral liturgy; these would include the rosary, stations of the cross, processions, prayers to the Virgin and other saints. In this last regard, it should be noted that liturgical prayer is always directed to the Father, through the Son, in the power of the Holy Spirit, which is to say that it is Trinitarian; devotional prayer is often more directed toward particular saints.

Christian spirituality has also developed over the centuries as various spiritual writers have sought to respond to human needs they encountered and offered such people their insights and "system." Saints like Francis of Assisi, Dominic, Ignatius Loyola, Catherine of Siena, Teresa of Avila, John of the Cross, and Francis de Sales have all contributed to the science of spirituality with their different but complementary emphases, geared to particular circumstances or personality types. Certain religious orders were established to advance a special method of spiritual growth; in this century, Blessed Josemaría Escrivá produced a spirituality uniquely suited to lay people as they endeavored to attain sanctity in the midst of the world.

After prayer, self-denial has been ranked second in enabling one to progress in the Christian life. That can take many shapes from fasting and abstinence to virginity and even martyrdom. Ascetical practices are not intended to be negative, as such; rather, they should be perceived as attempts to gain self-control and to obtain a perspective on life which could not otherwise be had. Fasting, for example, is a common means of expressing one's sorrow for one's sins and thus a sign of love for God; it also enables one to realize that control over one's appetites is possible and desirable; finally, it gives one the opportunity to experience voluntarily what so many in the world endure through no personal choice. In this last instance, fasting is a work of human and Christian solidarity.

This brings us to the third pillar of spirituality—action on behalf of the poor and oppressed; once more, entire religious orders have been created to meet certain needs (e.g., the Trinitarians for the ransom of slaves; the Sisters of Charity for the comfort of the poor; Mother Teresa's Missionaries of Charity to aid the poorest of the poor and the dying). One should not imagine, however, that such social action either is limited to those in the vowed life or is an optional aspect of a Christian's being. All Christians without distinction—clergy, religious and laity alike—must build their spirituality on all three pillars if the construction is to weather the storms of trial and temptation and be faithful to the program of perfection set forth by Jesus Christ.

Sometimes when non-Christians hear about spirituality, they think primarily of visionaries or stigmatists. While acknowledging that extraordinary phenomena are indeed possible, Catholic spirituality does not highlight the extraordinary and even discourages them, for God is most generally found in the normal and even humdrum experiences of daily living. The Church makes her own the discovery of Elijah of old who learned that God was not in the earthquake or the fire, but in "a still small voice" (1 Kgs 19:12). It is the task of spirituality to help people hear that "still small voice" and to respond with love, devotion and faith.

Peter Stravinskas

Suffering

JEWISH VIEW:

The question of human suffering is connected to the wider question of theodicy, namely the relationship between God and the presence of evil within the world. The Bible has a variety of responses to the question of suffering. The over-arching rubric is that God is the Creator of all, and as Judge of the world he pays out according to our deeds. Among the prophets, Amos takes the position "Does disaster come…unless the Lord has done it?" (3:6). Likewise Jeremiah suggests that should you ask "Why have these things come upon me? (The answer is) it is for your great iniquity" (13:22). Lamentations offers the observation "Is it not from the mouth of the Most High that good and bad come?" (3:38). The Psalmist who asks "My God, my God, why have you forsaken me, why are you so far from helping me?" certainly expects that God knows about human suffering, and will bring relief (Ps 22:1 (22:2 H). We learn elsewhere that suffering is not an end in itself, rather that once the punishment is complete, and expiation has taken place, reward will come (Is 40:1–2).

The Book of Job wrestles at length with the question of human deprivation, and considers human faith within the midst of this suffering. Beginning in chapter 38 God "answers" Job, but these answers are really rhetorical statements—"Where were you when I laid the earth's foundations?" (38:4). "Shall a faultfinder debate with the Almighty?" (40:2). "Would you even question my justice, will you condemn me that you would be justified?" (40:8). Job learns to accept that God who is involved in cosmic responsibilities also cares enough about the human condition to provide a response, even if the answer is not necessarily satisfying.

An even terser explanation for human suffering is offered in the Book of Proverbs: "For the Lord reproves the one he loves" (3:12).

The Rabbinic writings of the Talmud and Midrash continue to address the (essentially unresolved, and perhaps unresolvable) question of human suffering. There are many, many Rabbinic statements about suffering. A famous dictum begins with the thought that perhaps you yourself are to blame. Examine your conduct; you may have brought this grief upon yourself. If your conduct truly is exemplary, the suffering may be divinely decreed. "When you see that suffering has come, examine your conduct...If you find wrongdoing in yourself, repent. If upon self-examination you find no wrongdoing, attribute your suffering to neglect of Torah study...If, having attempted to attribute your suffering to neglect of Torah, and this could not [have been the case], then you can be certain that the suffering comes from God, that they are 'chastenings of [God's] love.' 'For the Lord reproves the one he loves' (Proverbs 3:12)" (Babylonian Talmud *Berachot* 5a).

A variation of this idea is that suffering is really a gift from God. This is articulated in the *Sifre to Deuteronomy, Piska* 32. Through suffering, God provided three wonderful gifts to the people Israel: Torah, the Land of Israel, and the World-to-Come. "Rabbi Simeon ben Yohai says: Precious are chastisements, for three wonderful gifts which were coveted by the nations of the world were given to Israel, solely on the basis of suffering. These three are Torah, the Land of Israel and the World-to-Come. Torah, because it is written, 'for learning wisdom and chastisement' (Proverbs 1:2); and 'Happy is the person that you chastise, the person whom you instruct in your Torah' (Psalm 94:12). The Land of Israel because it is written, 'God chastens you...your God is bringing you to a good land' (Deuteronomy 8:5, 7). The World-to-Come is explained by the line, 'The commandment is a lamp and the Torah a light, and reproofs of discipline are the way of life' (Proverbs 6:23)." Elsewhere in the Rabbinic literature we learn that God suffers watching the sufferings of Israel (Babylonian Talmud *Hagigah* 5b and Midrash Lamentations *Rabbah* 1:45 ff).

In the Middle Ages such thinkers as Saadia (ninth century) and Nahmanides (thirteenth century) suggest that people have free will, and the question of suffering is beyond our ken and will be revealed only at the end of days, and/or that the righteous who suffer in this world will find their reward in the World-to-Come.

Moving to the modern world, there are those who have suggested that the sufferings of the Holocaust (the Shoah) are connected to the establishment of the State of Israel. While that may serve as an answer to some people, it certainly is not reflective of mainstream Jewish thought. The modern philosopher Richard Rubenstein, in facing the Holocaust, concludes that while "God is dead," there is an even greater need for reaffirming the Jewish religious community. His contemporary, Emil Fackenheim, explains that we do not and cannot know what God was doing at Auschwitz, nor can we know why God allowed such horror, but nonetheless we need to insist that God was at Auschwitz. The Holocaust and the reestablishment of the State of Israel are connected, for what the Shoah would seem to deny, the latter would seem to affirm: God's very presence in history. As William Styron explains in the novel *Sophie's Choice* (1979), the real question is not "Where was God" at Auschwitz, but rather "Where was man?" (513).

A most compelling answer to the question of God and the divine connection to human suffering in the world is formulated by Harold Kushner in his work *When Bad Things Happen to Good People* (1981). He writes, "I believe in God [but]...I recognize His limitations. He is limited in what He can do by laws of nature and by the evolution of human nature and human moral freedom....God does not cause our misfortunes. Some are caused by bad luck, some are caused by bad people, and some are simply an inevitable consequence of our being human and being mortal, living in a world of inflexible natural laws" (134). Kushner continues with the thought that "God has created a world in which many more good things than bad things happen" (138). Further, in terms of suffering, Kushner raises the issue that even more important than wondering about the origin of suffering is to ask to where does it lead? It might lead us to appreciate that there are people near us who do care, or it might inspire others to act in such a way as to bring repair to the world.

David Birnbaum in *God and Evil: A Unified Theodicy/Theology/ Philosophy* (1989) posits that "God is in a state of contracted real-time consciousness for the higher purpose, elected by man, of allowing the totality of [humans] to grow up in a state of bonafide personal freedom, so that they may grasp the totality of their potentialities" (163–164). He goes on to say that a "Deity exercising contraction of real-time consciousness for the greater good, man's freedom and potential, clearly—not inscrutably—commits no crimes of breach of covenant or complicity of silence. He is guilty only of the crime of increasing man's freedom—an option exercised by man at Eden" (166).

Bernard Malamud addressed the eternal question of suffering in his wonderful short story "Angel Levine" (from the collection *The Magic Barrel,* 1958). The central character, patterned on Biblical Job, is an old Jewish tailor named Manischevitz who questions the purpose of his anguish and distress. He wonders why "he had been given so much to suffer. A tailor. Certainly not a man of talent. Upon him suffering was largely wasted. It went nowhere, into nothing: into more suffering" (48–49). Through his affliction, however, Manischevitz learns about pity for others, and realizes that despite all he has endured, he still believes in God.

There are no answers to the question of human suffering that will satisfy all people. For some, the Biblical notion that "the Lord reproves the one he loves" serves as a healing balm. Others are comforted by the notion that the human suffering of the righteous in this world will find its reward in the World-to-Come. That God suffers when we do is another possible answer. A limited God or a self-limiting God is another response. Human suffering just may be the terrible price we pay for moral choice and freedom. In Malamud's story, the tailor may or may not find an answer for his question why he had been given so much to suffer. Yet his life experience tells him that nonetheless God does care about people. "If you said it, it was said. If you believed, you must say it. If you believed, you believed" (55). In the end, it comes down to a matter of faith.

David Zucker

CHRISTIAN VIEW:

Dictionaries define suffering in terms of pain or distress. Therefore, one can say that any experience (physical, psychological, spiritual or material) which has a negative impact on one's life (personal or communal) has to do with suffering. Man has struggled with the question or problem of suffering from time immemorial.

In some schools of thought, suffering is just a fact of life to be resisted (e.g., existentialism) or borne nobly (e.g., certain classical Greek philosophies); others would hold that a Supreme Being causes suffering, in order to demonstrate his sovereignty or to teach his creatures a lesson; yet others would subscribe to the theory that an all-good God is not the direct cause of the evil of suffering but merely permits or tolerates what is really caused either by the impersonal forces of nature or the misguided actions of human beings operating with free will. Interestingly enough, biblical warrant can be found for most of these approaches, in one form or another.

Christianity takes the data of human and Jewish reflection on the matter and interprets it in light of the paschal mystery of Jesus Christ, that is, his passion, death and resurrection, believing that this is the only way in which sense can be made of the phenomenon. For Christians, the paschal mystery of Jesus is both revelatory and salvific. What does that mean?

The death of Christ teaches and saves in a manner heretofore unknown to those who have confronted such questions. His innocent and patient endurance of agony and ignominy reveals the depths of God's love for man, inasmuch as Jesus as the God-Man or God-in-the-flesh unites divinity and humanity in his own Person. It is not an exaggeration to say that, in Christ, God literally loved the human race to death. And this completely free, unconditional, absolute form of love is exemplary; what Jesus did was not simply a personal act, never again to be repeated (although his death, like his life, has a once-for-all dimension to it). Indeed, Jesus invites and even demands that his followers pursue his way of suffering and do so with an attitude of calmness and even joy: "If any man would come after me, let him deny himself an take up his cross daily and follow me" (Lk 9:23); "Greater love has no man than this, that a man lay down his life for his friends" (Jn 15:13).

Christians are frequently invited to meditate on the death of Christ, which death was offered in atonement for the sins of the whole world, including one's own, leading to a deeper apprehension of the depravity of human sin and equally the depths of divine love. This type of introspection and sensing personal responsibility for the Passion of Jesus is designed to move the believer to repentance and also to commune lovingly with one's Savior who, remarkably, was willing to die for sinners, thus proclaiming the immensity of God's love (cf. Rom 5:8).

Because of the identity of the One who suffered and the way in which he accepted it, this experience was also redemptive, in the tradition of the Suffering Servant of Deutero-Isaiah. As a result, what would normally be ascribed to the realm of human wickedness or human tragedy (i.e., the untimely death of a just man) is instead seen as the greatest event in human history. For in and through Christ's passion and death, man learns the depths of God's love which has a transforming power to it; furthermore, in Christ, human beings who believe in him are given the ability to live and die like him. Not by accident, then, has the cross become the symbol par excellence of the Christian faith, so that Christians begin and end their prayer with the sign of the cross; they wear crosses; they top their church buildings with them. The Christian cannot be ashamed of the cross but, like St. Paul, declares: "But far be it from me to glory except in the cross of our Lord Jesus Christ, by which the world has been crucified to me, and I to the world" (Gal 6:14). Hence, the Catholic Church keeps in her calendar on September 14 the feast known as the Triumph of the Cross, for evil men did not have the final say: A gracious and loving God took sin and nailed it to the cross, which is how every other sinful act and situation should be handled according to Christian theology. Out of that seemingly negative experience shines forth the love of Almighty God who, as the liturgy says, takes the cross, the instrument of man's defeat, and makes of it the instrument of his victory: "Where life was lost, there life has been restored, through Jesus Christ our Lord."

Humanly speaking, all suffering is pointless, which St. Paul acknowledged quite frankly: "...but we preach Christ crucified, a stumbling block to Jews and folly to Gentiles" (1 Cor 1:23). Therefore, this point of view is inseparable from a faith perspective.

How does Christian theology envision the participation of Jesus' disciples in the reality of suffering? Christians do not avoid it at all costs; nor are they masochistic seekers of suffering. Their attitude should be that of Christ himself, which is described by the evangelists in a telling scene from his agony in the Garden of Gethsemane on the night before he died. We read in the Gospel according to St. Matthew that two times Jesus prayed to his heavenly Father for relief from the impending torment, but ended each petition with a fervent desire to conform his Will to the Father's, in the final analysis: "My Father, if it be possible, let this cup pass from me; nevertheless, not as I will, but as thou wilt" (26:39). Similarly, in his earthly life and ministry, when Jesus encountered the sufferings of others, his instinctive response was to alleviate their sufferings and those who endured these with them; and so, he gained a reputation as One Who healed the sick and even raised the dead, with the result that the people "glorified the God of Israel" (Mt 15:31).

What do Christians take from all this? First of all, suffering is generally to be seen as a negative or an evil, to be avoided or eliminated, whenever possible. Secondly, when suffering is inevitable, it should be regarded as coming from the hand of God who, we trust, intends to bring good from evil. Thirdly, suffering allows us to identify in a most personal and dramatic manner with the suffering Christ; once more, St. Paul is instructive in this case: "Now I rejoice in my sufferings for your sake, and in my flesh I complete what is lacking in Christ's afflictions for the sake of his body, that is, the Church..." (Col 1:24). In other words, the redemption of the world continues until each member of Christ's mystical body, his Church, suffers with him and in him, for the sake of all. In fact, certain schools of spirituality have asserted that being given a cross to bear is a sign of divine favor; while that can be true in particular circumstances, the great Spanish mystic and theologian of the sixteenth century, St. Teresa of Avila, remained cautious on that score and playfully told the Lord: "If that's the way you treat your friends, it's no wonder you have so few of them!"

And so, several things result in the practical order. Individually,

Christians imitate the example of their Lord who did not go out of his way to endure suffering but, once convinced that it was the Father's holy Will, embraced it willingly and lovingly. Believers in Jesus also accept their various crosses in union with Christ and seek to accomplish good in their difficulties or to allow good to flow from them. Holding that there are things more precious than life itself (e.g., truth, the honor of God), Christians submit to martyrdom rather than betray these ultimate realities, again in imitation of Jesus Christ. At times, suffering can be a punishment for personal sins, about which Jesus warned the paralytic (cf. Jn 5:14), while in other circumstances, suffering can be but a wonderful occasion "that the works of God might be made manifest" in recovery and new life (Jn 9:3).

Beyond that, we do not believe that we ever suffer alone but that Christ is intimately associated with the suffering of each of his brothers and sisters. This realization caused Pope John Paul II to reflect on the situation in this fashion: "If one becomes a sharer in the sufferings of Christ, this happens because Christ has opened his suffering to men, because he himself in his redemptive suffering has become, in a certain sense, a sharer in all human sufferings" (*Salvifici Doloris,* 20). Yet more, "those who share in the sufferings of Christ preserve in their own sufferings a very special particle of the infinite treasure of the world's Redemption, and can share this treasure with others (*ibid*, 27). On behalf of others, either individually or collectively, Christians are called to alleviate human suffering, as did their Lord when he walked this earth. Hence, it should come as no surprise that the largest systems of relief for widows, orphans, the poor, the oppressed, the sick and the dying have been begun and operated under Christian auspices. Clearly, this is what Pope John Paul II has in mind when he writes: "...suffering is present in the world in order to release love, to give birth to works of love toward neighbor, to transform the whole of human civilization into a 'civilization of love'" (*ibid*, 30).

Facing suffering, the Christian is never permitted to respond with bitterness toward God or with a desire for revenge toward human perpetrators. Toward God, the believer echoes the dying and trustful words of Jesus: "Father, into thy hands I commit my spirit" (Lk 24:46). And evil-doers are to be given the benefit of Christ's prayer for them on the cross: "Father, forgive them; for they know not what they do" (Lk 23:34). In the Christian scheme of things, to harbor resentment is to destroy the power of love to transform suffering into glory; from a psychological standpoint, obsession with evil done only concedes to the enemy the final triumph. We believe that the victory of Christ was total because of the quality and quantity of his love: he loved unconditionally and totally.

Is this hard to accomplish in one's personal life? Undoubtedly, which is precisely why so few people have successfully negotiated the task. But Christians should know that "God is faithful, and he will not let you be tempted beyond your strength, but with the temptation will also provide the way of escape, that you may be able to endure it" (1 Cor 10:13), and that God's "grace is sufficient...for my power is made perfect in weakness" (2 Cor 12:9). Finally, Christians look at human suffering *sub specie aeternitatis;* now this should not and cannot lead to an attitude of passivity before suffering (anxiously waiting for "pie in the sky"), but it does provide one with a unique reference point—even a still point. That is, all is viewed with an eye on the time of future vindication and glory, like Christ himself: "That I may know [Christ] and the power of his resurrection, and may share his sufferings, becoming like him in his death, that if possible, I may attain the resurrection from the dead" (Phil 3:11). And all this is predicated on a firm faith in the promise of Jesus to would-be disciples in every age: "...and I, when I am lifted up from the earth [on the cross], will draw all men to myself" (Jn 12:32). For Christians, therefore, suffering is truly revelatory and salvific, which is to say that it has value, meaning and purpose, because of him who endured it first and showed the way.

Peter Stravinskas

Tolerance—Pluralism

JEWISH VIEW:

Tolerance, and, even more so, pluralism, and clearly tolerance and pluralism within a religious context, are relatively new concepts in the history of societal, religious, and certainly Jewish thought. It is difficult to imagine what our Biblical forebears or our ancestors the Rabbis of the Talmudic era would have made of those ideas. Indeed, the concept of religious pluralism, the celebration of living in a society where there are many faiths which interact with each other with mutual respect, that fact as a *positive idea to be acclaimed* is very much a product of the late twentieth century. Tolerance itself, one group's "tolerance," its willingness to live alongside, to allow or "put up with"—technically to "endure," from the Latin root of the word tolerate—the burden of differences of the "other" is often keyed into the sense of strength of, or lack-of-outside-threat to, the majority culture. Pluralism, the recognition and even celebration of clear distinctions and dissimilarities between faith communities only takes place when there is no perceived threat to the viability of the majority culture. The obverse is also true: in order to participate in pluralistic activities the minority cultures likewise need to have a sense of self-confidence. To take pride in differing faith communities living in proximity with the other, to go as far as suggesting that one may learn from the experience of the other, is the very antithesis of triumphalism.

There are numerous examples in the Biblical and Talmudic literature which make it clear that from its earliest days, the people Israel lived alongside, and often among, their pagan neighbors. When they were a clear minority in the land of their habitation they had no choice. Yet even when the independent kingdoms were a reality, or later during the time of the Commonwealth, it is clear that there were, as the Torah phrase puts it, "strangers dwelling among" them. The strangers were "tolerated" either as the majority culture, or as the minority culture, but there certainly was no celebration of religious pluralism. If anything, we could describe the general pre-modern viewpoint of Judaism toward other religions as "triumphalistic." Israel was not unique in this attitude; many if not most religious communities felt that they possessed the true word from the deity or deities. This was particularly true of the monotheistic faiths. At some periods, when Israel had political power, or when at least it was projected that Israel would have political power, the command was clearly to dispossess the peoples of the Land, to utterly destroy their molten images and cult places, to figuratively tear up "root and branch" any forms of pagan worship (Num 33:52ff). This was the "ideal," and whether it was ever accomplished is highly problematic.

In Leviticus 17:8ff Moses is told quite clearly that while there may be non-Israelites, "strangers," living among the nation, these "others" are to be limited in their religious practices. They are to follow the laws and mores of the Israelites or face severe punishment. Leviticus 18 details various sexual offenses and concludes with unambiguous statements that the Israelites are to reject such abominable practices lest they be cut off from the Lord, and the land itself spew them out, as it vomited out the previous inhabitants. The Book of Deuteronomy (18:9–14; 29:16–20, 26–28) likewise shows no patience for the religious practices of the other nations all about.

Hosea's denunciation of religious syncretism and Baal worship among the inhabitants of the northern kingdom is the eighth century BCE (Hosea 4:12ff *et. al.*) is matched by the prophet Jeremiah's similar criticism in Jerusalem one hundred fifty years later (Jeremiah 2:20ff *et. al.*). Torah law and the prophets' words of censorship were not concerned merely that Israel had turned from God, an issue bad enough in itself, but that the religious and moral practices of our neighbors were oftentimes inherently immoral, frequently sexual in nature, but also involving child sacrifices (2 Kgs 16:3; Jer 7:31 *et. al.*).

Turning to the Rabbinic literature there was no dearth of idol worship in the lands where the Jews were living. This was of great concern to the rabbis. In *Sifre to Deuteronomy Piska* 54 we read that "the Sages have said that anyone who acknowledges idolatry denies the entire Torah, and anyone who denies idolatry acknowledges the whole Torah." Likewise in the Jerusalem Talmud it explains that in order to save a life, one may violate any laws except idolatry, sexual immorality and murder (*T.J. Shevi'it* 4.2). That same line of reasoning is found in the midrashic literature, where we read, "Everything may be used for *healing* except idolatry, sexual immorality and murder"

(*Midrash Exodus Rabbah* 16.2). In this particular midrash it explains that the prohibition also extends to all matters connected with idolatry.

The twin triumphs of Christianity as a religious and political force, and later the similar triumphs of Islam, both of which came about within the first millennium of the Common Era, required Jewish religious leaders to address their attitudes toward these traditions. The question was less whether Christianity and Islam would be tolerated in the sense of being allowed to exist (the Jews were in no position to debate that point; they themselves were the minority religion) but rather what would or could be the relationship between Jews and Christians, or Jews and Muslims.

David Novak has suggested that the twelfth century philosopher Maimonides (Moses ben Maimon, Spain and Egypt, 1135–1204) saw certain virtues in Christianity that he did not find in Islam, and likewise saw other values in Islam missing in Christianity. "Maimonides preferred Islamic monotheism over Christian Trinitarianism; but...he preferred the Christian canonization of the Old Testament over the Muslim rejection of it and total replacement of it as sacred Scripture with the Quran" (*Jewish-Christian Dialogue: A Jewish Justification,* 66 [1989]). This is not to suggest that Maimonides either participated in or would have endorsed the concept of open religious dialogue. Consonant with the thinking of pre-modern times, triumphalist might be a better description of how Maimonides regarded Judaism's position to its daughter religions. If anything, Maimonides, according to Novak, was very sympathetic to the idea of accepting converts from these faith communities. "Maimonides clearly believed that the conversion of both Christians and Muslims to Judaism is a desideratum that Jews ought to encourage and facilitate as much as possible" (*ibid.,* 65).

Moving to a more modern times, the Enlightenment in Europe brought about a greater amount of "tolerance" for the Jewish people in various lands. It is curious that literally within a few years of each other, on both sides of the Atlantic there would be specific statements made by two government leaders addressing Jews and the question of toleration. In 1782 the Austrian Emperor Joseph II issued his *Toleranzpatent* which guaranteed certain rights to the Jews of his realm. Less than a decade later, newly inaugurated President George Washington wrote that the Jews were fully protected under the laws of the new American republic. "It is now no more that toleration is spoken of, as if it were by the indulgence of one class of people that any other enjoyed the exercise of their natural rights. For happily the Government of the United States...gives bigotry no sanction, to persecution no assistance..." (Letter to Moses Seixas, 1790).

The Enlightenment is also the time of Moses Mendelssohn, the great

German-Jewish philosopher who took great pride in the fact that he had as his friends many who were not Jewish, who despite their differences in religious opinions, still sincerely loved one another. This "love" often had a different purpose, a hidden meaning which was to try to persuade the Jews to convert to Christianity. In place of forcing Jews to become apostates, the new ploy was to love them into seeing the light. This stratagem was tried on both sides of the Atlantic, in Europe as well as in America. That legacy is still felt today. For many Jews interfaith dialogue remains an area for concern: Is the openness of that dialogue but a veil for the deeper desire to bring about a conversion to Christianity? Years of successful dialogue should allay that concern. The facts are that dialogue results in the strengthening of the person's own faith, and that there are no statistics to suggest that dialogue results in apostasy on *any* side of the discussion.

The real danger of dialogue is that it forces us to examine our own deeply held beliefs and statements even as the dialogue takes place. That, however, is a worthwhile price for us to pay for the benefits of true dialogue. Indeed, as religious dialogue continues and widens its conversations beyond Judaism, Christianity and Islam, it will face new challenges, not the least of which will be to find common expression with traditions which are polytheistic and/or animistic in nature.

Religious pluralism is a relatively new concept. It is a significant step forward from the earlier notion of Tolerance. By its very nature tolerance carries with it an air of condescension, and allows for feelings of triumphalism. Religious pluralism, like a celebration of multi-cultural diversity, recognizes that there are many valid ways to approach, and to be in right relationship with, the Source of Being.

David J. Zucker

CHRISTIAN VIEW:

Christians reach into the past and retrieve a story. This story is constructed so that Christians have a clearer perception of where they came from and where they are going. Christian scholars pay close attention to the ways in which the memory of the Church was configured in the New Testament, because they are convinced that the remembered past in large measure determines the Church's perception of present demands and future promises. Consequently, the limits and the possibilities of tolerance and pluralism are tied to the memories which govern the Christian imagination and its ecclesiastical practice.

Christians have traditionally excavated the apostolic era and unearthed an image of a golden age, an era when the Church was pure, united and harmoniously in tune with the Spirit. This idealized portrait of its beginning conceals the intense rivalries and embittered disputes that animated the early Church. The romanticized picture of the early Church has proven captivating. Over and over again reformers in the Church have justified their innovations by insisting that they are simply restoring the lost glory of the apostolic Church. This practice disposes Christians to make an idol out of a past that never really existed. Furthermore, this idealization reinforces a suspicion of diversity and change and establishes uniformity and permanence as the essential norms (see Robert Wilken, *The Myth of Christian Beginnings*. Tolerance and the promises of pluralism have not grown naturally on this theological soil.

When people are threatened with extinction or even a serious defeat, they commonly resort to one of two basic survival strategies. They retreat, or they attack. The same is true of many communities. When the early churches were struggling to establish their own identities, they found themselves besieged by opponents from without and dissidents from within. To protect themselves, these communities sometimes sought refuge by withdrawing from their neighbors. They retreated into separate enclaves where they were better equipped to resolve internal disputes and to resist the onslaughts of the surrounding culture.

This separatist impulse frequently calcifies into an ideology of isolation, hardening the group's perception of outsiders even after the imminent danger recedes. For much of their history, Christians have isolated themselves from creative interfaith exchanges. Outsiders present an alternative way of life and therefore by their very presence challenge communal norms. Furthermore, when a community is convinced that nothing more can enrich the revelatory deposits carefully guarded within the tradition, there is little incentive to enter into dialogue. The tendency to stand apart and maintain a safe distance from others provides living proof that the idealized memories of the early Church continue to shape the attitudes of many Christians.

Religions are forged in the heat of conflict. The formation of the Church was no exception. Early Christians found themselves in an extremely vulnerable predicament. They struggled to defend themselves against the judgments of rabbinic authorities who cast doubt on the churches' proclamations. To outflank their Jewish opponents, Christians tried to seize the covenantal privileges of God's chosen people and define themselves as the "new Israel." In the process of a painful separation, Christians directed sharp and hostile words at Jewish people. While this polemical style of argumentation may be understandable within the literary and historical context of the first centuries of the common era, this approach became petrified in an ideology of contempt.

When a community perceives itself under siege, its imagination often turns apocalyptic. The world is then divided into warring camps. The forces of good and the forces of evil converge in a life and death struggle. In this cosmic battle, the children of light must sustain God's cause against the powers of Satan. Instead of retreating, this expectation often inspires the tactics of attack.

At various times and places, Christians have fallen prey to these ideological temptations. From the twelfth to the fifteenth century, the interfaith climate worsened in Europe. In an atmosphere powerfully charged with uncertainty and suspicion, Christians all too often demonized the Jews. The fantasy of a world conspiracy, an international plot to overthrow Christendom, convinced many Christians to identify the Jews as humanity's archetypal enemy. The examples of National Socialism and Soviet Communism remind us that this dangerous chimera is more than a medieval artifact. The myth can also assume a secular guise and perform its deadly work.

The almost instinctive strategies to retreat or attack are understandable when the survival of a community is at stake. Yet these tactics may prove self-destructive in our own time. Communities frozen into ideologies of isolation and hostility are incapable of listening to and learning from those who are different. They are driven by fear and distrust. Such communities will remain ignorant of others and antagonistic or at least indifferent to the plight of "the aliens in their midst." Religious intolerance can sink deep roots within the churches when these two approaches are theologically sanctioned. Christian theologians who have confronted the failure of the churches during the Holocaust have brought the shortcomings of these two strategies into sharp focus. These ideological patterns are increasingly viewed as highly dysfunctional in a religiously plural world.

Christians who want to lay theological foundations strong enough to support tolerance and religious pluralism are reexamining the biblical bedrock on which they must build. What they are finding presents a major challenge. After all, the first commandment to have no other gods can inspire a community to drive out the heathen, destroy their altars and vigilantly protect the borders against intruders. While prophetic exhortations to eliminate idolatry can provide an internal critique that recalls a community to its original vocation, the same words can also sound from a community with the sensibilities of Calvin's Geneva. Are monotheists called to shatter the idols of their neighbors? Are there conditions in which Christians are legitimately called to wage war on the religious life of their neighbors? Is religious intolerance always an ideological expression of exaggerated suspicion or even paranoia? Or, to push the question in another direction, does the impetus for interreligious hostility derive from the logic of monotheism itself? (David Lochhead, *The Dialogical Imperative.* Does the problem of intolerance emerge from the exclusive truth claims of the monotheist, or does the triumphalism of these believers develop from the distorted reception and misinterpretation of God's revelations and election?

The ways in which Christians have historically defined themselves have left little room for those who see the world differently. Tolerance was not a product of theological daring, but an unanticipated benefit of battle fatigue. By the time that the Treaty of Wesphalia was fashioned in 1648, the excesses of religious zealotry were everywhere apparent. Tolerance was imposed on religious communities by secular authorities because Christians were proving themselves incapable of getting along with one another much less with the non-Christian world. To increase the prospects of peaceful coexistence, efforts were made to domesticate religious passions by pushing belief out of the public arena. In light of all the conflicting truth claims within and between different faith traditions, philosophers of the Enlightenment argued that religion appeals to the masses of people because they are unable to arrive at the truth autonomously. Champions of this "enlightened" philosophy sought to tame the unruly forces of religion by transcending national, ethnic, and theological allegiances. They attempted to establish a universal foundation on which a new social order could be built. Therefore, when John Locke advocated the inclusion of Jews as citizens of the state in his groundbreaking *First Letter Concerning Toleration* (1689), his conclusions were the logical outgrowth of this new philosophical platform—we are all endowed with a common humanity.

As much as some bewail the corrosive influence of secularization on our religious traditions, the ideal of tolerance could not take hold until the control of the state and society was wrested from religious authorities. The emancipation of the Jews in Western Europe and the affirmation of the universal rights of people enshrined in the American Constitution were inconceivable apart from the independence achieved in philosophy, politics, economics, art and science from doctrinal and ecclesiastical constraints. The constriction of faith in the modern age, legally prescribed in the separation of the church and state (and reinforced through the privatization of religious belief and practice), compels Christians to consider some unnerving questions: Does civility among different believers only flourish in societies that refuse to take their theological convictions seriously? If, as R. Laurence Moore claims, "religious tolerance was not the free gift of a dominant religious group, but the product of uneasy arrangements made between groups that did not much like one another," what are the prospects for peaceful coexistence in a religiously plural world? (*Religious Outsiders and the Making of Americans*).

While Christians have traditionally highlighted those theological affirmations that distinguish them from the rest of the world, the religious position of liberals which grew out of the Enlightenment maintained that we are all the same. The theological implications of this affirmation are reflected in the adage that there are many ways to climb a mountain. Different religious traditions provide different routes to follow, but they all converge at the top. In other words, beneath the multiplicity lies a common essence. This theological picture denies the reality of religious pluralism by concealing the fact that the goals as well as the means which Christians, Jews, and Muslims, Hindus and Buddhists pursue are irreducibly distinct. Furthermore, this portrait of religious life can establish a dangerous expectation.

When post-Enlightenment liberals advocated "the emancipation" of the Jews in the latter half of the eighteenth century, they were convinced that a more tolerant environment would "ameliorate" the Jewish condition. Once the legal disabilities were removed, liberals in countries such as France and Germany expected that "the peculiar attachments" of the Jews would dissolve. Out of gratitude, the Jews would blend into the larger culture and finally become thoroughly assimilated. For Christian conservatives and liberals the objective was the same. Religious conservatives hoped to resolve the Jewish question through conversion to Christianity, while liberals expected the answer to come through total absorption of the Jewish population into the body politic. In both cases a world was anticipated that would be devoid of Jews. When the majority of Jews continued to hold fast to their traditions and the revolutionary dream was not realized, the resentment directed against this "clannish people" boiled over and fed the flames of modern antisemitism.

Tolerance strikes most Americans as a political and social necessity. Yet, a growing number of Christian theologians argue that the church needs to confront the limits of this secular ideal. The practice of tolerance, often translated into the motto "live and let live," depends upon a fragile and uncertain balance of power. The horrors which developed in the wake of the break-up of the former Yugoslavia demonstrate the precarious achievements of a tolerance imposed by secular authorities. Does tolerance generate respect for others? Does tolerance engender a religious disposition that welcomes the challenges posed by those who hold different beliefs? More often than not, tolerance registers as an intermediate step on the road to interreligious understanding. If tolerance simply "puts up with" and "endures" the presence of "outsiders," it will dissolve when political and economic conflicts erupt and require daring commitments on behalf of vulnerable neighbors.

Many Christians maintain that interfaith relationships based on mutuality and reciprocity depend upon a theological affirmation of religious pluralism. The pluralist claims that theological diversity is a gift which enhances our perception of ourselves, others, and the world. Though the concept is often soft and malleable in the hands of both its champions and critics, a growing number of Christians insist that they must find new ways of encountering others. Religious pluralism entails a theological disposition of receptivity, an aptitude for listening and learning from those who see the world in a different light. Religious pluralism points beyond the achievements of the past to a future in which different groups will each contribute different sounds and different melodies to the music.

Christians will have difficulty joining the symphony until they return to their place of origin. What Christians find at the beginning is a rich and complex variety. Songs of dissent and songs of assent filled the churches, then as now. What does it mean to belong to a tradition that is often animated by disagreement, a tradition that insisted that the canon includes not one, but four Gospels? Can Christians affirm the plurality within the Biblical witness and the subsequent reading of those stories? Do Christians have anything to learn from those who share the same Scriptures, yet read them in very different ways?

When Christians remember their founding not with the dream of returning to a lost horizon, but with the hope of going forward, they may move beyond mere tolerance and secure the promise of religious pluralism. Christian stories, liturgies, and songs express a yearning for things to come, a vision of a just world that lies ahead of them, not behind. The response to the challenges of religious pluralism will define the character of churches in the future and largely determine the kind of peace for which they pray.

Christopher Leighton

Tradition

JEWISH VIEW:

The first chapter of the *Ethics of the Fathers* (a tractate of the Mishnah) begins with the statement: "Moses received the Torah from Sinai and transmitted it to Joshua, Joshua to the Elders, the Elders to the Prophets. And the Prophets transmitted it to the men of the Great Assembly." This passage provides insight into the Jewish concept of tradition.

The primary teachings of Judaism were divinely revealed at Sinai. These teachings, as well as subsequent interpretations and elaborations, constitute the core of Jewish tradition. In its broader sense, tradition includes everything that has been taught and observed by committed Jews over the generations.

The teachings of Judaism have been communicated in an unbroken chain from generation to generation. The Hebrew term describing this process is *Shalshelet Hakabbalah*, the chain of tradition.

Hebrew words are vital in the understanding of the Jewish idea of tradition. *Kabbalah* means that which has been received. Moses received a body of knowledge from God: laws, interpretations of Scripture. Each generation of scholars received the authoritative traditions from its teachers, who received these traditions from their teachers, etc., going back to Moses. Maimonides, in his introduction to his commentary on the Mishnah, notes that there can be no dispute about a law whose origin is attributed to Moses. Legal controversies only occur in those areas where there is no authoritative tradition. If an authoritative rabbi states without reservation that he received a tradition which is *Halakhah lemosheh misinai*—a law from Moses at Sinai—then this tradition has the weight of law and is not subject to controversy. Such traditions have the same authority as the written Torah itself.

The Hebrew word *Masorah* signifies tradition in its general sense. It also refers specifically to the traditional manner of vocalizing the Hebrew biblical texts (i.e., the Masoretic text). Literally, *Masorah* means that which has been transmitted. A specific tradition may be called *Masoret*.

Dibrei Kabbalah, words which have been received, refers to teachings of the prophets. *Mipi Hashemuah*—according to what has been heard— refers to ancient traditions whose origins may not be known exactly. The very antiquity of these traditions gives them tremendous authority.

Kabbalah may refer to a specific tradition received from one's teacher. It may also be used to signify the entire content and process of tradition. *Kabbalah* is also the term which designates Jewish mysticism. It is significant that Jewish mystics did not see themselves as creating a new body of knowledge, but rather as receiving ancient mystical teachings which originated as far back as Adam himself.

Minhag is the Hebrew word designating custom. Customs are religious observances which have developed among Jews over the centuries. There is no claim that these customs are of divine origin, yet they play an important role in everyday Jewish life. Customs vary from community to community. The two largest divisions of customs are Sephardic (tracing back to the Jewish communities of medieval Spain) and Ashkenazic (tracing back to the medieval communities of Germany). In reality, almost every community developed customs, and these were passed on through the generations. *Minhag* plays a role in Jewish law. A well-known rabbinical statement is: *Minhag avoteinu beyadeinu,* the custom of our forefathers is in our hands. Since a particular custom was observed for generations, it becomes incumbent upon us to maintain it. Aside from the area of law, *minhag* plays an important psychological role among traditional Jews. Each person wants to be true to the *minhag* of his own family and community. This mentality of reverence for the past tends to make traditional Jews conservative, resistant to abrupt change.

The authority of rabbinic tradition has been the source of controversy among Jews at different times in Jewish history. The Sadducees rejected the authority of rabbinic tradition, dismissing the claim that God gave oral teachings to Moses which were transmitted accurately from generation to generation. The Karaites believed only in the divinity of the Bible, not in the authority of the rabbinical chain of tradition. Both the Sadducees and the Karaites, however, were relegated to the periphery of Jewish history, since the vast majority of Jews retained their respect not only for the written Torah but also for the oral tradition.

In modern times, tradition has again become the source of controversy among Jews. Reform Judaism has, by and large, rejected the authority of the rabbinical chain of tradition. The Reform movement has dropped the observance of many Jewish traditions, whether biblical, oral, or rabbinic. Orthodox Judaism has retained its commitment to Jewish tradition and its belief in the authority of the chain of tradition as passed down through the generations from the time of Moses. Conservative Judaism, while formally retaining the historic Jewish attitude, has tried to adapt tradition to modern social pressures. In Israel, the Conservatives call themselves the Traditional (Masoretic) Movement.

The word tradition, then, has a variety of meanings for Jews. It may refer to something quite specific, such as a law passed down from Moses, or it may refer generally to Jewish teachings and observances of past generations. For some Jews, tradition constitutes the foundation of their religious belief and observance; for others, tradition is something merely nostalgic and pleasant. Participants in Christian-Jewish dialogues must, therefore, not only be aware of the differences of meaning of "tradition" but also of the particular tendency of thought of those involved in the dialogue.

Marc Angel

CHRISTIAN VIEW:

The historical critical methods of interpretation, among them especially form criticism and tradition criticism, show that Scripture itself is in a large part the outcome of oral tradition. It is thus legitimate to refer to the Bible as Israel's tradition. It is, moreover, indispensable to read the text while keeping in mind its insertion in Jewish tradition as a whole, in general, and in the historical, social, and spiritual "setting in life" of that text in particular. Furthermore, one will never insist enough on the point that the Hebrew text is consonantal, so that its reading, through orally providing it with a vocalization, is already interpretation along traditional lines.

A second feature of utmost significance here is the realization that Jesus and the early Church are to be situated within Jewish tradition, and at no point outside of it. Even the Johannine embarrassingly heinous allusions to the negative attitude of "the Jews" toward Jesus are to be understood in the Jewish context as a "family affair." If it is true that there is a Christian tradition shaping up as soon as the Nazarene starts to teach, it is however well within the parameters of Israel's spiritual life, and with the deepest respect for that life. Jesus is only interested in addressing "the twelve tribes of Israel," and nothing of his ongoing protest makes any sense outside of the general Jewish problematic. Because of this, and despite repeated powerful attempts to "de-Judaize" Christianity for twenty centuries, the Church never rejected the "Old Testament," i.e., the traditional reference of the Gospel.

It is thus of fundamental importance to specify as pointedly as possible the attitude of Jesus and of the early Church vis-à-vis Jewish tradition. The truth of the matter is that, within the Tradition, only a certain tradition is found unacceptable. The distinction is crucial. When it is blurred or outright disregarded, Christianity is disfigured; it is alienated into a "new religion." Then the Jewish-Christian dialogue becomes a conversation between two autonomous religions, instead of Christianity remaining true to its origins of a Jewish sect existentially in relation with the rest of Israel's body.

From this perspective, the Sermon on the Mount in the Gospels (Matthew 5–7 and it Lukan parallel) occupies a prominent place. There, Jesus takes exception to the teaching of Pharisaic rabbis ("the elders"; cf. Mt 15:2; Mk 7:3, 5; Acts 6:14; Gal 1:14). The latter are also called "doctors of the law," i.e., learned exegetes of the sacred texts. Their concern is basic: to insure the survival of Judaism. Their method is sensical: to popularize the commandments and prohibitions of Torah through teaching the "oral Torah" or Pharisaic tradition. Their aim is pragmatic: to facilitate the performance of the *mitzvot* by all. Obviously, such an aim will be best reached by delineating with elementary precision the semantic areas covered by the law. For example, when the Torah says "thou shalt love thy neighbor" (Lev 19:18), this Commandment becomes practical only when it is known what is meant here by "love" and by "neighbor." It is the task of the "doctors of the law" to respond to those questions. In so doing, they establish a *tradition*.

Jesus rejects the casuistic definitions proposed by "the elders." Indeed, any attempt at delineating the field of the Torah's sway is to him repulsive. The "neighbor" includes also the non-neighbor, the enemy (Mt 5:43–45), and adultery goes much beyond the limits of technicity (Mt 5:27f). Quarrel of exegetical schools then? Yes, and much more. At stake is the very nature of Torah (cf. Law Halakha). The problem of definition of terms is largely belittled by Jesus raising the fundamental question: What is the Torah?

Clearly, for Jesus, Torah does not suffer attempts at definition of any kind. There cannot be a definition or delineation of love, of life, of "extravagance." Not only is it an impossibility, but it is blasphemy and sterilization. It reduces Torah to a "human tradition" (Col 2:8; cf. Gal 1:14) handled by man, object instead of subject, religious device of oppression (Mt 23:4; Lk 11:46;

Heb 12:1), instead of liberation. Now, whether or not the slave rejoices in being a slave changes nothing about his slavery. Tradition has produced death (Rom 7:5, 10, 13) while claiming to give life.

We must now balance condemnation with approbation. In the same Sermon on the Mount where he expresses anger against a casuistic tradition of the rabbis, Jesus affirms also the eternity and intangibility of Torah, of tradition (cf. Mt 5:17f; 7:12; 22:40). Jesus is shown respecting Jewish tradition (Mk 1:44); so also do Peter and John (Acts 3:1, etc.); so also does Paul (Rom 2:13, 25, 3:30; 7:12ff; 13:8, 10; 1 Cor 14:34; Gal 3:21, 24, 5:23). There is a "tradition of the elders" (Mt 15:2), which leads to transgressing the Commandment of God (15:3, 8) or the Word of God (Mk 7:13), and a tradition coming "from the Lord" (1 Cor 11:23).

This distinction is nothing new. In pre-Christian Israel, the prophets had indefatigably fought against a deceiving tradition and in behalf of the authentic tradition. The former was forwarded by false prophets, sometimes by the "Establishment" in Jerusalem with its royal ideology which often amounted to a civil religion. As the true prophets were all reformers, so were also Jesus and his early followers.

This living tradition shall never pass. It is the historical continuity and integrity of Israel into which the Church has inserted itself. Through the medium of that tradition, the good news has come down to us. God is one; he is Lord; he loves Israel. All the rest is commentary. There is only one tradition, one *Heilsgeschichie* (history of salvation). Ecclesiastical traditions may not substitute themselves to it. The Church's history is prolongation of Israel's history, or else it is as deceptive as it is foreign.

Boldly, the early Church saw in Jesus Christ *the* tradition of Israel. It is from this perspective that the nature of the "New Testament" is defined. The documents gathered by the Church as an authoritative collection of testimonies to the Christ event constitute the tradition accompanying the Scriptures. Judaism and Christianity share in common the latter; they differ on the former (cf. Bible). The dialogue between them is a confrontation of traditions about Scriptures, i.e., a confrontation of hermeneutics.

André Lacocque

Universalism

JEWISH VIEW:

Judaism's balance between universal and parochial thinking is found in the way Jews view the opening verses of the Hebrew Bible. Genesis begins not with Israel's history but with universal beginnings. This universalism is reflected by the Jewish choice to count its calendar years from creation itself. Although the Bible explicitly states that the calendar begins with the national event *par excellence,* the Exodus from Egypt, the universalism of later Judaism insisted on using as its starting point not parochial Jewish nationalism but the more universally relevant event of creation. The medieval Jewish biblical exegete Rashi (1040–1105), however, suggests that there is a parochial purpose to beginning the Bible with creation. God's creative power is retold to legitimate God's gift of the land of Israel to the Jews. The Creator of the world must have the right to dispose with it as he sees fit. Creation has a nationalistic implication as well as a universal one.

The dual themes of universalism and particularism are given even-handed weight from the biblical writings through later Judaism. The Bible pays attention to universal elements of world history, while focusing on the Jewish people. Israel's kingdoms, its exile, its heroes and leaders form the core of biblical narrative. At the same time a universal emphasis constantly surfaces. King Solomon declares the Jerusalem Temple to be "a house of prayer for all peoples" (Is 56:7). The Book of Jonah argues that God's concern reaches even to Israel's arch-rival Assyria. The prophetic messianic expectation envisions a transformed world which embraces both a victorious Israel and a universal human renewal. From the perspective of some prophets the triumphant Jerusalem cult will be universalized in the final days and draw its priests from all nations.

Jewish monotheism insists on the unity of all creation under its com-

225

mon dependency on the Creator. Human beings share a special unity—that provided by the Noahide covenant. Noah is seen as the prototypical human being—he has good intentions but wayward instincts. God determines that since "the devisings of man's mind are evil from his youth" (Gen 8:21) certain natural laws will be established to control all humanity. Judaism sees every human being as under these laws; all are measured by their fidelity to Noahide ideals. How a person lives determines his nearness to God, and the tradition claims that "whether Jew or Gentile, male or female, slave or free, according to their deeds does the *Shekhina* (God's indwelling presence) rest upon them" (*Seder Eliyahu Rabbah,* chapter 9). Monotheism can hardly come to any other conclusion. The fact of one deity means that God must be accessible to all of creation. As Abraham Joshua Heschel wrote, "For God is everywhere or nowhere, the father of all men or no man, everything or nothing." The test of God's reality lies in the divine connection with all being. Judaism is universalistic because unless God is the God of all the world, monotheism makes no sense.

God's link with humanity, the basis upon which the Noahide laws are founded, is the divine image planted in every human being. The Talmudic sage Ben Azzai claimed that the most important verse in the Bible from which all of Judaism flowed was: "This is the record of Adam's line: God created man. He made him in the likeness of God" (Gen 5:1). Genesis 8:20–9:17 explains the obligations flowing from this common divine heritage. Human beings are responsible for maintaining social order just as God establishes the natural order. Human relationships are to be based on recognition of the divine image within every person. Rabbinic thought amplified this brief review of humanistic principles and from seven basic Noahide laws expanded them by developing corollaries to them. Today this tradition of universal human ethics provides the basis on which many Jews address the social and political problems of national and international concern.

Rabbi Akiba, an older contemporary of Ben Azzai, considered the biblical verse "Love your neighbor as yourself" (Lev 19:18) to be the most basic and inclusive law. Much modern debate has sought to define whether "neighbor" in this verse refers only to Jews or to non-Jews as well (it has long been established that the New Testament suggestion of a Jewish teaching "hate your enemies" is a polemical misrepresentation of Judaism). Rabbinic evidence is ambivalent. Hillel's claim that the whole Torah can be summed up in the phrase "that which is hateful to you do not do to your neighbor" was addressed to a potential proselyte (TB *Makkoth* 23b). It can easily be interpreted as having a particularistic rather than universal significance.

The particularism of the Jewish neighbor lies in adherence to Torah.

Torah consists of those distinctive teachings given at Mount Sinai which render the Jews a nation apart. In addition to the Noahide laws the Jew must observe six hundred and thirteen commandments which cover all of personal and social life. Through these laws the Jew gains a specific identity and becomes recognizable among the nations of the world. These regulations create a "kingdom of priests" with special restrictions. The particularism of Torah is a particularism of task, of purpose, and of self-understanding. The Jew has a peculiar cultural and social identity defined by the Sinaitic covenant.

That Sinaitic covenant is a *complement* to the Noahide laws and not a substitute for it. Torah amplifies but does not replace human obligation. The Jew has universal duties rooted in the Noahide covenant which cannot be nullified by Torah laws. Judaism accepts the existence of multiple covenants and does not claim that a later covenant supersedes an earlier one. Universal covenant is coherent with many particular ones. The purpose of the particularistic laws is, in fact, the same as the universal ones. A famous rabbinic passage explains that Moses gave Israel six hundred and thirteen commandments; David reduced them to eleven, Isaiah to six, Micah to three, Amos to two, and Habbakuk to one: "The righteous shall live by his faith" (2:4). That final verse is interpreted as a universal one. It refers to the righteous of all nations, not merely to Jews, and is, indeed, a rabbinical principle (cf. TB *Sanhedrin* 10:1). So too Leviticus 18:5 which reads: "Keep my statutes and my ordinances, by doing which a man shall live," is interpreted universally. The verse does not mention Jews, priests or scholars but human beings. Any human being can find life by observing the Commandments. While as particularistic tools for Jewish self-identification Torah stresses Judaic culture, as ethical teachings about human duty the laws of Torah are universalistic.

Jewish particularism, then, is cultural rather than religious. Nevertheless Sinai has a religious significance. The Jew is distinguishable among the nations as a witness to the divine plan. God requires distinctive cultural subgroups for the good of all humanity. Rabbi Leo Baeck, whose heroic survival in a Nazi death camp made him a modern legend, claimed that "without minorities there can be no world-historic goal." Judaism insists that human society needs variety, that minority culture is part of the divine intention. Jewish particularism is religious even while being cultural because it expresses God's will for humanity.

The dialogue between Jews and Christians has often been marred by acrimonious charges on both sides. Jews have been branded as insular and parochial. Christians have been charged with religious imperialism. The balance between universalism and particularism in Jewish thought can be a model for meaningful discussion. Universalism may be rooted in a particularistic culture. Apparently parochial tendencies may have a universalistic goal. Dialogue can proceed when neither universalism nor particularism is given specific positive or negative values. Universalism may indeed be a disguise for religious imperialism. Particularism may also be an excuse for insularity and parochial self-isolation. When balance rather than evaluation is stressed, however, the positive aspects of both particularism and universalism can be discovered. Dialogue should aim at cultivating such a creative balance rather than at mutual incrimination and abusive judgment of other traditions.

S. Daniel Breslauer

CHRISTIAN VIEW:

For Christians, "universalism" usually means the doctrine that God loves all people and/or will save all people. Sometimes Christians have mistakenly opposed universalism to the doctrine of election, as if election were a privilege more than a vocation. Christians need to be more nuanced in their definition of universalism, and thus this term becomes an important agenda item for the Jewish-Christian dialogue. Perhaps the more frequent and accurate antonym for universalism is particularism.

Universalism is most often treated as an aspect of the greater topic of grace, particularly connected with the divine will that all be saved. The crucial New Testament passage in this regard is 1 Timothy 2:4a: "(God) desires all men to be saved and to come to the knowledge of the truth." The writer of this Epistle goes on to identify the truth with Christ. Closely related, then, to the doctrine that God wills all people to be saved is the doctrine of predestination. For those Christians who hold to a strict universalism, God wills all people to salvation and predestines that not one will be lost. Other Christians claim that predestination means that God wills that everyone be saved, but allows people, in their freedom, to choose otherwise (cf. also 1 Tim 4:10).

One particular Christian expression of a general theology of universalism was apocatastasis, the belief that at the end of time all creatures—believers and sinners alike—would be restored in Christ. The early Church condemned this absolute doctrine for two reasons. First, it denied that humans have the freedom to choose other than God. Second, the Church asserted that one cannot change one's mind after death. (It is interesting to note in this context that the Christian Church has never said that anyone in particular has gone to hell, but it has affirmed that certain holy people are indeed in heaven.)

Surely, from a Christian perspective, God's offer of grace and salvation is a universal one. But it has also been traditional for Christians to say that this offer is intimately linked with faith in Jesus as the Christ. That is, God's will that all be saved is not an anonymous one, but one which is appropriated through belief in Christ. This revelation, as grace, is offered to all people in some form. Saving grace can be appropriated only through faith, although faith is not always explicit or conscious. As Vatican II states: "Nor does Divine Providence deny the help necessary for salvation to those who, without blame on their part, have not yet arrived at an explicit knowledge of God, but who strive to live a good life, thanks to his grace" (*Dogmatic Constitution on the Church*, n.16).

A growing interest in a renewed Christian understanding of universalism has paralleled a rising awareness of religious pluralism. From the time when explorers and missioners discovered peoples who for centuries before them had not heard of Christ, Christians have found various ways to link faith in Christ and God's universal will that all be saved. Christian thinkers have tried to balance out the requirement of explicit faith in Jesus Christ for salvation, God's will that all be saved, and thousands upon thousands of people who have lived lives of integrity and love, but who did not believe in Christ. Theories of limbo, *fides implicita,* and lack of culpability because of "invincible ignorance" mark the theological journey through the ages. These systematic constructions bear witness to the faithfulness of Christian theologians who wished to remain faithful to the tradition while making "theological room" not only for Jews of good faith, but for all who lived according to their conscience.

A theory of apocatastasis, as defined above, does not concern itself with issues of "good conscience"; rather it focuses solely on the mercy and compassion of the Savior God who will restore all things in Christ. More recent efforts at some form of Christian universalism stop short of apocatastasis, not only because of the early Church's condemnation, but more so because apocatastasis does not allow for God's taking human freedom seriously. These more recent efforts have focused on the universal salvific will of God. Perhaps the most famous of these contemporary theories is that of Karl Rahner. He calls his theory "anonymous Christianity." Oversimplified, Rahner asserts that since all saving grace is from Christ, God must will that those who are saved through following their good conscience in other world religions are somehow linked positively with Christ and therefore are in some way "anonymous Christians." Rahner is quick to note that this understanding of how non-Christians are saved is not a missionary tactic but rather a way for Christians to understand how God can save all people and how, at the same time, Christ is the mediator of all salvation. One can guess the kind of negative reaction which Rahner's theory has provoked, but it must be said that Rahner seeks to maintain traditional Christian faith-tenets while allowing that all people can be saved. Among mainstream Christians, some variation of combining these principles—the necessity of Christ and salvation open to all—has been debated even if the results do not resemble Rahner's. However these principles are articulated, they will be found where Christians seek a new, contemporary understanding of universalism.

Intimately connected with the Christian doctrine of universalism will be the theology of mission. That is, if Christians hold to some form of universalism, what need is there for a mission of conversion? Some Christians, usually of a more liberal leaning, beginning with their belief in God's universal salvific grace, have moved to a mission (q.v.) posture of "presence" in place of a strategy of proselytism. Others, granting God's universal grace, nonetheless see Christian mission as bringing to explicit consciousness what is there already implicitly—namely, the presence of Christ's saving power. In the Jewish-Christian dialogue, particularly among more conservative, evangelical Christians, evangelization has been a very sensitive issue. Therefore, discussion on what Christians and Jews mean by universalism could prove to be a very fruitful enterprise.

It should be noted, too, that for Christians with a more conservative leaning, a well-developed doctrine of universalism is simply not available. While they would admit that God wills all people to be saved, they would continue that this necessarily requires an explicit conversion in faith to Jesus as one's personal Lord and Savior. Anything short of this would be for them a betrayal of their fundamental belief: that salvation is through Jesus Christ and through him alone. They would cite such passages as John 6:44, John 14:6, and Matthew 28:19f to support their position.

Thus, discussion of universalism is crucial to the Jewish-Christian dialogue, for it spells grave implications for the Christian mission and for the Christian understanding of the place of Jews in the history of salvation.

Michael McGarry

Notes on the Contributors

MARC D. ANGEL is Rabbi of Congregation Shearith Israel, the Spanish and Portuguese Synagogue of New York. He received his rabbinic ordination from Rabbi Isaac Elchanan Theological Seminary of Yeshiva University, New York. Rabbi Angel is active in a wide range of Jewish communal organizations. He has authored and edited thirteen books; the most recent ones are: *Voices in Exile: A Study in Sephardic Intellectual History* (1991); and a collection of essays, *Seeking God, Speaking Peace* (1994).

DAVID R. BLUMENTHAL holds the Jay and Leslie Cohen Chair of Judaic Studies at Emory University. He is active in the Jewish-Christian dialogue and has devoted academic courses and research to questions relating to the Holocaust. His book *Facing The Abusing God* appeared in 1993 (Westminister).

S. DANIEL BRESLAUER is Professor of Religious Studies at the University of Kansas. He was ordained at Hebrew Union College/Jewish Institute of Religion and is the author of two books and numerous articles in Jewish periodicals.

CELIA DEUTSCH, a Sister of Our Lady of Sion, teaches early Judaism and early Christianity in the Department of Religion at Barnard College/ Columbia University (New York City). She is a member of the Catholic-Jewish Relations Advisory Committee for the National Conference of Catholic Bishops, and writes and lectures on subjects pertaining to the dialogue.

RABBI LEON KLENICKI is Director of the Department of Interfaith Affairs of the Anti-Defamation League and teaches courses at Immaculate Conception Seminary in Huntington, New York, and is editor of *The Passover*

Celebration; Toward a Theological Encounter: Jewish Understandings of Christianity (Stimulus Books, 1991).

ANDRÉ LACOCQUE was born in Belgium and studied in Strasbourg and Montpellier, at the Rabbinical School of Paris, and at the Hebrew University in Jerusalem. In 1957 he received a Ph.D. and in 1961 a doctorate in theology from Strasbourg University. Dr. Lacocque held various pastoral positions in France and Belgium and was Professor of Old Testament at the Protestant Theological Seminary of Brussels. Since 1966, he has been Professor of Old Testament at the Chicago Theological Seminary and director of its Center for Jewish-Christian Studies. He also lectures at Spertus College of Judaism, Chicago. Dr. Lacocque is a member of various learned societies and has received research and publications grants.

CHRISTOPHER M. LEIGHTON is a Presbyterian minister. He received his Master of Divinity at Princeton Theological Seminary and a doctorate from Columbia University. He serves as Executive Director of the Institute for Christian-Jewish Studies in Baltimore, MD.

MICHAEL B. McGARRY, C.S.P. is pastor of Newman Hall/Holy Spirit Parish at the University of California, Berkeley. For seven years, he was rector of St. Paul's College, the Paulist Fathers' seminary in Washington, D.C. He serves on the Advisory Board for the Secretariat for Catholic-Jewish Relations of the National Conference of Catholic Bishops. He is the author of *Christology After Auschwitz*, as well as many articles on Jewish-Christian relations and Christian responses to the Shoah.

PHEME PERKINS is Professor of New Testament at Boston College. She received her Ph. D. in New Testament and Christian Origins from Harvard University. Professor Perkins has written many books on the New Testament and early Christianity, including *The Gnostic Dialogue* (Paulist, 1980) and *Gnosticism and the New Testament* (Fortress, 1993). She has served as the president of the Catholic Biblical Association of America and as New Testament editor for the Society of Biblical Literature Dissertation Series.

ALAN F. SEGAL is full professor in the Religion Department at Barnard College/Columbia University. He received a Ph.D. from Yale University in 1975, where he studied Comparative Religion, Judaica, Rabbinics and Christian Origins. Segal is a member of learned societies in this country as well as in England and Canada. His most recent publication are: *The Other*

Judaisms of Late Antiquity (Scholars Press) for the Brown University Judaica Series; and *Paul the Convert: The Apostasy and Apostolate of Saul of Tarsus* (Yale University Press).

THE REV. PETER M.J. STRAVINSKAS is Administrator of Holy Trinity Lithuanian R.C. Church in Newark, N.J. He serves as an adjunct professor of education at Seton Hall University in South Orange, N.J. Fr. Stravinskas is a contributing editor to the *National Catholic Register* and the founding editor of *The Catholic Answer*. He is the author of ten books and numerous articles.

DR. GEOFFREY WIGODER of Hebrew University's Institute of Contemporary Jewry, is Editor-in-Chief of the *Encyclopedia Judaica* and Vice-Chairman of the Israel Interfaith Organization, Jerusalem.

DAVID J. ZUCKER was ordained by the Hebrew Union College/Jewish Institute of Religion and earned his Ph. D. from the University of Birmingham, England. He is the Community Chaplain in Denver, Colorado, and also serves on the faculty of Regis University. Active in Jewish-Christian dialogue, he is director of the interreligous dialogue firm, Bridges for Understanding. His book, *Israel's Prophets: An Introduction*, was published by Paulist Press in 1994.

Index of Hebrew Terms

(Words in parentheses refer to article in which concept is mentioned)

234

General Index

(Words in parentheses refer to article in which concept is mentioned)

Indwelling (God)
Inerrancy (Bible)
Inspiration (Bible)
Intertestamental Period (Messiah)
Irreversibility (Covenant)
Israel of Flesh (Church/Synagogue)
Israel of God (Church/Synagogue,
    Creation, Christ)

J
Jesus (Christ, Love, Messiah,
    Mission, Prayer, Salvation)
Jerusalem (Exile)
Jew-Hatred (Antisemitism)
Jewish Descent (Covenant)
Judaizers (Pharisees)
Judgment (Eschatology)
Justice (Righteousness)
Justification (Justice, Righteousness,
    Sin)

K
Kairos (Revelation)
Kingdom of God (Eschatology,
    Christ, Jewish-Christian
    Dialogue, Messiah,
    Repentance)

L
Land (Israel, Messiah)
Last Supper (Sacrament)
Law (Love)
Liberation Theology (Ideology,
    Righteousness)
Liturgy (Bible, Church/Synagogue,
    Israel, Prayer)
Logos (God)
Lord's Prayer (Eschatology)
Love (God, Jewish-Christian
    Dialogue, Justice)

M
Marriage (Love, Sacrament)
Martyrdom (Afterlife, Eschatology,
    Holiness, Mission)
Masada (Martyrdom)
Mercy (Justice, Righteousness)
Merit (Justice, Pharisees)
Messiah (Afterlife, Antisemitism,
    Christ, Election, Eschatology,
    Exile, God, Israel, Salvation)
Mission (Universalism)
Monotheism (God, Messiah,
    Universalism)
Moral Theology (Sin)
Moses (Law, Revelation, Tradition)

N
National Redemption (Salvation)
Nature (Personhood, Revelation)
New Covenant (Church/Synagogue,
    Covenant)
New Creation (Creation)
Noah (Covenant, Universalism)
Nomos (Law)

O
Obedience (Law/Halakha)
Oral Torah (Bible, Law/Halakha,
    Tradition)
Ordination (Sacrament)
Original Sin (Repentance, Sin)

P
Palestine (Exile)
Particularism (Universalism)
Penance (Sacrament, Sin)
Penitence (Repentance)
People (Israel, Prayer)
People of God (Church/Synagogue,
    Covenant)

David Burrell and Yehezkel Landau, editors, *Voices from Jerusalem* (A Stimulus Book, 1991).

John Rousmaniere, *A Bridge to Dialogue: The Story of Jewish-Christian Relations*; edited by James A. Carpenter and Leon Klenicki (A Stimulus Book, 1991).

Michael E. Lodahl, *Shekhinah/Spirit* (A Stimulus Book, 1992).

George M. Smiga, *Pain and Polemic: Anti-Judaism in the Gospels* (A Stimulus Book, 1992).

Eugene J. Fisher, editor, *Interwoven Destinies: Jews and Christians Through the Ages* (A Stimulus Book, 1993).

Anthony Kenny, *Catholics, Jews and the State of Israel* (A Stimulus Book, 1993).

Eugene J. Fisher, editor, *Visions of the Other: Jewish and Christian Theologians Assess the Dialogue* (A Stimulus Book, 1994).

Vincent Martin, *A House Divided: The Parting of the Ways Between Synagogue and Church* (A Stimulus Book, 1995).

STIMULUS BOOKS are developed by Stimulus Foundation, a not-for-profit organization, and are published by Paulist Press. The Foundation wishes to further the publication of scholarly books on Jewish and Christian topics that are of importance to Judaism and Christianity.

Stimulus Foundation was established by an erstwhile refugee from Nazi Germany who intends to contribute with these publications to the improvement of communication between Jews and Christians.

Books for publication in this Series will be selected by a committee of the Foundation, and offers of manuscripts and works in progress should be addressed to:

Stimulus Foundation
c/o Paulist Press
997 Macarthur Boulevard
Mahwah, N.J. 07430